TUFF STUFF'S
COMPLETE GUIDE TO
STARTING LINEUP

A Pictorial History of Kenner Starting Lineup Figures

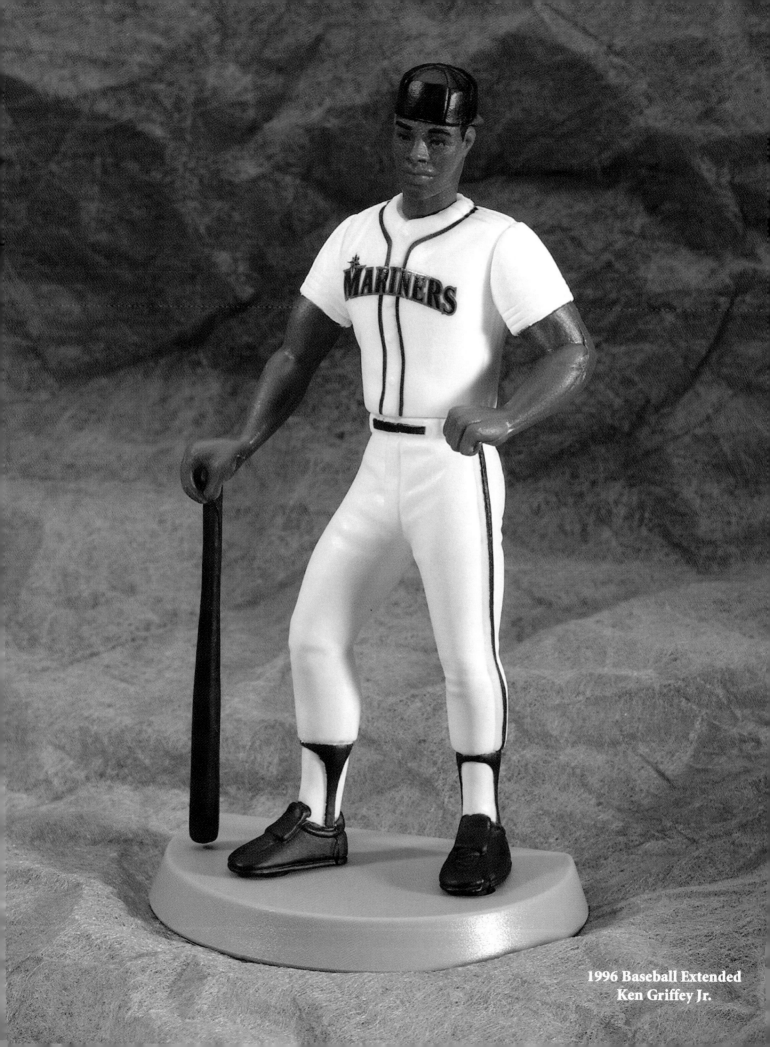

1996 Baseball Extended
Ken Griffey Jr.

TUFF STUFF'S
COMPLETE GUIDE TO
STARTING LINEUP

A Pictorial History of Kenner Starting Lineup Figures

By Jim Warren II

Editorial Director: Larry Canale
Copy Editor: Jerry Shaver
Proofreader: Sean Ryan

Art Director: Rick Whiteman
Designer: Gordon Schmidt

Tuff Stuff Books
Richmond, Va.
A division of Landmark Specialty Publications Inc.

ISBN: 0-930625-78-1
Library of Congress Catalog Number: 97-61495

Manufactured in the United States of America

Published by
Tuff Stuff Books
Richmond, Va.
A division of Landmark Specialty Publications Inc.

Front cover photo: Top (left to right) 1994 "Red" Rodman, 1996 Extended Ken Griffey Jr., 1993 Grant Fuhr.
Bottom (left to right) 1996 Convention Cal Ripken Jr., 1996 Far East Magic Johnson, 1989 Rod Woodson.

Acknowledgements

This book would never have been completed if it weren't for a patient friend—Charles Hungerford. I owe a debt of gratitude to Charles for which I will never be able to repay. Thank you, Charles, for allowing us to invade your home and shoot your entire collection.

I would like to give a special thanks to Jerry Shaver and Larry Canale for editing all of the copy when there was a host of other things that needed to be done. Thanks also to Tuff Stuff Publications president Frank Finn for his guidance.

Thanks to Jorge Chazo, John Harrelson, and Craig Anderson of Thurston Advertising and Photography Inc. for shooting each figure.

Thanks to Dennis Madigan, Melanie Haynie, and Andrew McCrum for their help in making sure we didn't damage any of Charles' figures and returning his home to the way we found it.

Thank you to Gordon Schmidt and Rick Whiteman for their creative flair in bringing these pages to life. Thanks to our "hired-gun" proofer, Sean Ryan.

I would like to thank Allan Miller and Elizabeth Smith of Antique Trader Books and Rick Spears, president of Landmark Specialty Publications, for their expertise. Without their help, this book would still be on the drawing board.

I also would like to thank Jim Hook, Bill Hartglass, Jack Farrah, and Jerri Bombadier of Kenner for all of their help and support in making this book a reality.

Thanks to Bud Tompkins, Chris Daugherty, O.J. Hart, Mathew Weiss, and Derek Hill for providing case assortment information and for allowing us to borrow the last few figures we needed to complete the photo shoot.

I would like to thank Jake Bower and Lindsay Pritchard who both suggested that a Kenner Starting Lineup pictorial was long overdue.

And finally, thanks to my wife, Cindi, for having the patience to let me follow my second love, sports.

Jim Warren II
June 1997

Contents

Football

Hockey

Multi-Sport

Foreword

How It All Began

By Jeff Clow

Collectors evolve and hobbies evolve, and the story of Starting Lineup action figures is a perfect example. Once considered a small niche in the overall sports collectibles hobby, Starting Lineups have evolved into one of the premier collectibles in the country. The reasons are many, but it begins and ends with the collector. And it's an incredible story.

Ten years ago, Kenner Products of Cincinnati took a retired athlete's idea and transformed 4-inch pieces of plastic into replicas of sports stars. The company tested the idea on children in a series of focus groups—and returned the highest scores ever recorded up to that point. The folks at Kenner were ecstatic and production began in earnest in 1987. A marketing whiz at Kenner by the name of Bruce Stein personally supervised the launch.

It was Stein who had started a chain reaction that resulted in the Starting Lineup concept. While looking over some furniture that he was contemplating buying from Pat McInally, Stein asked the former Cincinnati Bengal punter to come up with an idea for a new line of toys aimed primarily at young boys.

McInally was the right person to ask. A graduate of Harvard, he had recently started writing a column published in newspapers nationwide on kids and sports. McInally visited toy stores with Stein and the idea struck him: Most companies were producing action figures based on fictional heroes, like the popular G.I. Joe dolls. Why not a line based on real-life sports heroes instead? He posed the question to Stein, and from that chance occurrence a toy, a collectible, and ultimately a phenomenon was born.

What neither McInally nor Stein could predict, however, was that their line of boys' action figures would come to attract a much larger audience. Or that their regional distribution pattern would create an underground trading network that evolved into a full-fledged secondary market. Or that grown men and women would end up sleeping in their cars in store parking lots just to get the first shot at newly stocked Starting Lineups.

Both McInally and Stein were visionaries, but their original vision never could have drawn the picture of today's hobby.

And here's where the collector comes in.

The collector is the most fickle of humans. Show him something that is easy to obtain, and he turns up his nose. Show him something that he can't locate without some hard work, and his mind brightens. Show him something that combines his love of sports with his love of collecting, and he's apt to jump right in. Allow him to share his hobby with his kids, and you've got him hooked—big time. Does that sound like you? If it does, welcome to the club.

I speak from experience. When *Tuff Stuff* approached me to write this foreword, I actually had one of those flashbacks that people have in movies. You see, I was that collector that fell in love with Starting Lineups. I can distinctly remember the event that started it all. A friend of mine had suggested that a good way for a father and son to spend time together was to collect baseball cards. My son had just turned 5, and we started building sets. Then we chanced upon a dealer at a local card show who had a box of Starting Lineups. I had never seen one before and asked about them. The dealer informed me that they were brand new products, and that different players were available in different regions of the country. I bought my first piece—and we stopped at a toy store on the way home and bought more.

As I walked through my front door, my wife saw the packages and said, "You bought toys? I thought you were going to buy some cards…." "No, no," I explained to her, as only a husband can do when confronted by a questioning wife. "These aren't toys—they're collectibles!" Thus the journey began.

Soon the whole family was searching for Starting Lineup figures. First we wanted all the players from the local teams, and later, the regional teams. Then we heard about some dealers who specialized in Starting Lineups. We set up a trade for a couple of pieces we needed in exchange for some local players, and soon we had more than 70 different figures. By then we knew that 124 players comprised the whole set, and the search took on a life of its own.

Then, by chance, something else happened—something that would have great significance in the hobby, although at the time it seemed like a minor thing. I came across a publication named *Tuff Stuff* that was then publishing a newspaper-style monthly covering various aspects of sports collecting. Thumbing through the magazine, I saw that there was a price guide for everything under the sun—except Starting Lineup figurines. Because I was so hooked on these new collectibles, I wrote to Ernie White, then the publisher of *Tuff Stuff,* and asked why he didn't have a price guide for Starting Lineups. Didn't he know that Starting Lineups were being collected?

White wrote me back, and while he hadn't been aware that people were collecting Starting Lineups, he was interested enough in the idea to ask me to write an article about the young hobby. I was shocked. I hadn't suggested any such thing—I was simply hoping *Tuff Stuff* would start listing prices for some of the tougher pieces. I had never written anything for publication in my life. I had a good career going that had nothing whatsoever to do with journalism or collecting. But I really liked the hobby, so I sat down at my old

Smith-Corona typewriter and wrote my first article—"The Thrill of the Chase."

I talked about how my family and I piled in the station wagon and drove for hours in search of elusive Starting Lineup figures. I talked about the thrill of doing it as a family, and the fun we had running from store to store. I talked about 4-inch pieces of plastic that gave us a lot more enjoyment than we had ever imagined.

I wrote what I felt about the whole thing, and it struck a chord with others. Funny how chance can play such a big role in a hobby. Soon my mailbox was full of letters from people who'd had the same experiences I had.

Next thing I knew, the folks at *Tuff Stuff* called and asked whether I'd like to write a bimonthly column. Two months later, they called back and asked that I write it monthly. Soon *Tuff Stuff's* offices were being inundated with mail from Starting Lineup collectors. The column had tapped a vein in the collecting world that none of *Tuff Stuff's* competitors were aware of—and they were smart enough to see the trend. *Tuff Stuff* was the first to publish a price guide on Starting Lineups. The first to have a column devoted to the hobby. And the first to see the potential of an item that was dismissed by other publications as "just a toy."

As the hobby grew, it took on the momentum of a tidal wave. The first two years were a gradual buildup, and in 1990, the wave hit the mainland. Smart collectors were beginning to take notice of the truly limited production of Starting Lineups—not only the figures, but the cards that were packaged with each player. Whereas Topps might release several million copies of a player's card, Kenner was producing quantities in the tens of thousands—and sometimes even less.

And then Ken Griffey Jr. rode that tidal wave all the way in, and the hobby exploded almost overnight.

Griffey, the hottest young player on the planet in 1990, was packed only one figure per Starting Lineup case. When that fact became publicized, every person with even a remote interest in collecting sports-related items came out of the woodwork. The frenzy started, only to be followed by the frenzy surrounding the release of the first Kenner Hockey issue three years later. Collectors migrated from the sports card hobby

by the thousands.

The hobby evolved and the collector evolved. Old-timers recall being able to find hundreds of pieces hanging on toy-store shelves. Newcomers only remember having to fight through crowds in hopes of finding any figures at all. Fistfights broke out and stores changed their policies. Back-door deals and bribery of store employees became an industry-wide black eye. But the collector remained.

As the hobby continued to grow, the chase became even tougher, but Kenner avoided the temptation to overproduce, while continuing to issue new series and new sports. And through it all, *Tuff Stuff* became known as the industry's bible. Advertising in competitive publications carried the assumption that *Tuff Stuff* was *the* guide—and it is still not uncommon to see a dealer advertising his or her prices as 10 percent off *Tuff Stuff* in one of the magazine's many competitors.

Another figure appeared on the scene that helped influence the hobby. Jim Warren, now the price guide editor of *Tuff Stuff* and Tuff Stuff Publications, took over the Starting Lineup price guide four years ago and saw even greater potential than his predecessors had. With his encouragement, *Tuff Stuff* produced a publication entirely devoted to Starting Lineups—first as an annual, then as a quarterly, and then as a bimonthly. And now you're holding the first book ever produced about this phenomenon—a collector's item in its own right with photos of every piece produced by Kenner under the Starting Lineup brand name during the first 10 years.

What a story! From a minuscule hobby to an overwhelming success in 10 short years. From a single article to a reference manual that every serious collector will want to own. From 124 players to more than 2,000 different figures in circulation. From a kid's toy to a serious—and valuable—sports collectible. What a ride it has been—and what a ride it continues to be.

Welcome aboard.

Introduction

In 1988, Kenner—famous for making action figures for kids—released its first line of sports figures. The company called them Starting Lineups (SLUs), and they marked the beginning of what has become one of the most popular sports collectibles today.

In *Tuff Stuff* magazine, we've been covering this burgeoning market since the early 1990s. In this, the debut from Tuff Stuff Books, we have compiled the first comprehensive Starting Lineup book on the market. It's as complete as any collector could want: We've included photographs, pricing trends, and all of the information a Starting Lineup collector needs. Whether you've just started collecting SLUs or have been in it since the start, you should find this book to be an invaluable resource.

In compiling the images for this book, we've photographed every Starting Lineup figure Kenner issued in the United States through 1996—from the first baseball pieces of 1988 all the way through the '96 Basketball Extended set. Plus, we have included pictures of all of the Canadian Hockey and the Canadian Timeless Legends series. (The only photos you won't find here are the soccer figures Kenner issued in Europe. But that's another story....)

Along with each photo, we list the pictured piece's current value along with values from recent years. All of these prices come from *Tuff Stuff*. In our "1988 Baseball" chapter, for example, we list prices from July 1991 (when we began compiling SLU data), July 1994, and July 1997.

All of the prices we list are based on mint-in-box figures—SLUs that remain in perfect condition in their original packaging. We also present, on p. 11, an illustrated grading guide offering four levels of condition: "mint," "near-mint," "lesser," and "distressed." Along with each condition grade is an approximate percentage (of mint price) you should apply in order to determine your collection's value.

We also provide case assortment information with each set. Kenner distributes SLUs, of course, in cases. Stamped onto every case that leaves Kenner's factories is a product code number. At the end of each product code is a period followed by two digits. The number lets you know which assortment of players appears inside the box. We've listed—as frequently as possible—the last two numbers from each case.

Originally, Kenner issued SLUs in either all-star or team cases. The company distributed all-star cases nationally and the team cases locally. This distribution system made the challenge of completing sets especially difficult—and forced collectors to trade with each other. As a result, a secondary SLU market evolved.

Today, Kenner usually issues between two and five all-star case assortments per set, depending on the production run. This makes it easier for collectors, no matter where they're located, to complete sets.

One other note about this book: If you're looking for a specific player, use the index we've prepared (p. 183). It provides an alphabetical listing of every player who's appeared as a Starting Lineup figure.

Jim Warren II
Price Guide Editor, *Tuff Stuff*

Condition Guide

Mint (MT)—The package must have four perfect corners and the blister bubble cannot be creased, dented, or damaged in any way. The cardboard backing and hanging tab must be in perfect condition, showing no signs of wear. The prices listed are for figures in mint condition.

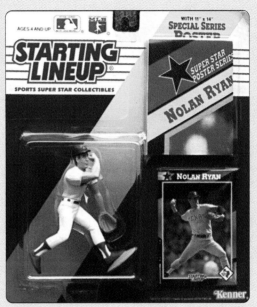

Near Mint (NM)—The package may have one slightly worn corner. The cardboard backing can have only a small, light surface crease. The blister bubble cannot be creased, dented, or damaged. Figures in near mint condition sell for approximately 70 to 80 percent of the listed price.

Lesser (L)—More than one corner shows wear, the hang tag has been damaged, and the backing board may have a few light creases. The blister bubble may have only a slight dent. Figures in lesser condition sell for 60 to 70 percent of the listed price.

Distressed (D)—Shows obvious handling. The hang tag has been damaged to the point where the figure cannot be hung by it. The package may be torn and the blister damaged, but the figure and card are unaffected. Distressed-condition packages sell for 50 to 60 percent of the listed price.

1988 BASEBALL

★ Set Price: $3,100.00 ★ Total Figures: 124 ★

In 1988, with licensing agreements firmly in place, Kenner was ready to make former Cincinnati Bengal punter/wide receiver Pat McInally's brainchild a reality, and Starting Lineups (SLUs) were born.

The revolutionary sports figures—fewer than 6 inches tall and individually packaged with a trading card—were assembled and readied for shipment. In order to appeal to the widest possible consumer base, Kenner came up with a unique distribution plan. The game's biggest stars would be packed in "all-star" cases and distributed nationally, while local fan favorites would be packed in "team" cases and distributed regionally. As a further enticement to collectors, Kenner added a special offer on many of its baseball packages. For $3.99 and five proofs of purchase, collectors could receive a baseball featuring facsimile autographs of many of the game's top stars.

A handful of figures are pictured with the baseball premium offer, while a majority are not. It is unknown which figures are available with or without the offer.

Ironically, these efforts—originally intended to make the Starting

Bob Welch and Mike Davis are listed on the back of the '88 Baseball package (above), but neither made it into the set. At left: Sid Bream.

Lineup product more appealing to consumers—have actually made the task of assembling an '88 Baseball set more difficult for collectors. Regional distribution made several of the pieces almost impos-

Case Assortments

AL ALL-STAR
George Bell (1)
Wade Boggs (3)
George Brett (3)
Roger Clemens (3)
Rickey Henderson (1)
Wally Joyner (3)
Eddie Murray (2)
Don Mattingly (3)
Kirby Puckett (2)
Alan Trammell (1)
Dave Winfield (2)

NL ALL-STAR
Gary Carter (2)
Eric Davis (2)
Andre Dawson (2)
Dwight Gooden (1)
Pedro Guerrero (2)
Tony Gwynn (1)
Dale Murphy (2)
Tim Raines (1)
Pete Rose (2)
Mike Schmidt (2)
Mike Scott (2)
Ozzie Smith (3)
Fernando Valenzuela (2)

TEAM CASES
Atlanta Braves
Ken Griffey Sr. (4)
Dale Murphy (7)
Ken Oberkfell (4)
Zane Smith (4)

Ozzie Virgil (5)

Baltimore Orioles
Mike Boddicker (4)
Terry Kennedy (4)
Fred Lynn (5)
Eddie Murray (6)
Cal Ripken Jr. (5)

Boston Red Sox
Wade Boggs (8)
Ellis Burks (1)
Roger Clemens (4)
Dwight Evans (4)
Jim Rice (7)

California Angles
Brian Downing (5)
Wally Joyner (7)
Donnie Moore (3)
Devon White (4)
Mike Witt (5)

Chicago Cubs
Jody Davis (4)
Andre Dawson (7)
Shawon Dunston (2)
Leon Durham (4)
Ryne Sandberg (5)
Rick Sutcliffe (3)

Chicago White Sox
Harold Baines (7)
Carlton Fisk (5)

Ozzie Guillen (4)
Gary Redus (3)
Greg Walker (5)

Cincinnati Reds
Buddy Bell (4)
Kal Daniels (5)
Eric Davis (10)
John Franco (5)

Cleveland Indians
Joe Carter (6)
Julio Franco (5)
Mel Hall (4)
Cory Snyder (5)
Pat Tabler (4)

Detroit Tigers
Willie Hernandez (3)
Jack Morris (6)
Matt Nokes (2)
Alan Trammell (7)
Lou Whitaker (6)

Houston Astros
Alan Ashby (4)
Kevin Bass (4)
Glenn Davis (4)
Billy Hatcher (4)
Nolan Ryan (4)
Mike Scott (4)

Kansas City Royals
George Brett (6)

Dan Quisenberry (4)
Bret Saberhagen (5)
Kevin Seitzer (5)
Danny Tartabull (4)

Los Angeles Dodgers
Pedro Guerrero (7)
Mike Marshall (2)
Steve Sax (7)
Franklin Stubbs (2)
Fernando Valenzuela (6)

Milwaukee Brewers
Rob Deer (5)
Ted Higuera (5)
Paul Molitor (5)
B.J. Surhoff (4)
Robin Yount (5)

Minnesota Twins
Tom Brunansky (3)
Gary Gaetti (5)
Kent Hrbek (5)
Kirby Puckett (5)
Jeff Reardon (2)
Frank Viola (5)

New York Mets
Gary Carter (4)
Lenny Dykstra (2)
Dwight Gooden (4)
Keith Hernandez (4)

Howard Johnson (1)
Kevin McReynolds (4)
Darryl Strawberry (5)

New York Yankees
Jack Clark (4)
Rickey Henderson (4)
Don Mattingly (6)
Willie Randolph (3)
Dave Righetti (3)
Dave Winfield (4)

Oakland Athletics & San Francisco Giants
Jose Canseco (3)
Carney Lansford (2)
Mark McGwire (4)
Dave Parker (2)
Will Clark (4)
Jeffrey Leonard (4)
Candy Maldonado (2)
Rick Reuschel (3)

Philadelphia Phillies
Steve Bedrosian (4)
Von Hayes (3)
Shane Rawley (4)
Juan Samuel (5)
Mike Schmidt (8)

Pittsburgh Pirates
Barry Bonds (5)

Bobby Bonilla (5)
Sid Bream (5)
Mike Dunne (4)
Andy Van Slyke (5)

San Diego Padres
Chris Brown (5)
Tony Gwynn (8)
John Kruk (5)
Benito Santiago (6)

Seattle Mariners
Alvin Davis (7)
Mark Langston (5)
Ken Phelps (7)
Jim Presley (5)

St. Louis Cardinals
Vince Coleman (6)
Tom Herr (4)
Willie McGee (6)
Ozzie Smith (7)
Todd Worrell (1)

Texas Rangers
Charlie Hough (4)
Pete Incaviglia (6)
Pete O'Brien (4)
Larry Parrish (6)
Ruben Sierra (4)

sible to find, and the autographed baseball promotion created a shortage of mint-in-box figures. Of course, at the time these figures hit the shelves, they were still considered toys, and consumers opened and played with them. All of these factors combine to make this one of the rarest and most difficult sets for collectors to complete today.

This series features many of the hobby's premier pieces, but none has had an impact on SLU collecting like the '88 Nolan Ryan. Credited by many as the piece that started the hobby, the '88 Ryan was the first Starting Lineup to reach $100 on the secondary market (in 1991). While a nationwide network of Kenner collectors had already emerged—started mainly by collectors trading regional pieces from different areas of the country—the success of the Ryan figure, once known as the "Holy Grail" of the SLU hobby, focused national attention on Starting Lineups and brought a whole new generation of collectors into the hobby. While the Ryan piece is no longer the most expensive SLU on the market, and baseball sets haven't appreciated as much as their counterparts in other sports, '88 Baseball is still a noteworthy set, and a great addition to any collection.

Alan Ashby

July '91	25.00
July '94	20.00
July '97	18.00

Harold Baines

July '91	12.00
July '94	15.00
July '97	15.00

Kevin Bass

July '91	12.00
July '94	14.00
July '97	12.00

Steve Bedrosian

July '91	12.00
July '94	14.00
July '97	15.00

Buddy Bell

July '91	12.00
July '94	20.00
July '97	18.00

George Bell

July '91	12.00
July '94	18.00
July '97	15.00

Mike Boddicker

July '91	12.00
July '94	18.00
July '97	120.00

Wade Boggs

July '91	12.00
July '94	26.00
July '97	35.00

Barry Bonds

July '91	25.00
July '94	70.00
July '97	100.00

Bobby Bonilla

July '91	20.00
July '94	22.00
July '97	20.00

Sid Bream

July '91	12.00
July '94	16.00
July '97	12.00

George Brett

July '91	20.00
July '94	52.00
July '97	75.00

Chris Brown
July '91 ....20.00
July '94 ....13.00
July '97 ....10.00

Tom Brunansky
July '91 ....25.00
July '94 ....24.00
July '97 ....22.00

Ellis Burks
July '91 ....45.00
July '94 ....35.00
July '97 ....40.00

Jose Canseco
July '91 ....70.00
July '94 ....30.00
July '97 ....32.00

Gary Carter
July '91 ....12.00
July '94 ....20.00
July '97 ....20.00

Joe Carter
July '91 ....12.00
July '94 ....30.00
July '97 ....35.00

Jack Clark
July '91 ....25.00
July '94 ....19.00
July '97 ....17.00

Will Clark
July '91 ....40.00
July '94 ....29.00
July '97 ....27.00

Roger Clemens
July '91 ....12.00
July '94 ....30.00
July '97 ....30.00

Vince Coleman
July '91 ....12.00
July '94 ....14.00
July '97 ....10.00

Kal Daniels
July '91 ....12.00
July '94 ....18.00
July '97 ....15.00

Alvin Davis
July '91 ....12.00
July '94 ....14.00
July '97 ....12.00

Eric Davis
July '91 ....15.00
July '94 ....10.00
July '97 ....10.00

Glenn Davis
July '91 ....12.00
July '94 ....15.00
July '97 ....12.00

Jody Davis
July '91 ....12.00
July '94 ....16.00
July '97 ....14.00

Andre Dawson
July '91 ....12.00
July '94 ....24.00
July '97 ....20.00

Rob Deer
July '91......................15.00
July '94......................15.00
July '97......................16.00

Brian Downing
July '91......................12.00
July '94......................14.00
July '97......................12.00

Mike Dunne
July '91......................12.00
July '94......................14.00
July '97......................10.00

Shawon Dunston
July '91......................20.00
July '94......................18.00
July '97......................15.00

Leon Durham
July '91......................12.00
July '94......................14.00
July '97......................14.00

Lenny Dykstra
July '91......................20.00
July '94......................30.00
July '97......................25.00

Dwight Evans
July '91......................15.00
July '94......................20.00
July '97......................20.00

Carlton Fisk
July '91......................30.00
July '94......................54.00
July '97......................75.00

John Franco
July '91......................12.00
July '94......................18.00
July '97......................16.00

Julio Franco
July '91......................15.00
July '94......................20.00
July '97......................18.00

Gary Gaetti
July '91......................12.00
July '94......................17.00
July '97......................15.00

Dwight Gooden
July '91......................12.00
July '94......................18.00
July '97......................10.00

Ken Griffey Sr.
July '91......................35.00
July '94......................25.00
July '97......................25.00

Pedro Guerrero
July '91......................12.00
July '94......................12.00
July '97......................10.00

Ozzie Guillen
July '91......................15.00
July '94......................20.00
July '97......................17.00

Tony Gwynn
July '91......................12.00
July '94......................32.00
July '97......................125.00

Mel Hall
July '91......................12.00
July '94......................14.00
July '97 ....12.00

Billy Hatcher
July '91......................25.00
July '94......................18.00
July '97 ....14.00

Von Hayes
July '91.....................20.00
July '94......................15.00
July '97 ....15.00

Rickey Henderson
July '91......................30.00
July '94 ....25.00
July '97 ....25.00

Keith Hernandez
July '91......................20.00
July '94......................18.00
July '97 ....15.00

Willie Hernandez
July '91......................20.00
July '94......................16.00
July '97 ....14.00

Tom Herr
July '91......................12.00
July '94......................15.00
July '97 ....10.00

Ted Higuera
July '91......................12.00
July '94......................18.00
July '97 ....15.00

Charlie Hough
July '91......................12.00
July '94......................18.00
July '97 ....18.00

Kent Hrbek
July '91......................12.00
July '94......................18.00
July '97 ....15.00

Pete Incaviglia
July '91......................12.00
July '94 ....20.00
July '97 ....18.00

Howard Johnson
July '91......................30.00
July '94 ....25.00
July '97 ....14.00

Wally Joyner
July '91.........................12.00
July '94......................14.00
July '97 ....12.00

Terry Kennedy
July '91......................20.00
July '94......................18.00
July '97 ....15.00

John Kruk
July '91......................12.00
July '94 ....35.00
July '97 ....30.00

Mark Langston
July '91......................20.00
July '94 ....27.00
July '97 ....30.00

Carney Lansford
July '91 .... 30.00
July '94 .... 22.00
July '97 .... 20.00

Jeffrey Leonard
July '91 .... 20.00
July '94 .... 15.00
July '97 .... 15.00

Fred Lynn
July '91 .... 20.00
July '94 .... 20.00
July '97 .... 20.00

Candy Maldonado
July '91 .... 16.00
July '94 .... 16.00
July '97 .... 12.00

Mike Marshall
July '91 .... 12.00
July '94 .... 18.00
July '97 .... 14.00

Don Mattingly
July '91 .... 12.00
July '94 .... 25.00
July '97 .... 35.00

Willie McGee
July '91 .... 12.00
July '94 .... 18.00
July '97 .... 16.00

Mark McGwire
July '91 .... 45.00
July '94 .... 40.00
July '97 .... 75.00

Kevin McReynolds
July '91 .... 20.00
July '94 .... 20.00
July '97 .... 15.00

Paul Molitor
July '91 .... 12.00
July '94 .... 35.00
July '97 .... 60.00

Donnie Moore
July '91 .... 25.00
July '94 .... 20.00
July '97 .... 20.00

Jack Morris
July '91 .... 12.00
July '94 .... 24.00
July '97 .... 24.00

Dale Murphy
July '91 .... 12.00
July '94 .... 15.00
July '97 .... 14.00

Eddie Murray
July '91 .... 12.00
July '94 .... 25.00
July '97 .... 85.00

Matt Nokes
July '91 .... 12.00
July '94 .... 15.00
July '97 .... 12.00

Pete O'Brien
July '91 .... 12.00
July '94 .... 14.00
July '97 .... 12.00

Ken Oberkfell

July '91......................12.00
July '94......................14.00
July '97......................12.00

Dave Parker

July '91......................35.00
July '94......................30.00
July '97......................25.00

Larry Parrish

July '91......................12.00
July '94......................13.00
July '97......................12.00

Ken Phelps

July '91......................20.00
July '94......................15.00
July '97......................12.00

Jim Presley

July '91......................12.00
July '94......................15.00
July '97......................12.00

Kirby Puckett

July '91......................12.00
July '94......................36.00
July '97......................75.00

Dan Quisenberry

July '91......................20.00
July '94......................18.00
July '97......................16.00

Tim Raines

July '91......................12.00
July '94......................16.00
July '97......................14.00

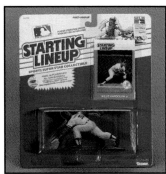

Willie Randolph

July '91......................12.00
July '94......................15.00
July '97......................14.00

Shane Rawley

July '91......................12.00
July '94......................15.00
July '97......................12.00

Jeff Reardon

July '91......................20.00
July '94......................25.00
July '97......................25.00

Gary Redus

July '91......................20.00
July '94......................15.00
July '97......................12.00

Rick Reuschel

July '91......................18.00
July '94......................15.00
July '97......................12.00

Jim Rice

July '91......................12.00
July '94......................25.00
July '97......................24.00

Dave Righetti

July '91......................12.00
July '94......................15.00
July '97......................15.00

Cal Ripken Jr.

July '91......................20.00
July '94......................125.00
July '97......................375.00

Pete Rose

July '91.......................20.00
July '94 ....30.00
July '97.......................70.00

Nolan Ryan

July '91.....................105.00
July '94 ....285.00
July '97 ....325.00

Bret Saberhagen

July '91.......................20.00
July '94 ....20.00
July '97 ....20.00

Juan Samuel

July '91.......................12.00
July '94 ....15.00
July '97 ....12.00

Ryne Sandberg

July '91.......................25.00
July '94 ....50.00
July '97 ....80.00

Benito Santiago

July '91.......................12.00
July '94 ....18.00
July '97 ....20.00

Steve Sax

July '91.......................15.00
July '94 ....15.00
July '97 ....13.00

Mike Schmidt

July '91.......................30.00
July '94 ....50.00
July '97 ....70.00

Mike Scott

July '91.......................12.00
July '94 ....12.00
July '97 ....10.00

Kevin Seitzer

July '91.......................20.00
July '94 ....17.00
July '97 ....14.00

Ruben Sierra

July '91.......................40.00
July '94 ....32.00
July '97 ....30.00

Ozzie Smith

July '91.......................12.00
July '94 ....24.00
July '97 ....80.00

Zane Smith

July '91.......................12.00
July '94 ....15.00
July '97 ....12.00

Cory Snyder

July '91.......................15.00
July '94 ....15.00
July '97 ....12.00

Darryl Strawberry

July '91.......................14.00
July '94 ....14.00
July '97 ....10.00

Franklin Stubbs

July '91.......................20.00
July '94 ....14.00
July '97 ....12.00

B.J. Surhoff
July '91......................12.00
July '94 ....20.00
July '97 ....20.00

Rick Sutcliffe
July '91......................12.00
July '94 ....17.00
July '97 ....17.00

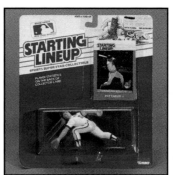

Pat Tabler
July '91......................12.00
July '94 ....14.00
July '97 ....12.00

Danny Tartabull
July '91......................20.00
July '94 ....18.00
July '97 ....17.00

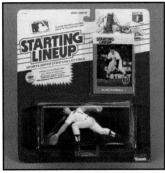

Alan Trammell
July '91......................12.00
July '94 ....18.00
July '97 ....20.00

Fernando Valenzuela
July '91......................12.00
July '94 ....12.00
July '97 ....10.00

Andy Van Slyke
July '91......................30.00
July '94 ....28.00
July '97 ....28.00

Frank Viola
July '91......................12.00
July '94 ....20.00
July '97 ....18.00

Ozzie Virgil
July '91......................15.00
July '94 ....14.00
July '97 ....12.00

Greg Walker
July '91......................12.00
July '94 ....15.00
July '97 ....12.00

Lou Whitaker
July '91......................12.00
July '94 ....24.00
July '97 ....24.00

Devon White
July '91......................15.00
July '94 ....30.00
July '97 ....30.00

Dave Winfield
July '91......................12.00
July '94 ....32.00
July '97 ....50.00

Mike Witt
July '91......................15.00
July '94 ....15.00
July '97 ....12.00

Todd Worrell
July '91......................20.00
July '94 ....20.00
July '97 ....18.00

Robin Yount
July '91......................45.00
July '94 ....75.00
July '97 ....75.00

1989 BASEBALL

★ **Set Price: $4,500.00** ★ **Total Figures: 168** ★

A year of disappointing sales forced Kenner to scale back production on '89 Baseball. The company greatly reduced its print run for all figures (including those shipped in the all-star cases), but it also limited production on several teams that had proven to be very poor sellers. The list of short-printed teams included the San Diego Padres, Chicago Cubs, Chicago White Sox, and California Angels. The latter is one of the hardest team sets to complete. Originally, Kenner had planned to distribute many of the

Angels figures directly through the team, but for unknown reasons, this plan was shelved.

Members of the Angels—with the exception of Wally Joyner, who was packed in both the team and all-star cases—are considered some of the most difficult pieces to acquire. But they're not the only ones; the '89 Baseball set is loaded with tough finds. The second-year figures of such hobby favorites as Tony Gwynn and Cal Ripken Jr. are even more difficult to obtain than their rookie SLUs. And several players who have since become super-

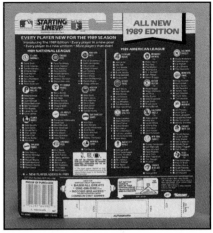

Because of production changes, several players are listed on the back of each package (pictured above) but were never actually released. Pictured at left is Bobby Bonilla.

stars were omitted from the '89 all-star cases and included only in their respective

Case Assortments

AL ALL-STAR
George Bell (1)
Wade Boggs (2)
Jose Canseco (2)
Roger Clemens (2)
Mike Greenwell (1)
Rickey Henderson (2)
Wally Joyner (1)
Don Mattingly (3)
Mark McGwire (3)
Paul Molitor (1)
Kirby Puckett (1)
Alan Trammell (1)
Frank Viola (1)
Dave Winfield (2)

NL ALL-STAR
Bobby Bonilla (1)
Will Clark (2)
Vince Coleman (2)
Eric Davis (2)
Andre Dawson (2)
Kirk Gibson (2)
Dwight Gooden (2)
Dale Murphy (1)
Tim Raines (1)
Ryne Sandberg (2)
Mike Scott (1)
Ozzie Smith (3)
Darryl Strawberry (1)

TEAM CASES
Atlanta Braves
Ron Gant (4)
Albert Hall (2)
Dion James (3)
Dale Murphy (6)
Gerald Perry (4)

Zane Smith (2)
Bruce Sutter (3)

Baltimore Orioles
Brady Anderson (5)
Cal Ripken Jr. (7)
Larry Sheets (6)
Pete Stanicek (6)

Boston Red Sox
Marty Barrett (3)
Wade Boggs (4)
Ellis Burks (3)
Roger Clemens (4)
Mike Greenwell (5)
Jim Rice (2)
Lee Smith (3)

California Angels
Chili Davis (4)
Jack Howell (3)
Wally Joyner (4)
Johnny Ray (3)
Dick Schofield (3)
Devon White (3)
Mike Witt (3)

Chicago Cubs
Damon Berryhill (2)
Andre Dawson (6)
Shawon Dunston (2)
Mark Grace (5)
Greg Maddux (2)
Ryne Sandberg (5)
Rick Sutcliffe (2)

Chicago White Sox
Harold Baines (5)
Ivan Calderon (3)
Ozzie Guillen (5)
Dan Pasqua (3)
Melido Perez (3)
Bobby Thigpen (3)
Greg Walker (3)

Cincinnati Reds
Kal Daniels (3)
Eric Davis (5)
Bo Diaz (3)
John Franco (3)
Danny Jackson (4)
Barry Larkin (3)
Chris Sabo (3)
Jeff Treadway (1)

Cleveland Indians
Joe Carter (4)
Mel Hall (4)
Brook Jacoby (4)
Doug Jones (4)
Cory Snyder (4)
Greg Swindell (4)

Detroit Tigers
Tom Brookens (1)
Mike Henneman (3)
Chet Lemon (3)
Jack Morris (4)
Matt Nokes (4)
Luis Salazar (1)
Alan Trammell (2)
Lou Whitaker (5)

Houston Astros
Kevin Bass (3)
Glenn Davis (5)
Billy Doran (3)
Billy Hatcher (3)
Mike Scott (3)
Dave Smith (4)
Gerald Young (3)

Kansas City Royals
George Brett (4)
Mark Gubicza (3)
Bo Jackson (4)
Bret Saberhagen (2)
Kevin Seitzer (3)
Kurt Stillwell (3)
Pat Tabler (2)
Danny Tartabull (3)

Los Angeles Dodgers
Kirk Gibson (5)
Orel Hershiser (2)
Mike Marshall (3)
Mike Scioscia (5)
John Shelby (3)
Fernando Valenzuela (6)

Milwaukee Brewers
Glenn Braggs (3)
Rob Deer (4)
Ted Higuera (3)
Paul Molitor (4)
Dan Plesac (3)
B.J. Surhoff (3)

Robin Yount (4)

Minnesota Twins
Gary Gaetti (4)
Dan Gladden (4)
Kent Hrbek (2)
Tim Laudner (3)
Kirby Puckett (4)
Jeff Reardon (2)
Frank Viola (4)

New York Mets
Gary Carter (2)
David Cone (2)
Lenny Dykstra (2)
Kevin Elster (2)
Dwight Gooden (4)
Keith Hernandez (2)
Gregg Jefferies (2)
Kevin McReynolds (2)
Randy Myers (2)
Darryl Strawberry (4)

New York Yankees
Rickey Henderson (3)
Al Leiter (3)
Don Mattingly (6)
Mike Pagliarulo (4)
Dave Righetti (2)
Don Slaught (2)
Dave Winfield (4)

Oakland Athletics
Jose Canseco (4)
Dennis Eckersley (2)

Carney Lansford (2)
Mark McGwire (4)
Dave Parker (3)
Terry Steinbach (2)
Dave Stewart (3)
Walt Weiss (2)
Bob Welch (2)

Philadelphia Phillies
Steve Bedrosian (4)
Phil Bradley (1)
Von Hayes (4)
Chris James (4)
Juan Samuel (4)
Mike Schmidt (5)
Milt Thompson (1)

Pittsburgh Pirates
Barry Bonds (4)
Bobby Bonilla (5)
Doug Drabek (3)
Mike LaValliere (3)
Jose Lind (2)
Andy Van Slyke (4)
Bob Walk (3)

St. Louis Cardinals
Tom Brunansky (3)
Vince Coleman (4)
Pedro Guerrero (3)
Willie McGee (3)
Tony Pena (3)
Terry Pendleton (3)
Ozzie Smith (4)
Todd Worrell (2)

San Diego Padres
Roberto Alomar (4)
Mark Davis (4)
Tony Gwynn (5)
John Kruk (4)
Benito Santiago (4)
Marvell Wynne (3)

San Francisco Giants
Brett Butler (5)
Will Clark (5)
Candy Maldonado (3)
Kevin Mitchell (4)
Robby Thompson (4)
Jose Uribe (3)

Seattle Mariners
Mickey Brantley (6)
Alvin Davis (6)
Mark Langston (4)
Rey Quinones (4)
Harold Reynolds (4)

Texas Rangers
Steve Buechele (5)
Scott Fletcher (4)
Pete Incaviglia (5)
Jeff Russell (4)
Ruben Sierra (6)

team cases. Players like Roberto Alomar and Greg Maddux are now almost impossible to find in any condition.

Decreased production, short-printing, and sheer size—a whopping 168 pieces—combine to make this set the most difficult Kenner baseball issue to complete. Collectors with enough patience—and money—to do it will find this set to be a real treasure. But with individual pieces priced at nearly $500, '89 Baseball remains beyond the reach of most collectors.

One interesting note is that Kenner never issued a Montreal Expos or Toronto Blue Jays team set in 1988 or 1989. The only Expos and Blue Jays in '88 and '89 were Tim Raines and George Bell. Both players in each set were only issued in the All-Star cases.

Roberto Alomar (R)
July '91 ....25.00
July '94 ....75.00
July '97 ....475.00

Brady Anderson (R)
July '91 ....9.00
July '94 ....24.00
July '97 ....180.00

Harold Baines
July '91 ....9.00
July '94 ....15.00
July '97 ....15.00

Marty Barrett (R)
July '91 ....9.00
July '94 ....14.00
July '97 ....14.00

Kevin Bass
July '91 ....9.00
July '94 ....12.00
July '97 ....10.00

Steve Bedrosian
July '91 ....9.00
July '94 ....10.00
July '97 ....12.00

George Bell
July '91 ....9.00
July '94 ....12.00
July '97 ....10.00

Damon Berryhill (R)
July '91 ....20.00
July '94 ....12.00
July '97 ....12.00

Wade Boggs
July '91 ....9.00
July '94 ....18.00
July '97 ....30.00

Barry Bonds
July '91 ....9.00
July '94 ....50.00
July '97 ....80.00

Bobby Bonilla
July '91 ....9.00
July '94 ....15.00
July '97 ....16.00

Phil Bradley (R)
July '91 ....35.00
July '94 ....22.00
July '97 ....22.00

Glenn Braggs (R)
July '91........................9.00
July '94......................14.00
July '97......................12.00

Mickey Brantley (R)
July '91......................20.00
July '94......................15.00
July '97......................12.00

George Brett
July '91......................22.00
July '94......................42.00
July '97......................70.00

Tom Brookens (R)
July '91........................9.00
July '94......................12.00
July '97......................12.00

Tom Brunansky
July '91........................9.00
July '94......................15.00
July '97......................12.00

Steve Buechele (R)
July '91........................9.00
July '94......................18.00
July '97......................18.00

Ellis Burks
July '91......................20.00
July '94......................20.00
July '97 ....25.00

Brett Butler (R)
July '91........................9.00
July '94......................18.00
July '97 ....20.00

Ivan Calderon (R)
July '91........................9.00
July '94......................18.00
July '97......................18.00

Jose Canseco
July '91......................12.00
July '94......................15.00
July '97 ....24.00

Gary Carter
July '91........................9.00
July '94......................15.00
July '97......................18.00

Joe Carter
July '91........................9.00
July '94......................16.00
July '97 ....20.00

Will Clark
July '91........................9.00
July '94......................18.00
July '97 ....22.00

Roger Clemens
July '91........................9.00
July '94 ....25.00
July '97 ....30.00

Vince Coleman
July '91........................9.00
July '94......................12.00
July '97......................10.00

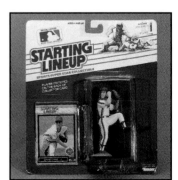

David Cone (R)
July '91......................20.00
July '94......................20.00
July '97 ....35.00

Kal Daniels

July '91 ....9.00
July '94 ....18.00
July '97 ....12.00

Alvin Davis

July '91 ....9.00
July '94 ....20.00
July '97 ....15.00

Chili Davis (R)

July '91 ....9.00
July '94 ....50.00
July '97 ....140.00

Eric Davis

July '91 ....9.00
July '94 ....10.00
July '97 ....10.00

Glenn Davis

July '91 ....9.00
July '94 ....12.00
July '97 ....10.00

Mark Davis (R)

July '91 ....9.00
July '94 ....12.00
July '97 ....30.00

Andre Dawson

July '91 ....9.00
July '94 ....18.00
July '97 ....20.00

Rob Deer

July '91 ....9.00
July '94 ....10.00
July '97 ....10.00

Bo Diaz (R)

July '91 ....9.00
July '94 ....15.00
July '97 ....14.00

Billy Doran (R)

July '91 ....20.00
July '94 ....19.00
July '97 ....20.00

Doug Drabek (R)

July '91 ....9.00
July '94 ....22.00
July '97 ....30.00

Shawon Dunston

July '91 ....9.00
July '94 ....17.00
July '97 ....15.00

Lenny Dykstra

July '91 ....9.00
July '94 ....18.00
July '97 ....30.00

Dennis Eckersley (R)

July '91 ....9.00
July '94 ....50.00
July '97 ....90.00

Kevin Elster (R)

July '91 ....9.00
July '94 ....13.00
July '97 ....12.00

Scott Fletcher (R)

July '91 ....9.00
July '94 ....12.00
July '97 ....12.00

John Franco
July '91 ....9.00
July '94 ....14.00
July '97 ....12.00

Gary Gaetti
July '91 ....9.00
July '94 ....14.00
July '97 ....12.00

Ron Gant (R)
July '91 ....9.00
July '94 ....70.00
July '97 ....225.00

Kirk Gibson (R)
July '91 ....9.00
July '94 ....15.00
July '97 ....12.00

Dan Gladden (R)
July '91 ....9.00
July '94 ....16.00
July '97 ....14.00

Dwight Gooden
July '91 ....9.00
July '94 ....15.00
July '97 ....10.00

Mark Grace (R)
July '91 ....30.00
July '94 ....30.00
July '97 ....40.00

Mike Greenwell (R)
July '91 ....9.00
July '94 ....12.00
July '97 ....10.00

Mark Gubicza (R)
July '91 ....9.00
July '94 ....10.00
July '97 ....10.00

Pedro Guerrero
July '91 ....9.00
July '94 ....10.00
July '97 ....10.00

Ozzie Guillen
July '91 ....9.00
July '94 ....20.00
July '97 ....24.00

Tony Gwynn
July '91 ....30.00
July '94 ....36.00
July '97 ....200.00

Albert Hall (R)
July '91 ....20.00
July '94 ....13.00
July '97 ....14.00

Mel Hall
July '91 ....9.00
July '94 ....10.00
July '97 ....12.00

Billy Hatcher
July '91 ....9.00
July '94 ....12.00
July '97 ....10.00

Von Hayes
July '91 ....9.00
July '94 ....10.00
July '97 ....12.00

Rickey Henderson
July '91......................22.00
July '94......................18.00
July '97......................15.00

Mike Henneman (R)
July '91........................9.00
July '94......................10.00
July '97......................10.00

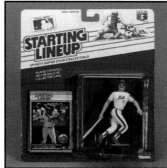

Keith Hernandez
July '91........................9.00
July '94......................10.00
July '97......................12.00

Orel Hershiser (R)
July '91......................25.00
July '94......................20.00
July '97......................20.00

Ted Higuera
July '91........................9.00
July '94......................20.00
July '97......................20.00

Jack Howell (R)
July '91........................9.00
July '94......................50.00
July '97....................100.00

Kent Hrbek
July '91........................9.00
July '94......................12.00
July '97......................14.00

Pete Incaviglia
July '91........................9.00
July '94......................14.00
July '97......................12.00

Bo Jackson (R)
July '91......................70.00
July '94......................30.00
July '97......................25.00

Danny Jackson (R)
July '91........................9.00
July '94......................14.00
July '97......................14.00

Brook Jacoby (R)
July '91........................9.00
July '94......................10.00
July '97......................10.00

Chris James (R)
July '91........................9.00
July '94......................10.00
July '97......................12.00

Dion James (R)
July '91........................9.00
July '94......................12.00
July '97......................15.00

Gregg Jefferies (R)
July '91......................25.00
July '94......................24.00
July '97......................32.00

Doug Jones (R)
July '91......................15.00
July '94......................16.00
July '97......................18.00

Wally Joyner
July '91........................9.00
July '94......................13.00
July '97......................14.00

John Kruk

July '91.......................9.00
July '94.....................30.00
July '97.....................40.00

Mark Langston

July '91.....................25.00
July '94.....................28.00
July '97.....................26.00

Carney Lansford

July '91.......................9.00
July '94.....................20.00
July '97.....................20.00

Barry Larkin (R)

July '91.....................30.00
July '94.....................30.00
July '97.....................75.00

Tim Laudner (R)

July '91.......................9.00
July '94.....................14.00
July '97.....................15.00

Mike LaValliere (R)

July '91.......................9.00
July '94.....................10.00
July '97.....................10.00

Al Leiter (R)

July '91.......................9.00
July '94.....................12.00
July '97.....................15.00

Chet Lemon (R)

July '91.......................9.00
July '94.....................14.00
July '97.....................14.00

Jose Lind (R)

July '91.....................25.00
July '94.....................18.00
July '97.....................20.00

Greg Maddux (R)

July '91.......................9.00
July '94.....................40.00
July '97...................375.00

Candy Maldonado

July '91.......................9.00
July '94.....................12.00
July '97.....................12.00

Mike Marshall

July '91.......................9.00
July '94.....................11.00
July '97.....................10.00

Don Mattingly

July '91.......................9.00
July '94.....................16.00
July '97.....................27.00

Willie McGee

July '91.......................9.00
July '94.....................15.00
July '97.....................15.00

Mark McGwire

July '91.....................15.00
July '94.....................18.00
July '97.....................36.00

Kevin McReynolds

July '91.......................9.00
July '94.....................18.00
July '97.....................18.00

Kevin Mitchell (R)
July '91 ....20.00
July '94 ....19.00
July '97 ....20.00

Paul Molitor
July '91 ....9.00
July '94 ....30.00
July '97 ....35.00

Jack Morris
July '91 ....9.00
July '94 ....20.00
July '97 ....20.00

Dale Murphy
July '91 ....9.00
July '94 ....13.00
July '97 ....13.00

Randy Myers (R)
July '91 ....9.00
July '94 ....18.00
July '97 ....18.00

Matt Nokes (R)
July '91 ....9.00
July '94 ....10.00
July '97 ....10.00

Mike Pagliarulo (R)
July '91 ....9.00
July '94 ....13.00
July '97 ....10.00

Dave Parker
July '91 ....25.00
July '94 ....24.00
July '97 ....25.00

Dan Pasqua (R)
July '91 ....9.00
July '94 ....18.00
July '97 ....15.00

Tony Pena (R)
July '91 ....9.00
July '94 ....15.00
July '97 ....18.00

Terry Pendleton (R)
July '91 ....9.00
July '94 ....28.00
July '97 ....25.00

Melido Perez (R)
July '91 ....9.00
July '94 ....20.00
July '97 ....27.00

Gerald Perry (R)
July '91 ....9.00
July '94 ....16.00
July '97 ....16.00

Dan Plesac (R)
July '91 ....9.00
July '94 ....10.00
July '97 ....10.00

Kirby Puckett
July '91 ....9.00
July '94 ....30.00
July '97 ....60.00

Rey Quinones (R)
July '91 ....22.00
July '94 ....18.00
July '97 ....18.00

Tim Raines
July '91 ....9.00
July '94 ....11.00
July '97 ....11.00

Johnny Ray (R)
July '91 ....22.00
July '94 ....50.00
July '97 ....120.00

Jeff Reardon
July '91 ....9.00
July '94 ....25.00
July '97 ....30.00

Harold Reynolds (R)
July '91 ....20.00
July '94 ....20.00
July '97 ....20.00

Jim Rice
July '91 ....9.00
July '94 ....15.00
July '97 ....16.00

Dave Righetti
July '91 ....9.00
July '94 ....14.00
July '97 ....16.00

Cal Ripken Jr.
July '91 ....20.00
July '94 ....78.00
July '97 ....400.00

Jeff Russell (R)
July '91 ....9.00
July '94 ....20.00
July '97 ....18.00

Bret Saberhagen
July '91 ....9.00
July '94 ....20.00
July '97 ....16.00

Chris Sabo (R)
July '91 ....25.00
July '94 ....20.00
July '97 ....20.00

Luis Salazar (R)
July '91 ....18.00
July '94 ....15.00
July '97 ....15.00

Juan Samuel
July '91 ....9.00
July '94 ....13.00
July '97 ....10.00

Ryne Sandberg
July '91 ....9.00
July '94 ....28.00
July '97 ....50.00

Benito Santiago
July '91 ....9.00
July '94 ....20.00
July '97 ....25.00

Mike Schmidt
July '91 ....65.00
July '94 ....65.00
July '97 ....75.00

Dick Schofield (R)
July '91 ....9.00
July '94 ....50.00
July '97 ....120.00

Mike Scioscia (R)
July '91 ....9.00
July '94 ....15.00
July '97 ....20.00

Mike Scott
July '91 ....9.00
July '94 ....12.00
July '97 ....10.00

Kevin Seitzer
July '91 ....9.00
July '94 ....14.00
July '97 ....12.00

Larry Sheets (R)
July '91 ....9.00
July '94 ....12.00
July '97 ....12.00

John Shelby (R)
July '91 ....9.00
July '94 ....12.00
July '97 ....10.00

Ruben Sierra
July '91 ....9.00
July '94 ....32.00
July '97 ....30.00

Don Slaught (R)
July '91 ....9.00
July '94 ....12.00
July '97 ....12.00

Dave Smith (R)
July '91 ....9.00
July '94 ....14.00
July '97 ....10.00

Lee Smith (R)
July '91 ....9.00
July '94 ....30.00
July '97 ....70.00

Ozzie Smith
July '91 ....9.00
July '94 ....24.00
July '97 ....50.00

Zane Smith
July '91 ....9.00
July '94 ....14.00
July '97 ....12.00

Cory Snyder
July '91 ....9.00
July '94 ....15.00
July '97 ....12.00

Pete Stanicek (R)
July '91 ....9.00
July '94 ....10.00
July '97 ....10.00

Terry Steinbach (R)
July '91 ....40.00
July '94 ....18.00
July '97 ....18.00

Dave Stewart (R)
July '91 ....9.00
July '94 ....21.00
July '97 ....25.00

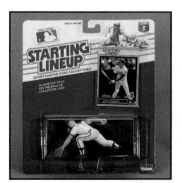

Kurt Stillwell (R)
July '91 ....9.00
July '94 ....10.00
July '97 ....12.00

Darryl Strawberry
July '91 ....9.00
July '94 ....10.00
July '97 ....10.00

B.J. Surhoff
July '91 ....9.00
July '94 ....18.00
July '97 ....18.00

Rick Sutcliffe
July '91 ....9.00
July '94 ....18.00
July '97 ....16.00

Bruce Sutter (R)
July '91 ....9.00
July '94 ....25.00
July '97 ....30.00

Greg Swindell (R)
July '91 ....9.00
July '94 ....18.00
July '97 ....18.00

Pat Tabler
July '91 ....9.00
July '94 ....13.00
July '97 ....13.00

Danny Tartabull
July '91 ....9.00
July '94 ....15.00
July '97 ....12.00

Bobby Thigpen (R)
July '91 ....9.00
July '94 ....25.00
July '97 ....30.00

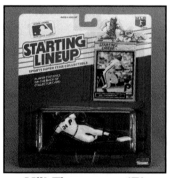

Milt Thompson (R)
July '91 ....25.00
July '94 ....15.00
July '97 ....15.00

Robby Thompson (R)
July '91 ....9.00
July '94 ....15.00
July '97 ....15.00

Alan Trammell
July '91 ....9.00
July '94 ....15.00
July '97 ....15.00

Jeff Treadway (R)
July '91 ....32.00
July '94 ....35.00
July '97 ....40.00

Jose Uribe (R)
July '91 ....9.00
July '94 ....12.00
July '97 ....12.00

Fernando Valenzuela
July '91 ....9.00
July '94 ....13.00
July '97 ....14.00

Andy Van Slyke
July '91 ....9.00
July '94 ....17.00
July '97 ....16.00

Frank Viola
July '91 ....9.00
July '94 ....14.00
July '97 ....10.00

Bob Walk (R)

July '91 ....9.00
July '94 ....12.00
July '97 ....12.00

Greg Walker

July '91 ....9.00
July '94 ....20.00
July '97 ....18.00

Walt Weiss (R)

July '91 ....25.00
July '94 ....32.00
July '97 ....30.00

Bob Welch (R)

July '91 ....15.00
July '94 ....20.00
July '97 ....20.00

Lou Whitaker

July '91 ....9.00
July '94 ....20.00
July '97 ....20.00

Devon White

July '91 ....9.00
July '94 ....50.00
July '97 ....140.00

Dave Winfield

July '91 ....9.00
July '94 ....24.00
July '97 ....30.00

Mike Witt

July '91 ....9.00
July '94 ....40.00
July '97 ....120.00

Todd Worrell

July '91 ....9.00
July '94 ....16.00
July '97 ....14.00

Marvell Wynne (R)

July '91 ....9.00
July '94 ....18.00
July '97 ....32.00

Gerald Young (R)

July '91 ....9.00
July '94 ....12.00
July '97 ....12.00

Robin Yount

July '91 ....9.00
July '94 ....62.00
July '97.....................75.00

1990 BASEBALL

★ **Set Price: $1,600.00** ★ **Total Figures: 87** ★
★ **Extended Set: $200.00** ★ **Total Figures: 9** ★

As an incentive to increase sales, Kenner incorporated a few changes in its 1990 baseball product. Each piece was packaged with not one, but two trading cards: a regular card and a "rookie" card commemorating the respective player's first year in the major leagues. In addition, the company issued several of the more popular players in more than one pose, and developed the first baseball extended series.

Kenner again scaled back production for teams that had poor sales during the previous two years. Only 15 of the previous 24 team cases were issued. Of these team cases that were actually issued, the Baltimore Orioles, Cincinnati Reds, Detroit Tigers, New York Mets, New York Yankees, Oak-

land Athletics, and Pittsburgh Pirates were produced in much smaller quantities. Wally Backman, Nick Esasky, and Gary Pettis are considered short-printed pieces. All three switched teams via free agency before the season began, but because each player had already been produced in his old uniform, Kenner opted to issue them as one-packs in their original team's cases.

Kenner issued four players in multiple poses. Will Clark and Don Mattingly appeared in both the "bat in hand" pose (showing the player ready to drop his bat after swinging) and the "power" pose (depicting the player following through on a swing). Mark Grace was also featured in the "power" pose as well as the standard "batting" pose, and Darryl Strawberry was issued in both the "batting" and "jumping fielder" poses. At the time of the series' release, Kenner announced that Fred McGriff

Again, Kenner lists several players on the back of its '90 Baseball package (above) that were never issued. Barry Bonds is pictured at left.

would also appear in two different poses, but no second pose was ever produced.

When '90 Baseball was first released, much collector anticipation centered on the rookie piece of Jim Abbott. At the time, Abbott was entering his second year in the majors and had already led the U.S. team to a gold medal in the 1988 Olympics. Although Kenner had announced that '90 Baseball would feature an Abbott figure, no

Case Assortments

AL ALL-STAR		TEAM CASES	Cincinnati	Gary Sheffield (6)	Dave Righetti (3)	Andy Van Slyke (7)
Wade Boggs	Mark Grace	**Baltimore**	**Reds**	Robin Yount (7)	Steve Sax (4)	**St. Louis**
Jose Canseco (2)	Orel Hershiser (2)	**Orioles**	Todd Benzinger (3)		Dave Winfield (3)	**Cardinals**
Roger Clemens	Gregg Jefferies	Jeff Ballard (8)	Eric Davis (4)	**Minnesota Twins**		Vince Coleman (4)
Mike Greenwell	Kevin Mitchell (2)	Cal Ripken Jr. (8)	Rob Dibble (3)	Allan Anderson (6)	**Oakland**	Pedro Guerrero (6)
Ken Griffey Jr.	Chris Sabo (2)	Mickey Tettleton (8)	Barry Larkin (5)	Wally Backman (1)	**Athletics**	Joe Magrane (6)
Rickey Henderson	Ryne Sandberg		Paul O'Neill (4)	Gary Gaetti (4)	Jose Canseco (5)	Jose Oquendo (4)
Bo Jackson (4)	Mike Scott	**Boston Red Sox**	Chris Sabo (5)	Kent Hrbek (6)	Dennis Eckersley (3)	Ozzie Smith (4)
Don Mattingly (2)	Ozzie Smith	Wade Boggs (5)		Kirby Puckett (7)	Dave Henderson (3)	
Fred McGriff	Darryl Strawberry (2)	Ellis Burks (4)	**Detroit Tigers**		Rickey Henderson (4)	**San Francisco**
Mark McGwire (3)		Roger Clemens (5)	Matt Nokes (4)	**New York Mets**	Mark McGwire (5)	**Giants**
Paul Molitor	**EXTENDED**	Nick Esasky (1)	Gary Pettis (1)	Ron Darling (2)	Dave Stewart (4)	Steve Bedrosian (5)
Kirby Puckett	Jim Abbott (3)	Mike Greenwell (5)	Alan Trammell (9)	Dwight Gooden (4)		Will Clark (8)
Cal Ripken Jr.	Sandy Alomar Jr. (2)	Jody Reed (4)	Lou Whitaker (10)	Gregg Jefferies (3)	**Philadelphia**	Kevin Mitchell (7)
Nolan Ryan (2)	Jose Canseco (3)			Howard Johnson (4)	**Phillies**	Rick Reuschel (4)
Steve Sax (2)	Joe Carter (1)	**Chicago Cubs**	**Los Angeles**	Kevin McReynolds (3)	Lenny Dykstra (6)	
	Ken Griffey Jr. (4)	Damon Berryhill (2)	**Dodgers**	Juan Samuel (2)	Von Hayes (6)	
NL ALL-STAR	Bo Jackson (4)	Andre Dawson (4)	Orel Hershiser (8)	Darryl Strawberry (4)	Tom Herr (6)	
Will Clark (2)	Ben McDonald (2)	Mark Grace (4)	Eddie Murray (8)	Frank Viola (2)	Ricky Jordan (6)	
Vince Coleman	Nolan Ryan (3)	Greg Maddux (2)	Willie Randolph (8)			
Eric Davis (2)	Jerome Walton (2)	Ryne Sandberg (3)		**New York**	**Pittsburgh**	
Andre Dawson		Rick Sutcliffe (2)	**Milwaukee**	**Yankees**	**Pirates**	
Andres Galarraga		Jerome Walton (3)	**Brewers**	Jessie Barfield (4)	Barry Bonds (5)	
Kirk Gibson (2)		Mitch Williams (4)	Chris Bosio (5)	Roberto Kelly (4)	Bobby Bonilla (6)	
Dwight Gooden (2)			Paul Molitor (6)	Don Mattingly (6)	John Smiley (6)	

such piece appeared in the AL all-star cases. Because of Abbott's handicap (he was born without a right hand), a special mold had to be produced for his SLU and a delay in production forced Kenner to exclude his piece from the initial run of the set.

The delay of the Abbott piece led to the development of the highly successful baseball extended series. Rather than simply cancel production of the figure, Kenner decided to issue a smaller baseball set—with a much more limited production run—later in the season. The extended set featured Abbott along with Jose Canseco, Bo Jackson, Nolan Ryan, and Jerome Walton in poses identical to those in their regular '90 issues. Ken Griffey Jr. appeared in the "fielding" pose rather than the "sliding" pose, and new pieces of Sandy Alomar Jr., Joe Carter, and Ben McDonald—none of whom made it in the regular 1990 set—were produced. All of the extended pieces were released with or without an extended sticker.

It's estimated that Kenner issued only 3,000 extended case assortments. Carter was the short-print and was packed one per case, meaning that Kenner made only 3,000 Carter figures. The success of the extended series gave a much-needed boost to SLU sales—and has helped make the entire set a landmark series in the history of Starting Lineup collecting.

Allan Anderson (R)
July '91 ....6.00
July '94 ....12.00
July '97 ....12.00

Wally Backman (R)
July '91 ....40.00
July '94 ....15.00
July '97 ....15.00

Jeff Ballard (R)
July '91 ....6.00
July '94 ....10.00
July '97 ....12.00

Jessie Barfield (R)
July '91 ....6.00
July '94 ....10.00
July '97 ....10.00

Steve Bedrosian (R)
July '91 ....6.00
July '94 ....12.00
July '97 ....10.00

Todd Benzinger (R)
July '91 ....6.00
July '94 ....13.00
July '97 ....14.00

Damon Berryhill (R)
July '91 ....6.00
July '94 ....12.00
July '97 ....12.00

Wade Boggs
July '91 ....6.00
July '94 ....22.00
July '97 ....25.00

Barry Bonds
July '91 ....6.00
July '94 ....40.00
July '97 ....75.00

Bobby Bonilla
July '91 ....6.00
July '94 ....18.00
July '97 ....15.00

Chris Bosio (R)
July '91 ....6.00
July '94 ....14.00
July '97 ....15.00

Ellis Burks
July '91 ....6.00
July '94 ....14.00
July '97 ....15.00

Jose Canseco
July '91 ....6.00
July '94 ....15.00
July '97 ....16.00

Will Clark (bat in hand)
July '91 ....6.00
July '94 ....14.00
July '97 ....20.00

Will Clark (power)
July '91 ....6.00
July '94 ....25.00
July '97 ....22.00

Roger Clemens
July '91 ....6.00
July '94 ....20.00
July '97 ....25.00

Vince Coleman
July '91 ....6.00
July '94 ....10.00
July '97 ....10.00

Ron Darling (R)
July '91 ....6.00
July '94 ....10.00
July '97 ....10.00

Eric Davis
July '91 ....6.00
July '94 ....12.00
July '97 ....12.00

Andre Dawson
July '91 ....6.00
July '94 ....16.00
July '97 ....18.00

Rob Dibble (R)
July '91 ....15.00
July '94 ....16.00
July '97 ....16.00

Lenny Dykstra
July '91 ....25.00
July '94 ....26.00
July '97 ....25.00

Dennis Eckersley
July '91 ....20.00
July '94 ....35.00
July '97 ....60.00

Nick Esasky (R)
July '91 ....40.00
July '94 ....20.00
July '97 ....24.00

Gary Gaetti
July '91 ....6.00
July '94 ....12.00
July '97 ....12.00

Andres Galarraga (R)
July '91 ....6.00
July '94 ....20.00
July '97 ....30.00

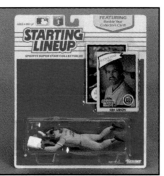

Kirk Gibson
July '91 ....6.00
July '94 ....10.00
July '97 ....10.00

Dwight Gooden
July '91 ....6.00
July '94 ....14.00
July '97 ....12.00

Mark Grace (batting)
July '91......................15.00
July '94......................15.00
July '97......................18.00

Mark Grace (power)
July '91......................30.00
July '94......................22.00
July '97......................22.00

Mike Greenwell
July '91........................6.00
July '94......................10.00
July '97......................10.00

Ken Griffey Jr. (R) (sliding)
July '91......................50.00
July '94......................64.00
July '97....................100.00

Pedro Guerrero
July '91........................6.00
July '94......................10.00
July '97......................10.00

Von Hayes
July '91........................6.00
July '94......................10.00
July '97......................10.00

Dave Henderson (R)
July '91........................6.00
July '94......................13.00
July '97......................13.00

Rickey Henderson
July '91......................22.00
July '94......................14.00
July '97......................15.00

Tom Herr
July '91........................6.00
July '94......................11.00
July '97......................10.00

Orel Hershiser
July '91........................6.00
July '94......................15.00
July '97......................18.00

Kent Hrbek
July '91........................6.00
July '94......................10.00
July '97......................12.00

Bo Jackson
July '91......................22.00
July '94......................12.00
July '97......................12.00

Gregg Jefferies
July '91......................15.00
July '94......................15.00
July '97......................15.00

Howard Johnson
July '91......................20.00
July '94......................15.00
July '97......................12.00

Ricky Jordan (R)
July '91........................6.00
July '94......................14.00
July '97......................12.00

Roberto Kelly (R)
July '91......................18.00
July '94......................18.00
July '97......................15.00

Barry Larkin
July '91.......................15.00
July '94.....................25.00
July '97.....................55.00

Greg Maddux
July '91.......................6.00
July '94.....................26.00
July '97...................450.00

Joe Magrane (R)
July '91.......................6.00
July '94.....................12.00
July '97.....................10.00

Don Mattingly (bat in hand)
July '91.......................6.00
July '94.....................14.00
July '97.....................20.00

Don Mattingly (power)
July '91.......................6.00
July '94.....................18.00
July '97.....................24.00

Fred McGriff (R)
July '91.......................6.00
July '94.....................30.00
July '97.....................50.00

Mark McGwire
July '91.......................6.00
July '94.....................15.00
July '97.....................22.00

Kevin McReynolds
July '91.....................20.00
July '94.....................12.00
July '97.....................10.00

Kevin Mitchell
July '91.......................6.00
July '94.....................10.00
July '97.....................12.00

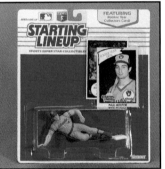

Paul Molitor
July '91.......................6.00
July '94.....................24.00
July '97.....................28.00

Eddie Murray
July '91.......................6.00
July '94.....................30.00
July '97...................150.00

Matt Nokes
July '91.......................6.00
July '94.....................15.00
July '97.....................15.00

Paul O'Neill (R)
July '91.......................6.00
July '94.....................20.00
July '97.....................30.00

Jose Oquendo (R)
July '91.......................6.00
July '94.....................10.00
July '97.....................10.00

Gary Pettis
July '91.....................40.00
July '94.....................20.00
July '97.....................20.00

Kirby Puckett
July '91.......................6.00
July '94.....................30.00
July '97.....................40.00

Willie Randolph
July '91 ....6.00
July '94 ....16.00
July '97 ....14.00

Jody Reed (R)
July '91 ....6.00
July '94 ....15.00
July '97 ....15.00

Rick Reuschel
July '91 ....6.00
July '94 ....12.00
July '97 ....12.00

Dave Righetti
July '91 ....6.00
July '94 ....10.00
July '97 ....10.00

Cal Ripken Jr.
July '91 ....6.00
July '94 ....52.00
July '97 ....180.00

Nolan Ryan
July '91 ....25.00
July '94 ....36.00
July '97 ....54.00

Chris Sabo
July '91 ....6.00
July '94 ....10.00
July '97 ....12.00

Juan Samuel
July '91 ....18.00
July '94 ....14.00
July '97 ....12.00

Ryne Sandberg
July '91 ....15.00
July '94 ....30.00
July '97 ....35.00

Steve Sax
July '91 ....6.00
July '94 ....10.00
July '97 ....10.00

Mike Scott
July '91 ....6.00
July '94 ....10.00
July '97 ....10.00

Gary Sheffield (R)
July '91 ....20.00
July '94 ....28.00
July '97 ....35.00

John Smiley (R)
July '91 ....6.00
July '94 ....13.00
July '97 ....13.00

Ozzie Smith
July '91 ....6.00
July '94 ....20.00
July '97 ....40.00

Dave Stewart
July '91 ....6.00
July '94 ....15.00
July '97 ....15.00

Darryl Strawberry
(batting)
July '91 ....6.00
July '94 ....8.00
July '97 ....10.00

Darryl Strawberry
(fielding)
July '91 ....6.00
July '94 ....8.00
July '97 ....10.00

Rick Sutcliffe
July '91 ....6.00
July '94 ....14.00
July '97 ....14.00

Mickey Tettleton (R)
July '91 ....6.00
July '94 ....18.00
July '97 ....20.00

Alan Trammell
July '91 ....6.00
July '94 ....12.00
July '97 ....14.00

Andy Van Slyke
July '91 ....6.00
July '94 ....18.00
July '97 ....20.00

Frank Viola
July '91 ....18.00
July '94 ....15.00
July '97 ....12.00

Jerome Walton (R)
July '91 ....15.00
July '94 ....8.00
July '97 ....10.00

Lou Whitaker
July '91 ....6.00
July '94 ....14.00
July '97 ....15.00

Mitch Williams
July '91 ....15.00
July '94 ....13.00
July '97 ....15.00

Dave Winfield
July '91 ....6.00
July '94 ....28.00
July '97 ....45.00

Robin Yount
July '91 ....25.00
July '94 ....54.00
July '97 ....70.00

Jim Abbott (R)
July '91 ....22.00
July '94 ....25.00
July '97 ....20.00

Sandy Alomar Jr. (R)
July '91 ....25.00
July '94 ....14.00
July '97 ....20.00

Joe Carter
July '91 ....30.00
July '94 ....30.00
July '97 ....35.00

Ken Griffey Jr. (jumping)
July '91 ....35.00
July '94 ....50.00
July '97 ....120.00

Ben McDonald (R)
July '91 ....20.00
July '94 ....20.00
July '97 ....24.00

1991 BASEBALL

★ Set Price: $450.00 ★ Total Figures: 46 ★
★ Extended Set: $150.00 ★ Total Figures: 10 ★

This may be the weakest baseball set produced by Kenner to date—it's certainly the least popular with collectors. From top to bottom, 1991 Baseball is plagued with problems. Player selection—a lack of key veterans such as Cal Ripken Jr. coupled with a mediocre rookie crop—is downright poor. The collector coin included as a premium isn't very attractive.

And then there's the incredible overemphasis on Bo Jackson. Kenner issued this set at the height of Jackson's popularity (for evidence, see the case assortments listed on this page). Not only was Jackson double-packed in each of the AL cases, but in the two NL cases—one of the few times Kenner has ever issued a player in a case for a league in which he never played—and the Extended case (in his new White Sox uniform). Bo knew overproduction, and this, coupled with his subsequent fall from the limelight, weakened an already lackluster issue.

Along with the standard trading card included with each figure, '91 Baseball featured a steel collector coin that promptly rusted while many of the figures were still on the shelves. In order to rectify this problem, Kenner replaced the steel coin with an aluminum one during production of the Extended series. While all of the regular issues contain the steel coin, the Extended figures appear with either coin, and the easiest way to tell them apart (in the absence of rust) is with a magnet.

The Extended set offers collectors very little, with the Dave Justice rookie and the new Ken Griffey Jr. piece being the only figures of note. The Nolan Ryan figure is the same as his regular piece, but the back of his card was updated to include stats through the first half of the '91 season. There is a different UPC code on the back to distinguish between the regular and Extended piece.

The '91 Baseball set was issued primarily through the two different all-star cases, with only eight team cases being released. Lack of success in certain cities, as well as the burgeoning popularity of SLU-collecting nationwide, led Kenner

The back of the '91 Baseball package (above) includes an offer for a limited edition poster. Pictured at left is Doug Drabek.

to begin moving away from the concept of regional issues and to focus more on national distribution.

Case Assortments

AL CASE	NL CASE	TEAM CASES	Oakland Athletics
Jim Abbott	Delino DeShields	**Chicago Cubs**	Jose Canseco (5)
Sandy Alomar Jr.	Lenny Dykstra	Andre Dawson (3)	Rickey Henderson (4)
Jose Canseco (3)	Dwight Gooden	Shawon Dunston (3)	Mark McGwire (4)
Cecil Fielder (2)	Mark Grace	Mark Grace (4)	Dave Stewart (3)
Ken Griffey Jr. (2)	Bo Jackson (2)	Ryne Sandberg (6)	
Ozzie Guillen	Gregg Jefferies		**Pittsburgh Pirates**
Rickey Henderson	Barry Larkin	**Cincinnati Reds**	Barry Bonds (5)
Bo Jackson (2)	Ramon Martinez	Jack Armstrong (4)	Bobby Bonilla (5)
Don Mattingly	Kevin Mitchell	Tom Browning (3)	Doug Drabek (6)
Mark McGwire	Chris Sabo	Barry Larkin (3)	
Nolan Ryan	Ryne Sandberg	Chris Sabo (5)	**San Francisco Giants**
	Benito Santiago		Will Clark (5)
AL CASE		**Detroit Tigers**	Kevin Mitchell (5)
Sandy Alomar Jr.	**NL CASE**	Cecil Fielder (11)	Matt Williams (6)
Jose Canseco (2)	Will Clark (2)	Alan Trammell (5)	
Cecil Fielder (2)	Eric Davis		**EXTENDED**
Ken Griffey Jr. (2)	Delino DeShields	**New York Mets**	George Bell
Kelly Gruber	Lenny Dykstra	John Franco (3)	Vince Coleman
Rickey Henderson	Mark Grace	Gregg Jefferies (2)	Glenn Davis
Bo Jackson (2)	Bo Jackson (2)	Howard Johnson (2)	Ken Griffey Jr. (3)
Kevin Maas	Barry Larkin	Dave Magadan (2)	Ken Griffey Sr.
Don Mattingly	Kevin Maas	Darryl Strawberry (2)	Bo Jackson (2)
Mark McGwire	Kevin Mitchell	Frank Viola (3)	Dave Justice (2)
Kirby Puckett	Chris Sabo		Tim Raines
Nolan Ryan	Ryne Sandberg	**New York Yankees**	Nolan Ryan (2)
	Benito Santiago	Roberto Kelly (3)	Darryl Strawberry (2)
NL CASE	Darryl Strawberry	Kevin Maas (5)	
Will Clark (2)	Todd Zeile	Don Mattingly (5)	
Eric Davis		Steve Sax (3)	

Jim Abbott
July '91 ....6.00
July '94 ....15.00
July '97 ....15.00

Sandy Alomar Jr.
July '91 ....6.00
July '94 ....10.00
July '97 ....16.00

Jack Armstrong (R)
July '91 ....6.00
July '94 ....12.00
July '97 ....14.00

Barry Bonds
July '91 ....6.00
July '94 ....28.00
July '97 ....35.00

Bobby Bonilla
July '91 ....6.00
July '94 ....14.00
July '97 ....14.00

Tom Browning
July '91 ....6.00
July '94 ....10.00
July '97 ....10.00

Jose Canseco
July '91 ....6.00
July '94 ....10.00
July '97 ....14.00

Will Clark
July '91 ....6.00
July '94 ....12.00
July '97 ....16.00

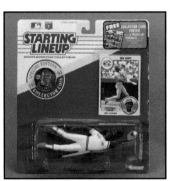

Eric Davis
July '91 ....6.00
July '94 ....8.00
July '97 ....8.00

Andre Dawson
July '91 ....6.00
July '94 ....16.00
July '97 ....14.00

Delino DeShields (R)
July '91 ....6.00
July '94 ....16.00
July '97 ....14.00

Doug Drabek
July '91 ....6.00
July '94 ....15.00
July '97 ....16.00

Shawon Dunston
July '91 ....6.00
July '94 ....12.00
July '97 ....12.00

Lenny Dykstra
July '91 ....6.00
July '94 ....15.00
July '97 ....16.00

Cecil Fielder (R)
July '91 ....10.00
July '94 ....11.00
July '97 ....18.00

John Franco
July '91 ....6.00
July '94 ....10.00
July '97 ....10.00

Dwight Gooden
July '91 ....6.00
July '94 ....10.00
July '97 ....9.00

Mark Grace
July '91 ....6.00
July '94 ....12.00
July '97 ....12.00

Ken Griffey Jr. (power)
July '91 ....20.00
July '94 ....16.00
July '97 ....25.00

Kelly Gruber (R)
July '91 ....6.00
July '94 ....10.00
July '97 ....10.00

Ozzie Guillen
July '91 ....6.00
July '94 ....15.00
July '97 ....12.00

Rickey Henderson
July '91 ....6.00
July '94 ....10.00
July '97 ....10.00

Bo Jackson (batting)
July '91 ....12.00
July '94 ....10.00
July '97 ....10.00

Gregg Jefferies
July '91 ....6.00
July '94 ....13.00
July '97 ....13.00

Howard Johnson
July '91 ....6.00
July '94 ....15.00
July '97 ....10.00

Roberto Kelly
July '91 ....6.00
July '94 ....14.00
July '97 ....10.00

Barry Larkin
July '91 ....6.00
July '94 ....10.00
July '97 ....20.00

Kevin Maas (R)
July '91 ....15.00
July '94 ....10.00
July '97 ....9.00

Dave Magadan (R)
July '91 ....6.00
July '94 ....9.00
July '97 ....9.00

Ramon Martinez
July '91 ....15.00
July '94 ....13.00
July '97 ....15.00

Don Mattingly
July '91 ....6.00
July '94 ....13.00
July '97 ....18.00

Ben McDonald
July '91 ....6.00
July '94 ....11.00
July '97 ....12.00

Mark McGwire
July '91 ....6.00
July '94 ....10.00
July '97 ....22.00

Kevin Mitchell
July '91 ....6.00
July '94 ....8.00
July '97 ....10.00

Kirby Puckett
July '91 ....6.00
July '94 ....20.00
July '97 ....25.00

Nolan Ryan
July '91 ....20.00
July '94 ....32.00
July '97 ....45.00

Chris Sabo
July '91 ....6.00
July '94 ....8.00
July '97 ....8.00

Ryne Sandberg
July '91 ....6.00
July '94 ....16.00
July '97 ....30.00

Benito Santiago
July '91 ....6.00
July '94 ....10.00
July '97 ....12.00

Steve Sax
July '91 ....6.00
July '94 ....13.00
July '97 ....12.00

Dave Stewart
July '91 ....6.00
July '94 ....13.00
July '97 ....13.00

Darryl Strawberry
July '91 ....10.00
July '94 ....10.00
July '97 ....10.00

Alan Trammell
July '91 ....6.00
July '94 ....15.00
July '97 ....16.00

Frank Viola
July '91 ....6.00
July '94 ....11.00
July '97 ....11.00

Matt Williams (R)
July '91 ....6.00
July '94 ....25.00
July '97 ....35.00

Todd Zeile (R)
July '91 ....15.00
July '94 ....20.00
July '97 ....15.00

George Bell
July '91 ....—
July '94 ....10.00
July '97 ....10.00

Vince Coleman
July '91 ....—
July '94 ....8.00
July '97 ....10.00

Glenn Davis
July '91 ....—
July '94 ....10.00
July '97 ....10.00

Ken Griffey Jr. (running)
July '91 ....—
July '94 ....16.00
July '97 ....35.00

Ken Griffey Sr.
July '91 ....—
July '94 ....16.00
July '97 ....20.00

Bo Jackson (diving)
July '91 ....—
July '94 ....16.00
July '97 ....18.00

Dave Justice
July '91 ....—
July '94 ....26.00
July '97 ....25.00

Tim Raines
July '91 ....—
July '94 ....13.00
July '97 ....13.00

Nolan Ryan
July '91 ....—
July '94 ....32.00
July '97 ....45.00

Darryl Strawberry
July '91 ....—
July '94 ....10.00
July '97 ....10.00

1992 BASEBALL

★ Set Price: $500.00 ★ Total Figures: 37 ★
★ Extended Set: $150.00 ★ Total Figures: 9 ★

Because baseball has traditionally been the most popular sport in terms of collectibles, Kenner produces considerably more baseball figures than those of any other sport. Multiple case assortments, not to mention the number of players included in each baseball issue, can be overwhelming. In fact, the sheer size of some of these sets has caused collectors to lose interest.

Kenner's '92 Baseball release is a good example of this. Unlike the mediocre '91 series, this is a solid set that has been overlooked in the hobby. While the idea of putting together this 37-figure regular set and nine-figure Extended series may seem expensive and time-consuming, it can be both fun and rewarding. And since most collectors show little interest in this issue, many figures can be bought for below book price.

Among the attractions in '92 Baseball is a great selection of rookie pieces. "The Big Hurt," Frank Thomas, is one of the premier first basemen in the game today. Then there's Tom Glavine, who has been one of

the most consistent pitchers of the '90s, winning more games since 1991 than any other pitcher. And don't forget 1996 American League MVP Juan Gonzalez, All-Star Craig Biggio, and slugger Matt Williams. Kenner complements these worthy rookies with the return of Cal Ripken Jr. and the inclusion of two poses for Ken Griffey Jr.

After Ripken broke Lou Gehrig's consecutive game streak, there was a run on Ripken figures that continues today. This Ripken piece has doubled since just months before he broke the record. If Griffey approaches Roger Maris' home run record, look for a similar run on Griffey figures by collectors.

The Extended series offers another Thomas rookie figure, produced in much smaller quantities than the regular Thomas. The only other rookie is pitcher Steve Avery, while Bret Saberhagen and Danny Tartabull are the shortprints. Like the regular figures, many of these pieces can be purchased for less than

The back of the '92 Baseball package (above) advertises the new Baseball Headline Collection. Pictured at left is Will Clark in the "jumping/fielding" pose.

book price.

The extended set also includes a figure of Tom Seaver, produced in honor of the pitcher's induction into the Hall of Fame (HOF). After the lackluster performance of the '89 Baseball Greats set, Kenner was reluctant to produce a complete series of former baseball players, choosing instead to feature recent HOF inductees in its regular sets. The popularity of the Seaver—and subsequent—HOF pieces ultimately led to the production of the first Cooperstown set in 1994.

Case Assortments

AL CASE		Bo Jackson (2)	Dave Justice
Ken Griffey Jr. (2)	Scott Erickson	Howard Johnson	Darryl Strawberry
Juan Gonzalez (2)	Cecil Fielder	Ramon Martinez (2)	
Rickey Henderson	Chuck Finley	Fred McGriff	**EXTENDED**
Bo Jackson	Ken Griffey Jr. (2)	Chris Sabo	Steve Avery (2)
(bat in hand)	Dave Henderson	Ryne Sandberg	Bobby Bonilla (2)
Kevin Maas (2)	Rickey Henderson	Matt Williams	Eric Davis (2)
Nolan Ryan (3)	Bo Jackson		Kirby Puckett (2)
Frank Thomas (3)	Brian McRae	**NL CASE**	Bret Saberhagen (1)
Ruben Sierra (2)	Cal Ripken Jr.	Craig Biggio	Tom Seaver (2)
	Nolan Ryan	Barry Bonds	Danny Tartabull (1)
AL CASE	Frank Thomas	Ivan Calderon	Frank Thomas (2)
Roberto Alomar		Will Clark	Todd Van Poppel (2)
Albert Belle	**NL CASE**	Tom Glavine	
Jose Canseco	George Bell	Tony Gwynn	
Roger Clemens	Rob Dibble	Felix Jose	
	Ken Griffey Jr. (5)		

Roberto Alomar
July '93 .... 15.00
July '95 .... 16.00
July '97 .... 25.00

George Bell
July '93 ....9.00
July '95 ....8.00
July '97 ....8.00

Albert Belle (R)
July '93 ....10.00
July '95 ....22.00
July '97 ....50.00

Craig Biggio (R)
July '93 ....10.00
July '95 ....10.00
July '97 ....12.00

Barry Bonds
July '93 ....17.00
July '95 ....25.00
July '97 ....25.00

Ivan Calderon
July '93 ....8.00
July '95 ....8.00
July '97 ....8.00

Jose Canseco
July '93 ....10.00
July '95 ....12.00
July '97 ....12.00

Will Clark
July '93 ....12.00
July '95 ....15.00
July '97 ....15.00

Roger Clemens
July '93 ....14.00
July '95 ....15.00
July '97 ....15.00

Rob Dibble
July '93 ....8.00
July '95 ....8.00
July '97 ....8.00

Scott Erickson (R)
July '93 ....9.00
July '95 ....8.00
July '97 ....8.00

Cecil Fielder
July '93 ....10.00
July '95 ....12.00
July '97 ....10.00

Chuck Finley (R)
July '93 ....8.00
July '95 ....8.00
July '97 ....8.00

Tom Glavine (R)
July '93 ....20.00
July '95 ....24.00
July '97 ....30.00

Juan Gonzalez (R)
July '93 ....20.00
July '95 ....28.00
July '97 ....40.00

Ken Griffey Jr. (bat in hand)
July '93 ....10.00
July '95 ....22.00
July '97 ....30.00

Ken Griffey Jr. (swinging)
July '93 ....12.00
July '95 ....24.00
July '97 ....30.00

Tony Gwynn
July '93 ....10.00
July '95 ....18.00
July '97 ....25.00

Dave Henderson
July '93 ....7.00
July '95 ....7.00
July '97 ....7.00

Rickey Henderson
July '93 ....8.00
July '95 ....10.00
July '97 ....10.00

Bo Jackson (running)
July '93 ....8.00
July '95 ....9.00
July '97 ....9.00

Bo Jackson (bat in hand)
July '93 ....8.00
July '95 ....12.00
July '97 ....10.00

Howard Johnson
July '93 ....10.00
July '95 ....10.00
July '97 ....10.00

Felix Jose (R)
July '93 ....13.00
July '95 ....12.00
July '97 ....12.00

Dave Justice
July '93 ....10.00
July '95 ....16.00
July '97 ....14.00

Kevin Maas
July '93 ....9.00
July '95 ....8.00
July '97 ....8.00

Ramon Martinez
July '93 ....8.00
July '95 ....8.00
July '97 ....8.00

Fred McGriff
July '93 ....9.00
July '95 ....15.00
July '97 ....20.00

Brian McRae (R)
July '93 ....9.00
July '95 ....9.00
July '97 ....9.00

Cal Ripken Jr.
July '93 ....28.00
July '95 ....38.00
July '97 ....75.00

Nolan Ryan
July '93 ....12.00
July '95 ....27.00
July '97 ....30.00

Chris Sabo
July '93 ....10.00
July '95 ....8.00
July '97 ....8.00

Ryne Sandberg
July '93 ....12.00
July '95 ....16.00
July '97 ....18.00

Ruben Sierra
July '93 ....12.00
July '95 ....14.00
July '97 ....14.00

Darryl Strawberry
July '93 ....9.00
July '95 ....10.00
July '97 ....10.00

Frank Thomas (fielding)
July '93 ....25.00
July '95 ....50.00
July '97 ....45.00

Matt Williams (R)
July '93 ....8.00
July '95 ....16.00
July '97 ....20.00

Steve Avery (R)
July '93 ....20.00
July '95 ....25.00
July '97 ....20.00

Bobby Bonilla
July '93 ....8.00
July '95 ....10.00
July '97 ....10.00

Eric Davis
July '93 ....10.00
July '95 ....8.00
July '97 ....8.00

Kirby Puckett
July '93 ....15.00
July '95 ....22.00
July '97 ....30.00

Bret Saberhagen
July '93 ....8.00
July '95 ....8.00
July '97 ....8.00

Tom Seaver
July '93 ....20.00
July '95 ....36.00
July '97 ....35.00

Danny Tartabull
July '93 ....10.00
July '95 ....7.00
July '97 ....10.00

Frank Thomas (batting)
July '93 ....22.00
July '95 ....50.00
July '97 ....65.00

Todd Van Poppel
July '93 ....18.00
July '95 ....15.00
July '97 ....12.00

1993 BASEBALL

★ **Set Price: $400.00** ★ **Total Figures: 38** ★
★ **Extended Set: $350.00** ★ **Total Figures: 7** ★

So far, '93 Baseball has received only modest interest from collectors. Like many of the other baseball sets, this one contains a larger number of figures than Kenner's corresponding issues for other sports. The size of the set—and a general decline in baseball interest following the strike of 1994—has kept demand for this series relatively low. But with many collectors returning to baseball, the '93 series could be a sleeper set.

After an unsuccessful flirtation with such premiums as collector coins and posters, Kenner returned to its traditional scheme of including only cards with its figures. The 1993 Baseball set offers two cards with each piece, a definite improvement over the previous two baseball issues.

Plus, this set has some great rookies. Players like Jeff Bagwell, Mike Mussina, John Smoltz, and Larry Walker—who were virtually ignored several years ago—are beginning to gain popularity in the hobby. Only after Smoltz was closing in on his first Cy Young award did collectors start to take notice. And players like Walker and Kevin Brown—who tossed a no-hitter in June 1997—are worth keeping an eye on.

While the regular set hasn't seen much fanfare, the Extended set is considered the best Kenner has ever issued. The Nolan Ryan retirement figure was one of baseball's most highly anticipated pieces at the time, trading for around $50 when it first hit store shelves.

At the time of the Extended set's release, the only other player drawing any collector interest was Carlton Fisk. And in 1993, Greg Maddux already owned one Cy Young award and had another on the way, but he was almost completely overlooked in the Kenner hobby. Three Cy Youngs later, Maddux has become the hottest figure in the set—and one of the most expensive Extended pieces in the hobby. Talk about a sleeper piece!

Because of constant production changes, the '93 Baseball package back (above) is the last one to provide a checklist of players.

Case Assortments

AL CASE .03	AL CASE .04
Roberto Alomar	Roberto Alomar
Roger Clemens	Carlos Baerga
Travis Fryman	Kevin Brown
Ken Griffey Jr. (2)	Jose Canseco (2)
Juan Guzman	Travis Fryman
Roberto Kelly	Juan Gonzalez
Shane Mack	Ken Griffey Jr. (2)
Jack McDowell	Jack McDowell
Mark McGwire	Mark McGwire
Mike Mussina	Kirby Puckett
Dean Palmer	Cal Ripken Jr.
Cal Ripken Jr.	Nolan Ryan
Nolan Ryan	Frank Thomas
Frank Thomas	Robin Ventura
Robin Ventura	
	NL CASE .03
	Barry Bonds (2)

Will Clark	Ken Griffey Jr.
Tom Glavine	Marquis Grissom
Ken Griffey Jr.	Ray Lankford (2)
Marquis Grissom	Fred McGriff (2)
Eric Karros	Terry Pendleton (2)
John Kruk	Bip Roberts
Ray Lankford	John Smoltz (2)
Barry Larkin (2)	
Terry Pendleton	**EXTENDED .02**
Ryne Sandberg	Barry Bonds (2)
Gary Sheffield	Carlton Fisk (2)
Andy Van Slyke	Bo Jackson (2)
Larry Walker	Greg Maddux (2)
	David Nied (2)
NL CASE .04	Nolan Ryan (4)
Jeff Bagwell	Benito Santiago (2)
David Cone (2)	
Tom Glavine (2)	

Roberto Alomar

July '93	6.00
July '95	9.00
July '97	15.00

Carlos Baerga (R)

July '93	12.00
July '95	22.00
July '97	15.00

Jeff Bagwell (R)

July '93	10.00
July '95	40.00
July '97	50.00

Barry Bonds

July '93	8.00
July '95	20.00
July '97	20.00

Kevin Brown (R)
July '93 ....6.00
July '95 ....6.00
July '97 ....15.00

Jose Canseco
July '93 ....6.00
July '95 ....10.00
July '97 ....12.00

Will Clark
July '93 ....7.00
July '95 ....8.00
July '97 ....8.00

Roger Clemens
July '93 ....8.00
July '95 ....10.00
July '97 ....12.00

David Cone
July '93 ....6.00
July '95 ....8.00
July '97 ....10.00

Travis Fryman (R)
July '93 ....6.00
July '95 ....8.00
July '97 ....8.00

Tom Glavine
July '93 ....7.00
July '95 ....14.00
July '97 ....24.00

Juan Gonzalez
July '93 ....8.00
July '95 ....15.00
July '97 ....20.00

Ken Griffey Jr.
July '93 ....6.00
July '95 ....20.00
July '97 ....24.00

Marquis Grissom (R)
July '93 ....6.00
July '95 ....7.00
July '97 ....10.00

Juan Guzman
July '93 ....8.00
July '95 ....8.00
July '97 ....8.00

Eric Karros (R)
July '93 ....9.00
July '95 ....12.00
July '97 ....16.00

Roberto Kelly
July '93 ....6.00
July '95 ....6.00
July '97 ....6.00

John Kruk
July '93 ....6.00
July '95 ....12.00
July '97 ....12.00

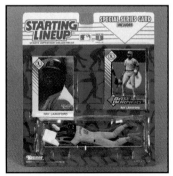

Ray Lankford (R)
July '93 ....6.00
July '95 ....6.00
July '97 ....10.00

Barry Larkin
July '93 ....6.00
July '95 ....6.00
July '97 ....15.00

Shane Mack (R)
July '93 ....6.00
July '95 ....6.00
July '97 ....6.00

Jack McDowell (R)
July '93 ....6.00
July '95 ....9.00
July '97 ....9.00

Fred McGriff
July '93 ....6.00
July '95 ....14.00
July '97 ....15.00

Mark McGwire
July '93 ....6.00
July '95 ....6.00
July '97 ....15.00

Mike Mussina (R)
July '93 ....10.00
July '95 ....22.00
July '97 ....24.00

Dean Palmer (R)
July '93 ....7.00
July '95 ....9.00
July '97 ....9.00

Terry Pendleton
July '93 ....6.00
July '95 ....6.00
July '97 ....6.00

Kirby Puckett
July '93 ....7.00
July '95 ....15.00
July '97 ....20.00

Cal Ripken Jr.
July '93 ....10.00
July '95 ....25.00
July '97 ....40.00

Bip Roberts (R)
July '93 ....6.00
July '95 ....9.00
July '97 ....9.00

Nolan Ryan
July '93 ....10.00
July '95 ....30.00
July '97 ....35.00

Ryne Sandberg
July '93 ....6.00
July '95 ....12.00
July '97 ....15.00

Gary Sheffield
July '93 ....9.00
July '95 ....9.00
July '97 ....10.00

John Smoltz (R)
July '93 ....10.00
July '95 ....10.00
July '97 ....50.00

Frank Thomas
July '93 ....8.00
July '95 ....18.00
July '97 ....20.00

Andy Van Slyke
July '93 ....6.00
July '95 ....6.00
July '97 ....6.00

Robin Ventura (R)
July '93 ....7.00
July '95 ....10.00
July '97 ....15.00

Larry Walker (R)
July '93 ....7.00
July '95 ....8.00
July '97 ....18.00

Barry Bonds
July '93 ....—
July '95 ....22.00
July '97 ....24.00

Carlton Fisk
July '93 ....—
July '95 ....20.00
July '97 ....35.00

Bo Jackson
July '93 ....—
July '95 ....10.00
July '97 ....10.00

Greg Maddux
July '93 ....—
July '95 ....36.00
July '97 ....160.00

David Nied (R)
July '93 ....—
July '95 ....16.00
July '97 ....15.00

Nolan Ryan (retirement)
July '93 ....—
July '95 ....100.00
July '97 ....160.00

Benito Santiago
July '93 ....—
July '95 ....10.00
July '97 ....10.00

1994 BASEBALL

★ **Set Price: $450.00** ★ **Total Figures: 57** ★
★ **Extended Set: $140.00** ★ **Total Figures: 8** ★

The 1994 Baseball series has received little collector attention, but not because of any flaws in the set itself. The series couldn't have been released under any worse conditions: Major League Baseball's sticky labor negotiations and eventual strike. Practically every day during the shortened season of 1994, fans and collectors were reading reports detailing the collapse of negotiations between the owners and players. Shortly after the All-Star break, talks broke down completely, and in August, the worst strike in baseball history began. But even before the strike, baseball was waning in the hobby as the explosion of the NBA drew collector attention from the National Pastime.

Now, in the post-strike era—as the troubled sport struggles to regain fan and collector interest—series like '94 Baseball are beginning to get a second look. In fact, this set does have plenty of potential. Almost half of the players are Starting Lineup rookies. The game's top two catchers—Mike Piazza of the Los Angeles Dodgers and Ivan Rodriguez of the Texas Rangers—show up in their very first pieces. The set also includes rookie figures of All-Star second baseman Chuck Knoblauch of the Minnesota Twins, first baseman Mo Vaughn of the Boston Red Sox, and pitching aces Randy Johnson, Kevin Appier, and Alex Fernandez. Most of these rookies can be obtained for less than $20, a bargain considering their talent.

Kenner again produced the Extended set in much smaller quantities than the regular series. Kenny Lofton—one of the best leadoff hitters in the game today—steals the show, just as

The '94 Baseball back (above) offers the first Starting Lineup Collector Club piece—Shaquille O'Neal. Pictured at left is Jay Bell.

he does on the field. Packed two per case (as all of the '94 Extended figures were), the Lofton piece is relatively hard to find. And while most of the other players draw only modest interest, the rookie piece of Rafael Palmeiro and the second figure of Juan Gonzalez still command attention.

Baseball's recent efforts toward improving fan relations and recovering from its 1994 setbacks are a step in the right direction and the future appears to be stable—for now. If baseball's health continues to improve, look for quality issues like the '94 series to become increasingly popular with collectors.

Case Assortments

AL CASE .09	Ken Griffey Jr.	Frank Thomas	Tommy Greene
Wade Boggs	Brian Harper	Greg Vaughn	Brian Harvey
Joe Carter	Mark Langston		Dave Justice (2)
Roger Clemens	Don Mattingly	**NL CASE .01**	Eric Karros
David Cone	Mike Mussina	Steve Avery (2)	Darryl Kile
Ken Griffey Jr.	John Olerud	Jeff Bagwell	Mike Piazza
Randy Johnson	Tim Salmon	Barry Bonds (2)	Jose Rijo
Chuck Knoblauch	Frank Thomas	John Burkett	Ryne Sandberg
Paul Molitor	Mo Vaughn	Darren Daulton	Curt Schilling
Mike Mussina		Delino DeShields	Matt Williams
Cal Ripken Jr.	**AL CASE .11**	Andres Galarraga	
Ivan Rodriguez	Kevin Appier	Charlie Hayes	**EXTENDED**
Tim Salmon	Carlos Baerga	Dave Hollins	Steve Carlton (2)
Frank Thomas (2)	Albert Belle	Gregg Jefferies	Will Clark (2)
Robin Ventura	Wade Boggs	Orlando Merced	Lenny Dykstra (2)
Dave Winfield	Roger Clemens	Mike Piazza	Juan Gonzalez (2)
	Chad Curtis	Gary Sheffield	Kenny Lofton (2)
AL CASE .10	Ken Griffey Jr.	Robby Thompson	Fred McGriff (2)
Kevin Appier	Chris Hoiles		Rafael Palmeiro (2)
Carlos Baerga	Randy Johnson	**NL CASE .03**	Gary Sheffield (2)
Albert Belle	Jimmy Key	Jeff Bagwell	
Joe Carter	John Olerud	Derek Bell	
Roger Clemens	Tony Phillips	Jay Bell	
Alex Fernandez	Cal Ripken Jr.	Barry Bonds	
Cecil Fielder	J.T. Snow	Mark Grace	

Kevin Appier (R)
July '95 ....7.00
July '96 ....7.00
July '97 ....8.00

Steve Avery
July '95 ....8.00
July '96 ....8.00
July '97 ....10.00

Carlos Baerga
July '95 ....10.00
July '96 ....12.00
July '97 ....10.00

Jeff Bagwell
July '95 ....18.00
July '96 ....18.00
July '97 ....20.00

Derek Bell (R)
July '95 ....7.00
July '96 ....10.00
July '97 ....10.00

Jay Bell (R)
July '95 ....7.00
July '96 ....7.00
July '97 ....10.00

Albert Belle
July '95 ....10.00
July '96 ....12.00
July '97 ....12.00

Wade Boggs
July '95 ....12.00
July '96 ....12.00
July '97 ....10.00

Barry Bonds
July '95 ....10.00
July '96 ....10.00
July '97 ....10.00

John Burkett (R)
July '95 ....7.00
July '96 ....7.00
July '97 ....7.00

Joe Carter
July '95 ....7.00
July '96 ....7.00
July '97 ....7.00

Roger Clemens
July '95 ....10.00
July '96 ....10.00
July '97 ....10.00

David Cone
July '95 ....7.00
July '96 ....10.00
July '97 ....10.00

Chad Curtis (R)
July '95 ....13.00
July '96 ....12.00
July '97 ....10.00

Darren Daulton (R)
July '95 ....13.00
July '96 ....13.00
July '97 ....10.00

Delino DeShields
July '95 ....7.00
July '96 ....7.00
July '97 ....8.00

Alex Fernandez (R)
July '95 ....10.00
July '96 ....10.00
July '97 ....14.00

Cecil Fielder
July '95 ....7.00
July '96 ....7.00
July '97 ....8.00

Andres Galarraga
July '95 ....10.00
July '96 ....10.00
July '97 ....10.00

Mark Grace
July '95 ....7.00
July '96 ....7.00
July '97 ....8.00

Tommy Greene (R)
July '95 ....8.00
July '96 ....8.00
July '97 ....8.00

Ken Griffey Jr.
July '95 ....20.00
July '96 ....20.00
July '97 ....24.00

Brian Harper (R)
July '95 ....8.00
July '96 ....8.00
July '97 ....8.00

Brian Harvey (R)
July '95 ....14.00
July '96 ....12.00
July '97 ....8.00

Charlie Hayes (R)
July '95 ....8.00
July '96 ....8.00
July '97 ....8.00

Chris Hoiles (R)
July '95 ....16.00
July '96 ....16.00
July '97 ....12.00

Dave Hollins (R)
July '95 ....8.00
July '96 ....8.00
July '97 ....8.00

Gregg Jefferies
July '95 ....7.00
July '96 ....7.00
July '97 ....7.00

Randy Johnson (R)
July '95 ....8.00
July '96 ....20.00
July '97 ....28.00

Dave Justice
July '95 ....8.00
July '96 ....10.00
July '97 ....10.00

Eric Karros
July '95 ....8.00
July '96 ....10.00
July '97 ....8.00

Jimmy Key (R)
July '95....................15.00
July '96....................14.00
July '97 ....12.00

Darryl Kile (R)
July '95 ....8.00
July '96 ....8.00
July '97 ....8.00

Chuck Knoblauch (R)

July '95 ....8.00
July '96 ....8.00
July '97 ....15.00

Mark Langston

July '95 ....8.00
July '96 ....8.00
July '97 ....8.00

Don Mattingly

July '95 ....15.00
July '96 ....15.00
July '97 ....15.00

Orlando Merced (R)

July '95 ....8.00
July '96 ....8.00
July '97 ....8.00

Paul Molitor

July '95 ....12.00
July '96 ....12.00
July '97 ....10.00

Mike Mussina

July '95 ....12.00
July '96 ....12.00
July '97 ....10.00

John Olerud (R)

July '95 ....25.00
July '96 ....15.00
July '97 ....12.00

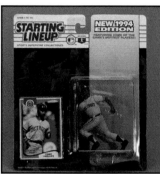

Tony Phillips (R)

July '95 ....7.00
July '96 ....7.00
July '97 ....7.00

Mike Piazza (R)

July '95 ....42.00
July '96 ....45.00
July '97 ....55.00

Jose Rijo (R)

July '95 ....8.00
July '96 ....8.00
July '97 ....8.00

Cal Ripken Jr.

July '95 ....20.00
July '96 ....35.00
July '97 ....40.00

Ivan Rodriguez (R)

July '95 ....15.00
July '96 ....15.00
July '97 ....12.00

Tim Salmon (R)

July '95 ....20.00
July '96 ....16.00
July '97 ....15.00

Ryne Sandberg

July '95 ....16.00
July '96 ....16.00
July '97 ....20.00

Curt Schilling (R)

July '95 ....8.00
July '96 ....8.00
July '97 ....8.00

Gary Sheffield

July '95 ....7.00
July '96 ....7.00
July '97 ....7.00

J.T. Snow (R)
July '95 ....16.00
July '96 ....14.00
July '97 ....16.00

Frank Thomas
July '95 ....16.00
July '96 ....16.00
July '97 ....18.00

Robby Thompson
July '95 ....7.00
July '96 ....7.00
July '97 ....7.00

Greg Vaughn (R)
July '95 ....8.00
July '96 ....8.00
July '97 ....10.00

Mo Vaughn (R)
July '95 ....14.00
July '96 ....15.00
July '97 ....20.00

Robin Ventura
July '95 ....7.00
July '96 ....7.00
July '97 ....7.00

Matt Williams
July '95 ....10.00
July '96 ....10.00
July '97 ....10.00

Dave Winfield
July '95 ....14.00
July '96 ....14.00
July '97 ....14.00

Steve Carlton
July '95 ....32.00
July '96 ....32.00
July '97 ....30.00

Will Clark
July '95 ....15.00
July '96 ....15.00
July '97 ....12.00

Lenny Dykstra
July '95 ....13.00
July '96 ....13.00
July '97 ....12.00

Juan Gonzalez
July '95 ....16.00
July '96 ....16.00
July '97 ....25.00

Kenny Lofton (R)
July '95 ....25.00
July '96 ....32.00
July '97 ....60.00

Fred McGriff
July '95 ....12.00
July '96 ....12.00
July '97 ....15.00

Rafael Palmeiro (R)
July '95 ....15.00
July '96 ....15.00
July '97 ....20.00

Gary Sheffield (power)
July '95 ....12.00
July '96 ....12.00
July '97 ....12.00

1995 BASEBALL

★ Set Price: $400.00 ★ Total Figures: 48 ★

★ Extended Set: $300.00 ★ Total Figures: 9 ★

This was an up-and-down year for both baseball and Starting Lineup figures. The Spring of 1995 opened with baseball's strike in its ninth month and the owners threatening to field teams of "replacement" players. When the strike was finally settled, baseball had to shorten its season, and many disgruntled fans opted to give up on the game altogether.

With fan support of the National Pastime at an all-time low, Kenner's release of the regular '95 series went almost entirely unnoticed. The introduction of a new catcher's throwing pose for the figures of Mike Piazza, Darren Daulton, Javy Lopez, and Rick Wilkins couldn't save this set, which had a decent rookie selection and most of the key veterans. Fans and collectors alike simply decided to spend their money on other pursuits.

Then Cal Ripken Jr. played in his 2,131st consecutive game, breaking Lou Gehrig's record. So while Kenner's regular '95 set received only mild attention, the Extended set—released later in the season—became hot. And even though fan support for the sport was still low, Ripken's pursuit of Gehrig's "unbreakable" record began bringing people back to baseball. The highlight of the Extended set, of course, is the Ripken "Streak" piece. Kenner depicts Ripken wearing a Baltimore Orioles uniform from 1982—the year the streak began—and the package features a sticker with May 30, 1982—the day it all started.

While Ripken-mania fueled the initial success of the 1995 Extended set, its other strengths have kept it at the top of many want lists. In fact, two years after this set hit store shelves, the hype surrounding the Ripken piece has cooled and the Alex Rodriguez rookie piece is sizzling. The series also features a rookie figure of Manny Ramirez, the second-year piece of Kenny Lofton, and another pose for Piazza. The excellent assortment of popular, talented players has kept this set's secondary-market value strong. The 1995 Ex-tended rivals the 1993 issue as the best Extended set Kenner has released.

The '95 Baseball package back shows only a handful of the actual pieces released. At left is Vinny Castilla in the new "sliding" pose.

Case Assortments

AL CASE .06
- Carlos Baerga
- Albert Belle
- Jay Buhner
- Jose Canseco
- Joe Carter
- Will Clark
- Cecil Fielder
- Ken Griffey Jr.
- Brian McRae
- Troy Neel
- Paul O'Neill
- Cal Ripken Jr. (2)
- Tim Salmon
- Frank Thomas
- Mo Vaughn

AL CASE .07
- Carlos Baerga
- Geronimo Berroa
- Joe Carter
- Will Clark
- Roger Clemens
- Carlos Delgado
- Juan Gonzalez
- Ken Griffey Jr.
- Bob Hamelin
- Randy Johnson
- Mike Mussina
- Paul O'Neill
- Cal Ripken Jr.
- Tim Salmon
- Frank Thomas
- Mo Vaughn

AL CASE .08
- Jim Abbott
- Albert Belle
- Scott Cooper
- John Franco
- Juan Gonzalez
- Jeffrey Hammonds
- Randy Johnson
- Chuck Knoblauch
- Paul Molitor
- Mike Mussina
- Dave Nilsson
- John Olerud
- Kirby Puckett (2)
- Mickey Tettleton
- Frank Thomas

NL CASE .04
- Moises Alou
- Jeff Bagwell
- Barry Bonds
- Andujar Cedeno
- Darren Daulton
- Cliff Floyd
- Jeff Kent
- Ryan Klesko
- John Kruk
- Ray Lankford
- Al Martin
- Raul Mondesi
- Mike Piazza
- Reggie Sanders
- Sammy Sosa
- Andy Van Slyke

NL CASE .05
- Moises Alou
- Jeff Bagwell
- Dante Bichette
- Barry Bonds
- Chuck Carr
- Jeff Conine
- Tony Gwynn
- Jeff King
- John Kruk
- Barry Larkin
- Javy Lopez
- Mike Piazza
- Deion Sanders
- Sammy Sosa
- Rick Wilkins
- Matt Williams

EXTENDED .00
- Jose Canseco (2)
- Rusty Greer
- Kenny Lofton
- Tom Pagnozzi
- Mike Piazza
- Manny Ramirez
- Cal Ripken Jr. (3)
- Alex Rodriguez (2)
- Mike Schmidt (2)

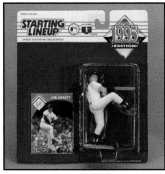

Jim Abbott

July '95 ....12.00
July '96 ....12.00
July '97 ....10.00

Moises Alou (R)

July '95 ....16.00
July '96 ....12.00
July '97 ....12.00

Carlos Baerga

July '95 ....8.00
July '96 ....10.00
July '97 ....8.00

Jeff Bagwell

July '95 ....8.00
July '96 ....10.00
July '97 ....12.00

Albert Belle

July '95 ....8.00
July '96 ....10.00
July '97 ....10.00

Geronimo Berroa (R)

July '95 ....15.00
July '96 ....12.00
July '97 ....10.00

Dante Bichette (R)

July '95 ....13.00
July '96 ....16.00
July '97 ....16.00

Barry Bonds

July '95 ....10.00
July '96 ....10.00
July '97 ....12.00

Jay Buhner

July '95 ....15.00
July '96 ....16.00
July '97 ....16.00

Jose Canseco

July '95 ....10.00
July '96 ....10.00
July '97 ....10.00

Chuck Carr (R)

July '95 ....14.00
July '96 ....14.00
July '97 ....10.00

Joe Carter

July '95 ....8.00
July '96 ....8.00
July '97 ....8.00

Andujar Cedeno (R)

July '95 ....15.00
July '96 ....15.00
July '97 ....10.00

Will Clark

July '95 ....8.00
July '96 ....8.00
July '97 ....8.00

Roger Clemens

July '95 ....10.00
July '96 ....10.00
July '97 ....10.00

Jeff Conine (R)

July '95 ....15.00
July '96 ....10.00
July '97 ....10.00

Scott Cooper (R)
July '95 ....15.00
July '96 ....15.00
July '97 ....10.00

Darren Daulton
July '95 ....8.00
July '96 ....10.00
July '97 ....10.00

Carlos Delgado (R)
July '95 ....20.00
July '96 ....15.00
July '97 ....12.00

Cecil Fielder
July '95 ....8.00
July '96 ....8.00
July '97 ....8.00

Cliff Floyd (R)
July '95 ....20.00
July '96 ....15.00
July '97 ....10.00

Julio Franco
July '95 ....8.00
July '96 ....8.00
July '97 ....8.00

Juan Gonzalez
July '95 ....12.00
July '96 ....12.00
July '97 ....10.00

Ken Griffey Jr.
July '95 ....15.00
July '96 ....18.00
July '97 ....28.00

Tony Gwynn
July '95 ....8.00
July '96 ....8.00
July '97 ....14.00

Bob Hamelin (R)
July '95 ....15.00
July '96 ....12.00
July '97 ....10.00

Jeffrey Hammonds
July '95 ....15.00
July '96 ....15.00
July '97 ....12.00

Randy Johnson
July '95 ....15.00
July '96 ....15.00
July '97 ....15.00

Jeff Kent (R)
July '95 ....15.00
July '96 ....15.00
July '97 ....10.00

Jeff King (R)
July '95 ....13.00
July '96 ....13.00
July '97 ....10.00

Ryan Klesko (R)
July '95 ....16.00
July '96 ....20.00
July '97 ....45.00

Chuck Knoblauch
July '95 ....8.00
July '96 ....8.00
July '97 ....10.00

John Kruk
July '95 ....10.00
July '96 ....10.00
July '97 ....10.00

Ray Lankford
July '95 ....8.00
July '96 ....8.00
July '97 ....8.00

Barry Larkin
July '95 ....8.00
July '96 ....8.00
July '97 ....12.00

Javy Lopez (R)
July '95 ....20.00
July '96 ....24.00
July '97 ....40.00

Al Martin (R)
July '95 ....13.00
July '96 ....10.00
July '97 ....10.00

Brian McRae
July '95 ....8.00
July '96 ....8.00
July '97 ....8.00

Paul Molitor
July '95 ....8.00
July '96 ....8.00
July '97 ....8.00

Raul Mondesi (R)
July '95 ....25.00
July '96 ....32.00
July '97 ....32.00

Mike Mussina
July '95 ....8.00
July '96 ....8.00
July '97 ....8.00

Troy Neel (R)
July '95 ....13.00
July '96 ....10.00
July '97 ....10.00

Dave Nilsson (R)
July '95 ....15.00
July '96 ....10.00
July '97 ....10.00

John Olerud
July '95 ....8.00
July '96 ....8.00
July '97 ....8.00

Paul O'Neill
July '95 ....10.00
July '96 ....10.00
July '97 ....10.00

Mike Piazza
July '95 ....14.00
July '96 ....15.00
July '97 ....25.00

Kirby Puckett
July '95 ....10.00
July '96 ....10.00
July '97 ....10.00

Cal Ripken Jr.
July '95 ....15.00
July '96 ....32.00
July '97 ....40.00

Tim Salmon
July '95 ....8.00
July '96 ....10.00
July '97 ....10.00

Deion Sanders
July '95 ....8.00
July '96 ....8.00
July '97 ....8.00

Reggie Sanders (R)
July '95 ....8.00
July '96 ....10.00
July '97 ....10.00

Sammy Sosa (R)
July '95 ....12.00
July '96 ....12.00
July '97 ....15.00

Mickey Tettleton
July '95 ....8.00
July '96 ....8.00
July '97 ....8.00

Frank Thomas
July '95 ....10.00
July '96 ....10.00
July '97 ....12.00

Andy Van Slyke
July '95 ....10.00
July '96 ....10.00
July '97 ....10.00

Mo Vaughn
July '95 ....8.00
July '96 ....8.00
July '97 ....10.00

Rick Wilkins (R)
July '95 ....10.00
July '96 ....10.00
July '97 ....10.00

Matt Williams
July '95 ....8.00
July '96 ....8.00
July '97 ....10.00

Jose Canseco
July '95 ....—
July '96 ....16.00
July '97 ....10.00

Rusty Greer
July '95 ....—
July '96 ....15.00
July '97 ....10.00

Kenny Lofton
July '95 ....—
July '96 ....40.00
July '97 ....60.00

Tom Pagnozzi
July '95 ....—
July '96 ....15.00
July '97 ....10.00

Mike Piazza
July '95 ....—
July '96 ....25.00
July '97 ....30.00

Manny Ramirez
July '95 ....—
July '96 ....45.00
July '97 ....70.00

Cal Ripken Jr. (streak)
July '95 ....—
July '96 ....80.00
July '97 ....100.00

Alex Rodriguez
July '95 ....—
July '96 ....25.00
July '97 ....120.00

Mike Schmidt
July '95 ....—
July '96 ....16.00
July '97 ....15.00

1996 BASEBALL

★ **Set Price: $750.00** ★ **Total Figures: 56** ★
★ **Extended Set: $180.00** ★ **Total Figures: 16** ★

By the start of the 1996 season, Major League Baseball was beginning to return to normal. With a labor agreement between the owners and players in place and their disputes behind them for the time being, the hard part began—trying to bring back the many fans and collectors who lost interest because of the strike.

Kenner hoped that the popularity of the previous year's Extended set would fuel collector interest in its 1996 issues. It got off to a great start by producing the highly anticipated rookie pieces of Chipper Jones, Hideo Nomo, and Derek Jeter.

It's no secret that Jones is the hot rookie in the set. He was a one-pack in the National League .05 case, which was the last case to be released. The piece quickly rose to a secondary-market price of $100, and now trades regularly for around $150. If Jones continues to produce for the Atlanta Braves, this price could be a bargain.

Jeter, the promising young shortstop

for the New York Yankees, drew modest interest from collectors—until the Yankees won the World Series and he was voted AL Rookie of the Year. Almost overnight, his rookie piece went from $25 to $60; it now trades for around $100.

When the 1996 Kenner season first began, Nomo—the '95 NL Rookie of the Year—was receiving most of the attention from collectors. He appeared in two poses: one that depicts him in a Dodgers road uniform at the start of his wind-up, the other featuring the home jersey in the middle of his corkscrew delivery.

The three big rookies weren't the only players generating collector interest in '96 Baseball. Cal Ripken Jr. was also issued with two different poses, and for the first time Kenner used a different card with each pose. The "diving" Ripken included a fielding card, while the "sliding" piece card captured him running the bases. Kenner made several mistakes during the card insertion process, however, and both figures can be found with either card. Apparently, the error and cor-

Again, the baseball package (above) shows only a few of the figures that were actually released. At left is the hot rookie piece of Chipper Jones.

rect versions were produced in similar quantities; as a result, there's no significant price difference between them on the secondary market.

Four-time Cy Young Award winner Greg Maddux is the subject of another popular non-rookie piece in 1996 Baseball. Maddux, who hadn't been featured in a Starting Lineup figure since the '93 Extended set, had become one of the hottest players in the hobby. His two other pieces—'89 and '90—were beyond the price range of most collectors, leaving collectors who wanted a Maddux piece scrambling to get his '96 figure while it was still affordable.

Case Assortments

AL CASE .00	Ken Griffey Jr.	Jeff Manto	Sammy Sosa (2)	NL CASE .05	EXTENDED .00	EXTENDED .01
Albert Belle (2)	Ozzie Guillen	Edgar Martinez	Ryan Thompson	Craig Biggio (2)	Moises Alou	Moises Alou
Will Clark (2)	Mark McGwire	Eddie Murray	Larry Walker	Rico Brogna	Garret Anderson (2)	Carlos Baerga
Ken Griffey Jr. (2)	Eddie Murray (2)	Cal Ripken Jr. (2)	Matt Williams (2)	Vinny Castilla (2)	Carlos Baerga	Dante Bichette
Ozzie Guillen	Paul O'Neill	Ivan Rodriguez (2)		Shawon Dunston	Dante Bichette	Jeff Conine
Paul O'Neill (2)	Kirby Puckett	Jim Thome	**NL CASE .04**	Jim Eisenreich	Joe Carter	Chad Curtis
Kirby Puckett (2)	Cal Ripken Jr. (2)	John Valentin	Jeff Bagwell	Marquis Grissom	Jeff Conine	Juan Gonzalez
Cal Ripken Jr. (2)	Frank Thomas	Mo Vaughn	Barry Bonds (2)	Brian Hunter	Chad Curtis	Ken Griffey Jr. (2)
Terry Steinbach	Jim Thome		Lenny Dykstra	Chipper Jones	Ken Griffey Jr. (2)	Dave Justice
Frank Thomas (2)		**NL CASE .03**	Ron Gant (2)	Hideo Nomo (2)	Eric Karros	Eric Karros
	AL CASE .02	Jeff Bagwell	Brian Hunter	Deion Sanders (2)	Barry Larkin	Barry Larkin
AL CASE .01	David Cone	Ken Caminiti	Greg Maddux (2)	Ozzie Smith	Don Mattingly (2)	Don Mattingly (2)
Roberto Alomar	Marty Cordova	Wil Cordero (2)	Hideo Nomo (2)	Rondell White	Hal Morris	Denny Neagle (2)
Ricky Bones	Jim Edmonds	Charles Johnson (2)	Mike Piazza (2)		Rafael Palmeiro	Rafael Palmeiro
Marty Cordova	Gary Gaetti	Fred McGriff (2)	Ozzie Smith			
Jim Edmonds (2)	Derek Jeter (2)	Raul Mondesi (2)	Larry Walker (2)			

Roberto Alomar
July '95 ....—
July '96 ....8.00
July '97 ....10.00

Jeff Bagwell (black bat)
July '95 ....—
July '96 ....10.00
July '97 ....10.00

Jeff Bagwell (white bat)
July '95 ....—
July '96 ....15.00
July '97 ....15.00

Albert Belle
July '95 ....—
July '96 ....8.00
July '97 ....10.00

Craig Biggio
July '95 ....—
July '96 ....8.00
July '97 ....8.00

Barry Bonds
July '95 ....—
July '96 ....8.00
July '97 ....10.00

Rickey Bones (R)
July '95 ....—
July '96 ....10.00
July '97 ....10.00

Rico Brogna (R)
July '95 ....—
July '96 ....10.00
July '97 ....10.00

Ken Caminiti (R)
July '95 ....—
July '96 ....8.00
July '97 ....20.00

Vinny Castilla (R)
July '95 ....—
July '96 ....8.00
July '97 ....12.00

Will Clark
July '95 ....—
July '96 ....8.00
July '97 ....8.00

David Cone
July '95 ....—
July '96 ....8.00
July '97 ....10.00

Wil Cordero (R)
July '95 ....—
July '96 ....12.00
July '97 ....10.00

Marty Cordova (R)
July '95 ....—
July '96 ....12.00
July '97 ....12.00

Shawon Dunston
July '95 ....—
July '96 ....8.00
July '97 ....8.00

Lenny Dykstra
July '95 ....—
July '96 ....8.00
July '97 ....8.00

Jim Edmonds (R)
July '95 ....—
July '96 ....12.00
July '97 ....10.00

Jim Eisenreich (R)
July '95 ....—
July '96 ....8.00
July '97 ....8.00

Gary Gaetti
July '95 ....—
July '96 ....8.00
July '97 ....8.00

Ron Gant
July '95 ....—
July '96 ....8.00
July '97 ....8.00

Ken Griffey Jr.
July '95 ....—
July '96 ....15.00
July '97 ....18.00

Marquis Grissom
July '95 ....—
July '96 ....8.00
July '97 ....12.00

Ozzie Guillen
July '95 ....—
July '96 ....8.00
July '97 ....8.00

Brian Hunter (R)
July '95 ....—
July '96 ....10.00
July '97 ....10.00

Derek Jeter (R)
July '95 ....—
July '96 ....15.00
July '97 ....100.00

Charles Johnson (R)
July '95 ....—
July '96 ....10.00
July '97 ....10.00

Chipper Jones (R)
July '95 ....—
July '96 ....30.00
July '97 ....160.00

Greg Maddux
July '95 ....—
July '96 ....20.00
July '97 ....35.00

Jeff Manto (R)
July '95 ....—
July '96 ....10.00
July '97 ....10.00

Edgar Martinez (R)
July '95 ....—
July '96 ....10.00
July '97 ....12.00

Fred McGriff
July '95 ....—
July '96 ....8.00
July '97 ....8.00

Mark McGwire
July '95 ....—
July '96 ....8.00
July '97 ....12.00

Raul Mondesi
July '95 ....—
July '96 ....10.00
July '97 ....10.00

Eddie Murray
July '95 ....—
July '96 ....10.00
July '97 ....12.00

Hideo Nomo (R) (white)
July '95 ....—
July '96 ....34.00
July '97 ....50.00

Hideo Nomo (R) (gray)
July '95 ....—
July '96 ....24.00
July '97 ....50.00

Paul O'Neill
July '95 ....—
July '96 ....8.00
July '97 ....8.00

Mike Piazza
July '95 ....—
July '96 ....12.00
July '97 ....18.00

Kirby Puckett
July '95 ....—
July '96 ....8.00
July '97 ....10.00

Cal Ripken Jr. (sliding)
July '95 ....—
July '96 ....25.00
July '97 ....30.00

Cal Ripken Jr. (fielding)
July '95 ....—
July '96 ....25.00
July '97 ....30.00

Cal Ripken Jr.
(sliding w/fielding)
July '95 ....—
July '96 ....30.00
July '97 ....30.00

Cal Ripken Jr.
(fielding w/sliding)
July '95 ....—
July '96 ....30.00
July '97 ....30.00

Ivan Rodriguez
July '95 ....—
July '96 ....8.00
July '97 ....10.00

Deion Sanders
July '95 ....—
July '96 ....8.00
July '97 ....8.00

Ozzie Smith
July '95 ....—
July '96 ....8.00
July '97 ....12.00

Sammy Sosa
July '95 ....—
July '96 ....8.00
July '97 ....8.00

Terry Steinbach
July '95 ....—
July '96 ....8.00
July '97 ....8.00

Frank Thomas
July '95 ....—
July '96 ....12.00
July '97 ....15.00

Jim Thome (R)
July '95 ....—
July '96 ....12.00
July '97 ....25.00

Ryan Thompson (R)
July '95 ....—
July '96 ....8.00
July '97 ....8.00

John Valentin (R)
July '95 ....—
July '96 ....8.00
July '97 ....8.00

Mo Vaughn
July '95 ....—
July '96 ....8.00
July '97 ....8.00

Larry Walker
July '95 ....—
July '96 ....8.00
July '97 ....10.00

Rondell White (R)
July '95 ....—
July '96 ....10.00
July '97 ....12.00

Matt Williams
July '95 ....—
July '96 ....8.00
July '97 ....8.00

Moises Alou
July '95 ....—
July '96 ....—
July '97 ....10.00

Garret Anderson (R)
July '95 ....—
July '96 ....—
July '97 ....12.00

Carlos Baerga
July '95 ....—
July '96 ....—
July '97 ....10.00

Dante Bichette
July '95 ....—
July '96 ....—
July '97 ....12.00

Joe Carter
July '95 ....—
July '96 ....—
July '97 ....10.00

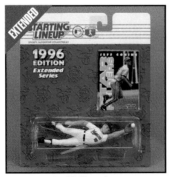

Jeff Conine
July '95 ....—
July '96 ....—
July '97 ....10.00

Chad Curtis
July '95 ....—
July '96 ....—
July '97 ....10.00

Juan Gonzalez
July '95 ....—
July '96 ....—
July '97 ....20.00

Ken Griffey Jr.
July '95 ....—
July '96 ....—
July '97 ....40.00

David Justice
July '95 ....—
July '96 ....—
July '97 ....15.00

Eric Karros
July '95 ....—
July '96 ....—
July '97 ....10.00

Barry Larkin
July '95 ....—
July '96 ....—
July '97 ....15.00

Don Mattingly
July '95 ....—
July '96 ....—
July '97 ....20.00

Hal Morris
July '95 ....—
July '96 ....—
July '97 ....8.00

Denny Neagle (R)
July '95 ....—
July '96 ....—
July '97 ....16.00

Rafael Palmeiro
July '95 ....—
July '96 ....—
July '97 ....12.00

1989 BASEBALL GREATS

★ **Set Price: $450.00** ★ **Total Figures: 10** ★

When Kenner began producing Starting Lineups, its original plan was to issue only yearly, standard sets of current basketball, football, and baseball players. It didn't take long, however, for the company to develop new ideas it wanted to bring to life—special series that would be issued in addition to the regular sets. The first of these were the 1989 Baseball Greats and the 1989 Basketball Slam Dunk series.

Kenner initially offered the Slam Dunk series as a mail-in promotion. But the company issued Baseball Greats—featuring some of the game's all-time best players—through its normal retail distribution channels. To differentiate this set from its standard baseball issue, Kenner developed a new packaging scheme featuring two figures and two cards in each package. The retail price was considerably higher than the usual SLU price. This factor, coupled with the lack of current athletes, prevented Baseball Greats from becoming popular upon its release. Kenner discontinued the series after only one year of production, and it wasn't until several years later—after the explosion of the Kenner hobby—that collectors began to appreciate this unique set.

The Babe Ruth/Lou Gehrig combination is available in three different variations. While Kenner originally intended for Ruth to be produced in the New York Yankees gray uniform and Gehrig in the white, both players were featured in either color. These pieces can be found in three different combinations: "white/gray" (Ruth in white, Gehrig in gray); "gray/white," or "regular" (Ruth in gray, Gehrig in white); and "white/white" (both players in white uniforms). The "white/white" variation, most hobbyists agree, is the shortest printed of the three.

The two other more popular combinations are the Mickey Mantle/Joe DiMaggio and the Hank Aaron/Carl Yastrzemski pieces.

The '89 Baseball Greats back advertises the new One-on-One set, which would be released later in the year. At left is Roberto Clemente.

Before the release of the 1997 Classic Doubles series, this was the only Mantle piece Kenner produced. The Mick's across-the-board popularity in the world of sports collectibles has kept interest in his SLU high. The Aaron/Yaz is a short print, and is one of the hardest pieces in this series to find.

Case Assortments

CASE	CASE
Babe Ruth/Lou Gehrig (4)	Mickey Mantle/Joe DiMaggio (4)
Johnny Bench/Pete Rose (3)	Don Drysdale/Reggie Jackson (2)
Ernie Banks/Billy Williams (2)	Hank Aaron/Carl Yastrzemski (1)
Stan Musial/Bob Gibson (1)	Willie McCovey/Willie Mays (3)
Roberto Clemente/Willie Stargell (2)	Hank Aaron/Eddie Mathews (2)

Ernie Banks/ Billy Williams

July '91	10.00
July '94	22.00
July '97	40.00

Johnny Bench/ Pete Rose

July '91	10.00
July '94	27.00
July '97	60.00

Don Drysdale/
Reggie Jackson
July '91......................10.00
July '94 ....25.00
July '97 ....60.00

Mickey Mantle/
Joe DiMaggio
July '91......................15.00
July '94 ....42.00
July '97 ....90.00

Eddie Mathews/
Hank Aaron
July '91......................10.00
July '94 ....24.00
July '97 ....50.00

Willie Mays/
Willie McCovey
July '91......................10.00
July '94 ....22.00
July '97 ....45.00

Stan Musial/
Bob Gibson
July '91......................16.00
July '94 ....25.00
July '97 ....40.00

Babe Ruth/Lou Gehrig
(white/gray)
July '91......................10.00
July '94 ....30.00
July '97 ....55.00

Babe Ruth/Lou Gehrig
(white/white)
July '91......................40.00
July '94 ....42.00
July '97......................70.00

Babe Ruth/Lou Gehrig
(gray/white)
July '91......................10.00
July '94 ....25.00
July '97 ....45.00

Willie Stargell/
Roberto Clemente
July '91......................10.00
July '94 ....22.00
July '97 ....55.00

Carl Yastrzemski/
Hank Aaron
July '91......................15.00
July '94 ....32.00
July '97 ....90.00

BASEBALL HEADLINE

★ **1991 Set Price: $180.00** ★ **Total Figures: 7** ★
★ **1992 Set Price: $140.00** ★ **Total Figures: 7** ★
★ **1993 Set Price: $175.00** ★ **Total Figures: 8** ★

Kenner produced its Baseball Headline series for only three years. While the idea was admirable, the figures themselves never caught on with collectors. The concept: Kenner took several headline stories from the previous season and turned them into collectibles. Everything from Nolan Ryan's 5,000th strikeout to Cecil Fielder's 50th home run to Cal Ripken Jr.'s pursuit of Lou Gehrig's consecutive game streak appeared as unique Starting Lineup pieces.

The real beauty behind these figures is that they're great to display. While most SLU purists cringe at the thought of opening a piece, in this case it's a must. With their attractive wood grain or black bases and reprints of the actual newspaper articles, Baseball Headlines are some of the most impressive-looking pieces Kenner has issued.

Unlike regular SLU issues, Headline pieces can be removed from their boxes without causing much damage to the package. And the box itself features a picture of the piece, so purists—who would never dream of opening the package—can still display the figures rather easily.

Most collectors have opted to complete their regular sets rather than collect these pieces. Recently, hobbyists who already have most of the baseball sets have begun to collect the headlines, which may indicate that these figures will soon become more popular.

Pictured at left is Nolan Ryan's 5,000th strikeout piece. Above, from top to bottom, are the '91, '92, and '93 Baseball Headline package backs.

Case Assortments

'91 Jose Canseco
July '91 ....17.00
July '94 ......15.00   July '97 .....18.00

'91 Will Clark
July '91 ....17.00
July '94 .....25.00   July '97 ....20.00

'91 Ken Griffey Jr.
July '91 ....20.00
July '94 .....36.00   July '97 ....55.00

'91 Rickey Henderson
July '91 ....20.00
July '94 .....20.00   July '97.....18.00

'91 Bo Jackson
July '91 ....17.00
July '94 ......15.00   July '97 .....15.00

'91 Don Mattingly
July '91 ....17.00
July '94 .....26.00   July '97 ....42.00

'91 Nolan Ryan
July '91 ....20.00
July '94 .....50.00   July '97 ....60.00

'92 George Brett
July '93 ....26.00
July '95 .....36.00   July '97 ....36.00

'92 Cecil Fielder
July '93 ....14.00
July '95 ......14.00   July '97 .....15.00

'92 Ken Griffey Jr.
July '93 ....17.00
July '95 .....22.00   July '97 ....35.00

'92 Rickey Henderson
July '93 ....15.00
July '95 ......15.00   July '97 .....15.00

'92 Bo Jackson
July '93 ....17.00
July '95 ......15.00   July '97 .....12.00

'92 Nolan Ryan
July '93 ....20.00
July '95 .....30.00   July '97 ....40.00

'92 Ryne Sandberg
July '93 ....23.00
July '95 .....30.00   July '97 ....32.00

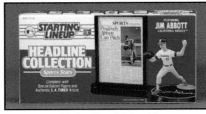

'93 Jim Abbott
July '93 ....13.00
July '95 ......14.00   July '97 .....14.00

'93 Roberto Alomar
July '93 ....13.00
July '95 ......14.00   July '97 .....14.00

'93 Tom Glavine
July '93 ....14.00
July '95 ......18.00   July '97 .....18.00

'93 Mark McGwire
July '93 ....12.00
July '95 ......14.00   July '97 ....25.00

'93 Cal Ripken Jr.
July '93 ....15.00
July '95 .....30.00   July '97 ....50.00

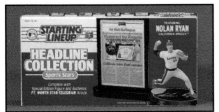

'93 Nolan Ryan
July '93 ....15.00
July '95 .....48.00   July '97 ....50.00

'93 Deion Sanders
July '93 ....12.00
July '95 ......14.00   July '97 ....20.00

'93 Frank Thomas
July '93 ....15.00
July '95 .....32.00   July '97 ....32.00

STADIUM STARS

★ **1993 Set Price: $175.00** ★ **Total Figures: 8** ★
★ **1994 Set Price: $180.00** ★ **Total Figures 8** ★
★ **1995 Set Price: $200.00** ★ **Total Figures: 9** ★
★ **1996 Set Price: $225.00** ★ **Total Figures: 11** ★

Kenner collectors have never quite embraced Stadium Stars figures. The series, which debuted in 1993, features star players posing atop a replica of their home stadiums. It's an interesting concept, but the high retail price point, $17.99, may have kept collectors away at first—seriously lessening the series' chances for success with later issues.

But despite mediocre collector interest in Stadium Stars, Kenner has continued to release a set each year since the line's debut. The 1993 issue consisted of only six figures, with the Nolan Ryan—his last Starting Lineup piece—and a short-printed Frank Thomas ranking as the most popular. The 1994 set offered two short-prints—Deion Sanders and Bo Jackson. Sanders can be found with or without a medallion necklace, but there are no reported price differences between the two versions.

Randy Johnson and Mark McGwire were the short-prints in the 1995 set. Both appeared in only one of the three cases and were packed only one to that case. The Greg Maddux Stadium Star became popular at the time of release because it was the least expensive Maddux piece available. While his figure is a one-pack in all three cases, it's still great piece to own.

In 1996, Kenner was unable to obtain the licensing to produce Dodger Stadium, Jacobs Field, or Camden Yards, but the company still wanted to expand the set to include Cal Ripken Jr., Mike Piazza, and Albert Belle. Anticipating that each of those players would make the All-Star team, Kenner produced their figures atop Veterans Stadium—the site of the 1996 All-Star game.

While the Stadium Stars series still hasn't caught fire, the fact that Kenner produced only three players twice—Ken Griffey Jr. and Frank Thomas in 1993 and 1995 and Darren Daulton in 1995 and 1996—gives it collecting potential for the future.

The back of the '96 Baseball Stadium Stars (above) shows all eight of the stadiums used in this set.

'93 Roger Clemens
July '93 ....25.00
July '95 ....25.00
July '97 ....25.00

'93 Cecil Fielder
July '93 ....18.00
July '95 ....16.00
July '97 ....20.00

Case Assortments

1993 BASEBALL STADIUM STARS
CASE .00
Roger Clemens
Cecil Fielder
Ken Griffey Jr. (2)
Nolan Ryan (2)
Ryne Sandberg
Frank Thomas

1994 BASEBALL STADIUM STARS
CASE .05
Barry Bonds (2)
Will Clark
Dennis Eckersley
Tom Glavine
Juan Gonzalez
Bo Jackson
Kirby Puckett

CASE .07
Barry Bonds (2)

Will Clark
Dennis Eckersley
Tom Glavine (2)
Juan Gonzalez
Kirby Puckett

CASE .08
Barry Bonds
Will Clark
Tom Glavine
Juan Gonzalez (2)
Kirby Puckett
Deion Sanders (2)

1995 BASEBALL STADIUM STARS
CASE .05
Lenny Dykstra
Randy Johnson
David Justice
Greg Maddux
Mark McGwire
Frank Thomas (2)

Mo Vaughn

CASE .06
Darren Daulton
Ken Griffey Jr. (2)
David Justice
Greg Maddux
Frank Thomas (2)
Mo Vaughn

CASE .07
Lenny Dykstra
Ken Griffey Jr. (2)
David Justice
Greg Maddux
Frank Thomas (2)
Mo Vaughn

1996 BASEBALL STADIUM STARS
CASE .01
Albert Belle
Jose Canseco

Javy Lopez
Mike Piazza
Cal Ripken Jr. (2)
Robin Ventura
Matt Williams

CASE .02
Jay Buhner
Darren Daulton
Mark Grace
Chuck Knoblauch
Javy Lopez
Mike Piazza
Cal Ripken Jr.
Matt Williams

CASE .03
Albert Belle (2)
Javy Lopez (2)
Mike Piazza (2)
Cal Ripken Jr. (2)

'93 Ken Griffey Jr.
July '93 ....18.00
July '95 ....24.00
July '97 ....35.00

'93 Nolan Ryan
July '93 ....30.00
July '95 ....40.00
July '97 ....60.00

'93 Ryne Sandberg
July '93 ....28.00
July '95 ....32.00
July '97 ....32.00

'93 Frank Thomas
July '93 ....32.00
July '95 ....45.00
July '97 ....50.00

'94 Barry Bonds
July '95 ....25.00
July '96 ....20.00
July '97 ....20.00

'94 Will Clark
July '95 ....20.00
July '96 ....18.00
July '97 ....18.00

'94 Dennis Eckersley
July '95 ....20.00
July '96 ....18.00
July '97 ....18.00

'94 Tom Glavine
July '95 ....20.00
July '96 ....20.00
July '97 ....25.00

'94 Juan Gonzalez
July '95 ....30.00
July '96 ....30.00
July '97 ....25.00

'94 Bo Jackson
July '95 ....38.00
July '96 ....60.00
July '97 ....55.00

'94 Kirby Puckett
July '95 ....20.00
July '96 ....30.00
July '97 ....20.00

'94 Deion Sanders
July '95 ....32.00
July '96 ....40.00
July '97 ....45.00

'95 Darren Daulton
July '95 ....28.00
July '96 ....28.00
July '97 ....35.00

'95 Lenny Dykstra
July '95 ....20.00
July '96 ....24.00
July '97 ....25.00

'95 Ken Griffey Jr.
July '95 ....24.00
July '96 ....24.00
July '97 ....30.00

'95 Randy Johnson
July '95 ....28.00
July '96 ....30.00
July '97 ....75.00

'95 Dave Justice
July '95 ....20.00
July '96 ....20.00
July '97 ....20.00

'95 Greg Maddux
July '95 ....22.00
July '96 ....50.00
July '97 ....60.00

'95 Mark McGwire
July '95 ....25.00
July '96 ....25.00
July '97 ....40.00

'95 Frank Thomas
July '95 ....25.00
July '96 ....25.00
July '97 ....30.00

'95 Mo Vaughn
July '95 ....20.00
July '96 ....20.00
July '97 ....30.00

'96 Albert Belle
July '95 ....—
July '96 ....20.00
July '97 ....20.00

'96 Jay Buhner
July '95 ....—
July '96 ....20.00
July '97 ....25.00

'96 Jose Canseco
July '95 ....—
July '96 ....20.00
July '97 ....20.00

'96 Darren Daulton
July '95 ....—
July '96 ....20.00
July '97 ....20.00

'96 Mark Grace
July '95 ....—
July '96 ....20.00
July '97 ....20.00

'96 Chuck Knoblauch
July '95 ....—
July '96 ....20.00
July '97 ....20.00

'96 Javy Lopez
July '95 ....—
July '96 ....20.00
July '97 ....35.00

'96 Mike Piazza
July '95 ....—
July '96 ....20.00
July '97 ....35.00

'96 Cal Ripken Jr.
July '95 ....—
July '96 ....20.00
July '97 ....55.00

'96 Robin Ventura
July '95 ....—
July '96 ....20.00
July '97 ....20.00

'96 Matt Williams
July '95 ....—
July '96 ....20.00
July '97 ....20.00

COOPERSTOWN COLLECTION

★ 1994 Set Price: $125.00 ★ Total Figures: 8 ★
★ 1995 Set Price: $100.00 ★ Total Figures: 10 ★
★ 1996 Set Price: $175.00 ★ Total Figures: 14 ★

Despite the poor returns on 1989's Baseball Greats set, Kenner was still interested in producing figures of the game's legends. Hoping to expand the appeal of the Starting Lineup line, encouraged by the success of several "HOF" figures (including Tom Seaver's 1992 Extended piece) and buoyed by the rapid growth of the vintage memorabilia market, Kenner decided to give the idea another shot in 1994. The result: its Cooperstown Collection. This time—after having learned from its mistakes with Baseball Greats—Kenner packaged the figures singly with a price point identical to regular SLUs.

The series became one of the more popular non-regular issues the company has ever produced.

The first series was an immediate success, and although it has since cooled down somewhat, it's still a strong set. The Reggie Jackson and Honus Wagner figures were short-printed, and the Jackie Robinson figure can be found with both his correct uniform number (42) and an error number (44). The latter is a popular piece, but extremely difficult to find.

The second set is slightly larger—10 as opposed to eight pieces—and Babe Ruth is the only repeated player. Harmon Killebrew and Eddie Mathews are the short-printed figures, appearing as one-packs in each case assortment.

In 1996, the SLU hobby experienced new players and a change in distribution. Kenner issued 10 of the 14 1996 Cooperstown Collection figures via the company's usual retail pattern, while the other four were exclusive pieces. The Richie Ashburn piece was available only at Clover stores in Philadelphia and sur-

The back of the 12-inch figures (below) show the many ways these figures can be displayed. At left is a '94 Cy Young. Above is the back of the '94 Cooperstown Collection.

Case Assortments

1994 COOPERSTOWN COLLECTION CASE .01	1995 COOPERSTOWN COLLECTION CASE .00		CASE .03	
Honus Wagner (1)	Rod Carew (1)	Harmon Killebrew (1)	Hank Aaron (3)	
Babe Ruth (3)	Dizzy Dean (2)	Eddie Mathews (1)	Grover Cleveland	
Reggie Jackson (2)	Don Drysdale (1)	Satchel Paige (2)	Alexander (1)	
Ty Cobb (2)	Bob Feller (2)	Babe Ruth (3)	Roberto Clemente (3)	
Jackie Robinson (2)	Whitey Ford (1)		Jimmy Foxx (2)	
Cy Young (2)	Bob Gibson (2)	1996 COOPERSTOWN COLLECTION CASE .02	Hank Greenberg (2)	
Lou Gehrig (2)	Harmon Killebrew (1)		Joe Morgan (2)	
Willie Mays (2)	Eddie Mathews (1)		Mel Ott (1)	
	Satchel Paige (2)	Grover Cleveland	Robin Roberts (1)	
CASE .03	Babe Ruth (3)	Alexander (1)	Jackie Robinson (1)	
Honus Wagner (2)		Roberto Clemente (3)		
Babe Ruth (3)	CASE .01	Hank Greenberg (1)	1996 12-INCH COOPERSTOWN COLLECTION CASE	
Reggie Jackson (1)	Rod Carew (2)	Rogers Hornsby (2)		
Ty Cobb (2)	Dizzy Dean (1)	Joe Morgan (3)		
Jackie Robinson (2)	Don Drysdale (2)	Mel Ott (2)	Lou Gehrig (2)	
Cy Young (2)	Bob Feller (1)	Robin Roberts (1)	Babe Ruth (2)	
Lou Gehrig (2)	Whitey Ford (2)	Jackie Robinson (2)	Honus Wagner (1)	
Willie Mays (2)	Bob Gibson (1)		Cy Young (1)	

rounding areas. Rod Carew's figure was available only at the 17th Annual Sports Collectors Convention in Anaheim, Calif. Kenner distributed Steve Carlton's piece only at the Major League Baseball All-Star FanFest in Philadelphia. And Killebrew's SLU was made available only at Tuff Stuff's 8th Annual Summer Classic.

Kenner also experimented with a completely different type of SLU—12-inch, fully articulated figures wearing cloth uniforms. Ruth appeared in two different uniforms—the New York Yankees (distributed to all retail outlets) and the Boston Red Sox (available only at Kay-Bee toy stores). The Wagner piece was exclusive to Toys R Us.

Collectors have shown little interest in these figures. All of these pieces can be found for the issue price on the secondary market.

'94 Ty Cobb

July '95	16.00
July '96	16.00
July '97	16.00

'94 Lou Gehrig

July '95	16.00
July '96	16.00
July '97	16.00

'94 Reggie Jackson

July '95	35.00
July '96	36.00
July '97	36.00

'94 Willie Mays

July '95	16.00
July '96	16.00
July '97	16.00

'94 Jackie Robinson (#42)

July '95	16.00
July '96	16.00
July '97	16.00

'94 Babe Ruth

July '95	16.00
July '96	16.00
July '97	18.00

'94 Honus Wagner

July '95	35.00
July '96	36.00
July '97	36.00

'94 Cy Young

July '95	16.00
July '96	16.00
July '97	16.00

'95 Rod Carew

July '95	14.00
July '96	14.00
July '97	14.00

'95 Dizzy Dean

July '95	14.00
July '96	14.00
July '97	14.00

'95 Don Drysdale

July '95	14.00
July '96	14.00
July '97	14.00

'95 Bob Feller

July '95	14.00
July '96	14.00
July '97	14.00

'95 Whitey Ford
July '95 ....14.00
July '96 ....14.00
July '97 ....14.00

'95 Bob Gibson
July '95 ....14.00
July '96 ....14.00
July '97 ....14.00

'95 Harmon Killebrew
July '95 ....20.00
July '96 ....20.00
July '97 ....20.00

'95 Eddie Mathews
July '95 ....20.00
July '96 ....20.00
July '97 ....20.00

'95 Satchel Paige
July '95 ....14.00
July '96 ....14.00
July '97 ....14.00

'95 Babe Ruth
July '95 ....15.00
July '96 ....18.00
July '97 ....18.00

'96 Hank Aaron
July '95 ....—
July '96 ....10.00
July '97 ....20.00

'96 Grover Cleveland Alexander
July '95 ....—
July '96 ....10.00
July '97 ....10.00

'96 Richie Ashburn
(Clover)
July '95 ....—
July '96 ....—
July '97 ....20.00

'96 Rod Carew (National Sports Collectors Convention)
July '95 ....—
July '96 ....—
July '97 ....30.00

'96 Steve Carlton
(Major League Baseball FanFest)
July '95 ....—
July '96 ....—
July '97 ....30.00

'96 Roberto Clemente
July '95 ....—
July '96 ....10.00
July '97 ....16.00

'96 Jimmy Foxx
July '95 ....—
July '96 ....10.00
July '97 ....15.00

'96 Hank Greenberg
July '95 ....—
July '96 ....10.00
July '97 ....10.00

'96 Harmon Killebrew
(Tuff Stuff Summer Classic)
July '95 ....—
July '96 ....—
July '97 ....25.00

'96 Rogers Hornsby
July '95 ....—
July '96 ....10.00
July '97 ....15.00

'96 Joe Morgan
July '95 ....—
July '96 ....10.00
July '97 ....10.00

'96 Mel Ott
July '95 ....—
July '96 ....10.00
July '97 ....10.00

'96 Robin Roberts
July '95 ....—
July '96 ....10.00
July '97 ....15.00

'96 Jackie Robinson
July '95 ....—
July '96 ....10.00
July '97 ....18.00

'96 Ty Cobb 12"
July '95 ....—
July '96 ....—
July '97 ....25.00

'96 Lou Gehrig 12"
July '95 ....—
July '96 ....—
July '97 ....25.00

'96 Babe Ruth 12"
(Red Sox—Kay-Bee)
July '95 ....—
July '96 ....—
July '97 ....25.00

'96 Babe Ruth 12"
(Yankees)
July '95 ....—
July '96 ....—
July '97 ....25.00

'96 Honus Wagner 12"
(Toys R Us)
July '95 ....—
July '96 ....—
July '97 ....25.00

'96 Cy Young 12"
July '95 ....—
July '96 ....—
July '97 ....25.00

1988 BASKETBALL

★ Set Price: $5,000.00 ★ Total Figures: 85 ★

It's hard to believe, but sales of Kenner's first basketball issue were a huge disappointment for the company. After trying to complete a 124-piece baseball set and a 137-piece football series, most collectors showed little interest in the new 85-piece basketball set. Imagine living in Salt Lake City in 1988 and seeing multiple Jazz team cases just sitting on store shelves. Well, they did, and many collectors at the time opted to keep their $3.99 instead of grabbing one more Karl Malone.

Now, of course, all that has changed. The sport of basketball has seen a tremendous increase in popularity over the past several years, and this '88 issue has become one of the most sought-after sets in the Kenner marketplace today.

When the hobby exploded in the early '90s, collectors tried to go back and complete some of the older sets. The influx of new collectors and the passage of time, however, had already started to take a toll on '88 Basketball. As recently as 1991, the thought of paying $55 for Malone and $20 for John Stockton was considered ridiculous. But as collectors began to understand just how rare some of these pieces were, prices began to escalate.

Now that the Kenner hobby has reached the 10-year mark, this set is nearly impossible to complete. Players like Michael Jordan or Larry Bird that Kenner issued in the all-star cases or were multiple packs in the team cases can be obtained without too much difficulty. But at a minimum of $30 to $50 per common piece, collectors will find it very expensive to get started.

Then there are the high-dollar star pieces. Many of these players were relative unknowns at the time and thus were limited to regional issues. Their subsequent rise in status and increase in popularity—and price—makes these pieces fairly easy to find. But you can expect to pay top dollar to get players like Reggie

The '88 Basketball back (above) lists four more players than were actually produced. Pictured at left is Clyde Drexler.

Miller, Mark Price, Scottie Pippen, and—of course—any member of the Utah Jazz.

What really make this set impossible to complete, however, are the short-printed pieces of several non-all-stars. Players like Adrian Dantley, Vinnie Johnson, Rodney McCray, and Danny Schayes were one-packs in their respective team cases and are nearly impossible to find in any condition—let alone in top shape.

As time passes, this set will only become harder and harder to complete.

Case Assortments

ALL-STAR
Charles Barkley
Michael Jordan (5)
Larry Bird (3)
Kevin McHale
Danny Manning
Kareem Abdul-Jabbar (2)
Magic Johnson (3)
Dominique Wilkins (2)
Patrick Ewing (2)
Isiah Thomas (2)
Hakeem Olajuwon (2)

TEAM CASES
Atlanta Hawks
Doc Rivers (3)
Spud Webb (2)
Dominique Wilkins (5)
Kevin Willis (2)

Boston Celtics
Danny Ainge (2)
Larry Bird (4)
Dennis Johnson (1)
Kevin McHale (3)
Robert Parish (2)

Chicago Bulls
Michael Jordan (7)
John Paxson (2)
Scottie Pippen (3)

Cleveland Cavaliers
Brad Daugherty (4)
Ron Harper (4)
Mark Price (2)
John Williams (2)

Dallas Mavericks
Mark Aguirre (4)
Rolando Blackman (3)
Derek Harper (3)
Sam Perkins (2)

Detroit Pistons
Adrian Dantley (3)
Vinnie Johnson (2)
Bill Laimbeer (2)
Isiah Thomas (5)

Denver Nuggets
Michael Adams (3)
Alex English (4)
Lafayette Lever (3)
Danny Schayes (2)

Golden State Warriors
Winston Garland (2)
Rod Higgins (2)
Chris Mullin (3)
Ralph Sampson (5)

Houston Rockets
Joe Barry Carroll (3)
Eric "Sleepy" Floyd (3)

Rodney McCray (2)
Hakeem Olajuwon (4)

Indiana Pacers
Reggie Miller (2)
Chuck Person (4)
Steve Stipanovich (3)
Wayman Tisdale (3)

Los Angeles Clippers and Los Angeles Lakers
Danny Manning (2)
Reggie Williams (1)
Kareem Abdul-Jabbar (2)
Michael Cooper (1)
Magic Johnson (4)
James Worthy (2)

Milwaukee Bucks
Terry Cummings (4)
Sidney Moncrief (3)
Paul Pressey (2)
Jack Sikma (3)

New Jersey Nets and New York Knicks
Dennis Hopson (1)
Buck Williams (2)
Patrick Ewing (4)
Mark Jackson (3)
Gerald Wilkins (2)

Phoenix Suns
Tom Chambers (4)
Armon Gilliam (3)
Jeff Hornacek (2)
Eddie Johnson (3)

San Antonio Spurs
Walter Berry (3)

Philadelphia 76ers
Charles Barkley (5)
Maurice Cheeks (3)
Mike Gminski (2)
Cliff Robinson (2)

Sacramento Kings
Kenny Smith (5)
LaSalle Thompson (4)
Otis Thorpe (3)

Portland Trailblazers
Clyde Drexler (4)
Steve Johnson (2)
Terry Porter (2)
Kiki Vandeweghe (4)

Johnny Dawkins (3)
David Greenwood (2)
Alvin Robertson (4)

Seattle SuperSonics
Michael Cage (3)
Dale Ellis (4)
Xavier McDaniel (3)
Derrick McKey (2)

Utah Jazz
Thurl Bailey (3)
Mark Eaton (2)
Karl Malone (4)
John Stockton (3)

Washington Bullets
Bernard King (5)
Jeff Malone (5)
Moses Malone (2)

Karem Abdul-Jabbar
July '91......................35.00
July '94 ....32.00
July '97 ....52.00

Michael Adams
July '91......................18.00
July '94 ....25.00
July '97 ....35.00

Mark Aguirre
July '91......................12.00
July '94 ....24.00
July '97 ....35.00

Danny Ainge
July '91......................12.00
July '94 ....28.00
July '97 ....55.00

Thurl Bailey
July '91......................18.00
July '94 ....150.00
July '97 ....200.00

Charles Barkley
July '91......................12.00
July '94 ....36.00
July '97 ....75.00

Walter Berry
July '91......................12.00
July '94 ....20.00
July '97 ....40.00

Larry Bird
July '91......................12.00
July '94 ....36.00
July '97 ....65.00

Rolando Blackman
July '91......................12.00
July '94 ....20.00
July '97 ....35.00

Michael Cage
July '91......................12.00
July '94 ....20.00
July '97 ....35.00

Joe Barry Carroll
July '91......................12.00
July '94 ....20.00
July '97 ....35.00

Tom Chambers
July '91......................30.00
July '94 ....26.00
July '97 ....35.00

Maurice Cheeks
July '91......................12.00
July '94 ....20.00
July '97 ....35.00

Michael Cooper
July '91......................22.00
July '94 ....20.00
July '97 ....45.00

Terry Cummings
July '91......................12.00
July '94 ....20.00
July '97 ....35.00

Adrian Dantley
July '91......................12.00
July '94 ....50.00
July '97 ....100.00

Brad Daugherty
July '91......................20.00
July '94 ....32.00
July '97 ....40.00

Johnny Dawkins
July '91......................12.00
July '94 ....20.00
July '97 ....35.00

Clyde Drexler
July '91.....................25.00
July '94 ....54.00
July '97 ....100.00

Mark Eaton
July '91.....................20.00
July '94 ....130.00
July '97 ....200.00

Dale Ellis
July '91......................12.00
July '94 ....20.00
July '97 ....35.00

Alex English
July '91......................12.00
July '94 ....20.00
July '97 ....40.00

Patrick Ewing
July '91.....................12.00
July '94 ....28.00
July '97 ....45.00

Eric "Sleepy" Floyd
July '91.....................12.00
July '94 ....18.00
July '97 ....35.00

Winston Garland
July '91......................12.00
July '94 ....18.00
July '97 ....35.00

Armon Gilliam
July '91......................12.00
July '94 ....18.00
July '97 ....35.00

Mike Gminski
July '91......................12.00
July '94 ....18.00
July '97 ....35.00

David Greenwood
July '91......................20.00
July '94 ....18.00
July '97 ....35.00

Derek Harper
July '91......................12.00
July '94 ....20.00
July '97 ....35.00

Ron Harper
July '91......................12.00
July '94 ....20.00
July '97 ....35.00

Rod Higgins
July '91......................12.00
July '94 ....20.00
July '97 ....35.00

Dennis Hopson
July '91......................12.00
July '94 ....20.00
July '97 ....35.00

Jeff Hornacek
July '91......................20.00
July '94......................28.00
July '97......................45.00

Mark Jackson
July '91......................18.00
July '94......................20.00
July '97......................35.00

Dennis Johnson
July '91......................18.00
July '94......................25.00
July '97......................40.00

Eddie Johnson
July '91......................12.00
July '94......................20.00
July '97......................35.00

Magic Johnson
July '91......................18.00
July '94......................35.00
July '97......................75.00

Steve Johnson
July '91......................12.00
July '94......................18.00
July '97......................35.00

Vinnie Johnson
July '91......................20.00
July '94......................75.00
July '97....................120.00

Michael Jordan
July '91......................22.00
July '94......................32.00
July '97....................100.00

Bernard King
July '91......................12.00
July '94......................22.00
July '97......................40.00

Bill Laimbeer
July '91......................22.00
July '94......................40.00
July '97....................120.00

Lafayette Lever
July '91......................12.00
July '94......................20.00
July '97......................35.00

Jeff Malone
July '91......................12.00
July '94......................22.00
July '97......................35.00

Karl Malone
July '91......................65.00
July '94....................475.00
July '97....................650.00

Moses Malone
July '91......................28.00
July '94......................35.00
July '97......................70.00

Danny Manning
July '91......................12.00
July '94......................20.00
July '97......................35.00

Rodney McCray
July '91......................12.00
July '94......................20.00
July '97......................40.00

Xavier McDaniel
July '91......................35.00
July '94 ....20.00
July '97 ....35.00

Kevin McHale
July '91......................12.00
July '94 ....20.00
July '97 ....50.00

Derrick McKey
July '91 ....28.00
July '94 ....28.00
July '97 ....40.00

Reggie Miller
July '91......................25.00
July '94 ....25.00
July '97 ....225.00

Sidney Moncrief
July '91......................12.00
July '94 ....22.00
July '97 ....40.00

Chris Mullin
July '91......................12.00
July '94 ....36.00
July '97 ....50.00

Hakeem Olajuwon
July '91......................12.00
July '94 ....25.00
July '97.....................75.00

Robert Parish
July '91......................12.00
July '94 ....24.00
July '97 ....40.00

John Paxson
July '91......................12.00
July '94 ....22.00
July '97 ....40.00

Sam Perkins
July '91......................20.00
July '94 ....25.00
July '97 ....35.00

Chuck Person
July '91......................12.00
July '94 ....20.00
July '97 ....35.00

Scottie Pippen
July '91......................12.00
July '94 ....35.00
July '97 ....150.00

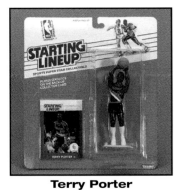

Terry Porter
July '91......................12.00
July '94 ....30.00
July '97 ....35.00

Paul Pressey
July '91......................12.00
July '94 ....20.00
July '97 ....40.00

Mark Price
July '91......................35.00
July '94 ....80.00
July '97 ....125.00

Doc Rivers
July '91......................12.00
July '94 ....20.00
July '97 ....35.00

Alvin Robertson
July '91.......................20.00
July '94.......................20.00
July '97.......................35.00

Cliff Robinson
July '91.......................12.00
July '94.......................24.00
July '97.......................35.00

Ralph Sampson
July '91.......................12.00
July '94.......................18.00
July '97.......................35.00

Danny Schayes
July '91.......................12.00
July '94.......................20.00
July '97.......................75.00

Jack Sikma
July '91.......................20.00
July '94.......................20.00
July '97.......................35.00

Kenny Smith
July '91.......................12.00
July '94.......................19.00
July '97.......................35.00

Steve Stipanovich
July '91.......................12.00
July '94.......................17.00
July '97.......................35.00

John Stockton
July '91.......................25.00
July '94.....................230.00
July '97.....................450.00

Isiah Thomas
July '91.......................12.00
July '94.......................22.00
July '97.......................35.00

LaSalle Thompson
July '91.......................12.00
July '94.......................20.00
July '97.......................35.00

Otis Thorpe
July '91.......................12.00
July '94.......................20.00
July '97.......................35.00

Wayman Tisdale
July '91.......................12.00
July '94.......................20.00
July '97.......................35.00

Kiki Vandeweghe
July '91.......................12.00
July '94.......................18.00
July '97.......................35.00

Spud Webb
July '91.......................30.00
July '94.......................25.00
July '97.......................35.00

Dominique Wilkins
July '91.......................12.00
July '94.......................32.00
July '97.......................40.00

Gerald Wilkins
July '91.......................12.00
July '94.......................20.00
July '97.......................35.00

Buck Williams
July '91........................12.00
July '94 ....20.00
July '97 ....35.00

John Williams
July '91........................12.00
July '94 ....22.00
July '97 ....35.00

Reggie Williams
July '91........................12.00
July '94........................16.00
July '97 ....35.00

Kevin Willis
July '91........................12.00
July '94 ....20.00
July '97 ....35.00

James Worthy
July '91........................12.00
July '94 ....24.00
July '97 ....40.00

1989 BASKETBALL

★ **Set Price: $125.00** ★ **Total Figures: 5** ★

The disappointing performance of Kenner's 1988 Basketball set forced the company to cancel most of its '89 figures. The company released just five players from only two teams—Rex Chapman, Dell Curry, and Kelly Tripucka from the newly formed Charlotte Hornets, and Ron Harper and Larry Nance from the Cleveland Cavaliers.

These figures were issued only in Hornets and Cavaliers team cases consisting of 12 figures each. Most of the cases were released regionally, and there were no all-star cases or any national distribution.

The front of the package is identical to the '88 set—red backing with a blue bordered card—while the back lists a projected lineup of 77 figures for the '89 set. Larry Nance was the only player Kenner actually released that was not listed on the package. Ron Harper is the only duplicate player from the '88 series. He appears here in a "jam" pose in a blue uniform instead of the "passing" pose in a white

uniform. Even the cards are different.

Because these five players have never achieved all-star status, most collectors overlook this set. The prices have seen only modest increases over the past several years, but keep in mind that these figures weren't released nationally and are becoming harder and harder to find.

The back of the '89 Basketball package (above) lists 77 figures of which only five players were actually produced. Pictured at left is Rex Chapman.

Case Assortments

CHARLOTTE HORNETS	CLEVELAND CAVALIERS
Rex Chapman (4)	Ron Harper (6)
Dell Curry (4)	Larry Nance (6)
Kelly Tripucka (4)	

Rex Chapman (R)
July '91......................18.00
July '94......................30.00
July '97......................30.00

Dell Curry (R)
July '91......................18.00
July '94......................18.00
July '97......................30.00

Ron Harper
July '91......................15.00
July '94......................18.00
July '97......................30.00

Larry Nance (R)
July '91......................15.00
July '94......................18.00
July '97......................30.00

Kelly Tripucka (R)
July '91......................18.00
July '94......................18.00
July '97......................30.00

1990 BASKETBALL

★ **Set Price: $550.00** ★ **Total Figures: 17** ★

The year 1990 brought new life to basketball SLUs. Disappointing sales left Kenner unable to afford any returns from retail outlets, so the company issued only 17 players with a much shorter production run than the 1988 Basketball set. Hoping to draw collector interest from the booming sports card hobby, Kenner included two trading cards with each figure. The strategy paid off, and sales increased as more and more people joined the ranks of SLU collecting. It was the beginning of the Starting Lineup hobby, although it would be several more years before Kenner collecting would gain full acceptance in the larger world of sports memorabilia.

Shortly after Kenner issued this series, the David Robinson rookie piece skyrocketed in popularity to rank alongside the '88 Nolan Ryan and the '90 Ken Griffey Jr. as the hobby's best-selling figures. Although demand for the Robinson piece has cooled over the past five years, several other pieces from this set have continued to increase in value. Figures of Charles

Barkley and Larry Bird, which were plentiful in the '88 set, were produced in much smaller quantities in 1990, and their relative scarcity has kept the value of their '90 figures high.

Two other players who have seen a lot of market activity are Karl Malone and John Stockton. The prohibitive price of their '88 figures—the two most expensive pieces in the hobby—has led collectors to pick up their '90 pieces instead. Until recently, you could get both for around $50. Now expect to pay that for each one.

As the popularity of the NBA continues to increase, Kenner's 1990 basketball issue remains a strong seller. The small quantity of players, limited print run, and relatively inexpensive price tag combine to make this set attractive to collectors who have given up on the '88 release. Don't be surprised if 1990 Basketball becomes much more difficult to complete in a few years.

Pictured above is the back of a '90 Basketball figure. Interestingly, it shows a different '91 Nolan Ryan Headliner than what was actually released. At left is Boston Celtic legend Larry Bird.

Case Assortments

NBA #67780	NBA #66790
Charles Barkley (2)	Larry Bird (4)
Clyde Drexler (2)	Tom Chambers
Joe Dumars	Patrick Ewing
Magic Johnson (4)	Michael Jordan (6)
Michael Jordan (6)	Karl Malone (3)
David Robinson (2)	Chris Mullin
Byron Scott	David Robinson (2)
John Stockton	Isiah Thomas (3)
Spud Webb (2)	James Worthy (3)
Dominique Wilkins (3)	

Charles Barkley

July '91	6.00
July '94	36.00
July '97	75.00

Larry Bird

July '91	6.00
July '94	40.00
July '97	75.00

Tom Chambers

July '91	15.00
July '94	16.00
July '97	15.00

Clyde Drexler

July '91	20.00
July '94	35.00
July '97	60.00

Joe Dumars (R)
July '91......................15.00
July '94......................14.00
July '97......................18.00

Patrick Ewing
July '91........................6.00
July '94......................32.00
July '97......................40.00

Magic Johnson
July '91........................6.00
July '94......................30.00
July '97......................50.00

Michael Jordan
July '91......................15.00
July '94......................35.00
July '97....................100.00

Karl Malone
July '91......................12.00
July '94......................25.00
July '97......................60.00

Chris Mullin
July '91........................6.00
July '94......................20.00
July '97......................22.00

David Robinson (R)
July '91......................35.00
July '94......................38.00
July '97......................60.00

Byron Scott
July '91......................15.00
July '94......................15.00
July '97......................20.00

John Stockton
July '91......................15.00
July '94......................22.00
July '97......................60.00

Isiah Thomas
July '91........................6.00
July '94......................18.00
July '97......................20.00

Spud Webb
July '91........................6.00
July '94......................14.00
July '97......................14.00

Dominique Wilkins
July '91........................6.00
July '94......................20.00
July '97......................30.00

James Worthy
July '91........................6.00
July '94......................14.00
July '97......................15.00

1991 BASKETBALL

★ Set Price: $500.00 ★ Total Figures: 16 ★

In the early 1990s, basketball continued to lag behind football and baseball in collector popularity. Consequently, Kenner decreased the number of players in its 1991 Basketball issue to 15 and again kept production numbers low.

In an effort to boost sales, and hoping to capitalize on Michael Jordan's popularity among fans of all sports, the company decided to produce two different '91 Jordan pieces. The first depicted the Bulls' star in a classic "shooting" pose, while the second was an all-new "jumping" pose. At the time this new pose was released,

Case Assortments

ALL-STAR CASE
Charles Barkley
Larry Bird (2)
Magic Johnson (3)
Michael Jordan (jumping) (7)
Michael Jordan (regular) (4)
Reggie Lewis
David Robinson (6)

ALL-STAR CASE
Derrick Coleman (2)
Clyde Drexler (2)
Joe Dumars
Patrick Ewing (3)
Michael Jordan (jumping) (3)
Michael Jordan (regular) (5)
Kevin Johnson (2)
Dennis Rodman
Isiah Thomas (3)
Spud Webb
Dominique Wilkins

most collectors were amazed at its detail and realism. Today, it remains one of Kenner's more popular basketball poses.

This set offers collectors little in the way of rookie pieces. Derrick Coleman and Kevin Johnson have played like All-Stars, but both have been hampered by injuries for most of their careers. And Reggie Lewis, unfortunately, never had a chance to live up to his potential. He died from heart disease at the age of 28.

Then there's Dennis Rodman. Whether you love him or hate him, his talent for manipulating the media combined with his championship rings has made him a focus of collector attention. Rodman's 1991 rookie SLU was a short-print and has become one of the hottest pieces in the hobby. Collectors should realize, however, that once Rodman retires, the value of his figures will most likely decline—unless he somehow worms his way into the Hall of Fame.

Kenner packaged its '91 Basketball set similarly to the baseball and football issues from that year. That means there's a coin included as a premium with each figure. Early on, after several reports of the baseball coins rusting while still in the package, Kenner decided to switch from a steel coin to an aluminium one. While it's unknown as to exactly when during the

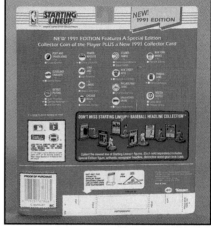

In '91, this Basketball piece was one of the pieces Kenner cut to remove the coin. A sticker was used to cover the hole.

production process this switch took place, it appears that the majority of 1991 Basketball figures were produced with the steel coin. Before releasing the figures to the general public, however, Kenner cut the back of most of the packages, replaced the steel coin with an aluminum version, and placed a sticker over the hole. Today, a significant number of figures have an unblemished card back—meaning Kenner didn't cut a hole to change the coin in every '91 piece. Reports indicate that these figures contain either the steel or the aluminum coin, and the only way to tell the difference is with a magnet, which will stick to the steel coin but not to the aluminium one.

Charles Barkley
July '92.......................11.00
July '94 ....35.00
July '97 ....100.00

Larry Bird
July '92.......................11.00
July '94 ....34.00
July '97 ....60.00

Derrick Coleman (R)
July '92.....................27.00
July '94 ....30.00
July '97 ....35.00

Clyde Drexler
July '92.....................15.00
July '94 ....25.00
July '97 ....30.00

Joe Dumars

July '92 ....11.00
July '94 ....10.00
July '97 ....12.00

Patrick Ewing

July '92 ....11.00
July '94 ....20.00
July '97 ....25.00

Kevin Johnson (R)

July '92 ....15.00
July '94 ....15.00
July '97 ....24.00

Magic Johnson

July '92 ....23.00
July '94 ....26.00
July '97 ....40.00

Michael Jordan (Jumping)

July '92 ....18.00
July '94 ....28.00
July '97 ....95.00

Michael Jordan (regular)

July '92 ....12.00
July '94 ....25.00
July '97 ....95.00

Reggie Lewis (R)

July '92 ....16.00
July '94 24,00
July '97 ....25.00

David Robinson

July '92 ....10.00
July '94 ....14.00
July '97 ....15.00

Dennis Rodman (R)

July '92 ....14.00
July '94 ....12.00
July '97 ....80.00

Isiah Thomas

July '92 ....12.00
July '94 ....12.00
July '97 ....15.00

Spud Webb

July '92 ....16.00
July '94 ....13.00
July '97 ....15.00

Dominique Wilkins

July '92 ....16.00
July '94 ....26.00
July '97 ....30.00

1992 BASKETBALL

★ Set Price: $1,000.00 ★ Total Figures: 30 ★

As Starting Lineup sales began to increase, so did the number of pieces in Kenner basketball sets. The 1992 hoop issue—which has nearly twice as many figures as the '91 set—features a few key rookies as well as two different pieces for Michael Jordan and David Robinson.

When '92 Basketball first hit store shelves, most of the collector interest centered on Charlotte Hornets forward Larry Johnson. Within just a few months of the set's release, L.J.'s piece was selling for around $90. At the time, Johnson was the star of a popular expansion team and was enjoying a great deal of media exposure and endorsement offers, so his short-printed rookie piece was red-hot. By 1997, though, injuries, a lack of success, and a trade to the New York Knicks had seriously diminished demand in this one-time superstar.

Meanwhile, another '92 piece began to steal the spotlight—the Magic Johnson jersey-color variation. Kenner's overseas production facility accidentally produced most of the Magic figures with the Los Angeles Lakers' purple (road) jerseys even though the company's designers had intended for that piece to appear with L.A.'s yellow (home) uniforms. Once Kenner realized the mistake, it immediately switched to the originally specified color.

Because so many figures had already been produced, however, Kenner opted to ship the "mistake" pieces as well. Only the later cases contained the yellow variation; it's estimated that fewer than 1,000 "yellow" Magics came off the production lines.

As a premium, Kenner included a poster with each 1992 Basketball figure. While the growth of the open-figure market has generated collector interest in some SLU premiums—most notably the cards—the same cannot be said for these posters. When unfolded, each one measures 13 by 11 inches, but it's unattractive because of the many creases.

Even so, this is still a great set to put together. And aside from the "yellow" Magic and the two Jordan figures, most of these pieces are relatively inexpensive. You can

The back of the '92 Basketball figures (above) show a Dikembe Mutumbo poster unfolded.

find more than half of '92 Basketball's 30 figures for less than $20 each, and the rest will cost between $30 and $60 apiece.

Case Assortments

ALL-STAR CASE			
Manute Bol	Chris Mullin	Joe Dumars	(regular)
Dee Brown	Dikembe Mutumbo	Patrick Ewing	David Robinson
Vlade Divac	Hakeem Olajuwon	Tim Hardaway	(warm-up)
Clyde Drexler	Scottie Pippen (3)	*Magic Johnson (2)	Dennis Rodman
Larry Johnson	David Robinson	Michael Jordan	John Stockton
Kevin Johnson	(regular)	(regular) (3)	
Magic Johnson	David Robinson	Michael Jordan	* Magic Johnson
Michael Jordan	(warm-up)	(warm-up) (3)	appears in either a
(regular) (3)	Isiah Thomas	Dan Majerle	purple or yellow jersey.
Michael Jordan		Dikembe Mutumbo	
(warm-up) (3)	**ALL-STAR CASE**	John Paxson	
Karl Malone	Charles Barkley	Scottie Pippen (2)	
Reggie Miller	Larry Bird	Mark Price	
	Derrick Coleman	David Robinson	

Charles Barkley
July '93 ....20.00
July '95 ....35.00
July '97 ....60.00

Larry Bird
July '93 ....20.00
July '95 ....40.00
July '97 ....50.00

Manute Bol (R)
July '93 ....10.00
July '95 ....8.00
July '97 ....10.00

Dee Brown (R)
July '93 ....12.00
July '95 ....14.00
July '97 ....14.00

Derrick Coleman
July '93 .... 15.00
July '95 .... 12.00
July '97 .... 12.00

Vlade Divac (R)
July '93 .... 11.00
July '95 .... 10.00
July '97 .... 15.00

Clyde Drexler
July '93 .... 15.00
July '95 .... 15.00
July '97 .... 24.00

Joe Dumars
July '93 .... 8.00
July '95 .... 10.00
July '97 .... 10.00

Patrick Ewing
July '93 .... 12.00
July '95 .... 22.00
July '97 .... 22.00

Tim Hardaway (R)
July '93 .... 22.00
July '95 .... 24.00
July '97 .... 32.00

Kevin Johnson
July '93 .... 10.00
July '95 .... 12.00
July '97 .... 12.00

Larry Johnson
July '93 .... 90.00
July '95 .... 70.00
July '97 .... 35.00

Magic Johnson (Purple)
July '93 .... 18.00
July '95 .... 32.00
July '97 .... 65.00

Magic Johnson (yellow)
July '93 .... 60.00
July '95 .... 240.00
July '97 .... 450.00

Michael Jordan (regular)
July '93 .... 12.00
July '95 .... 28.00
July '97 .... 120.00

Michael Jordan (warm up)
July '93 .... 18.00
July '95 .... 32.00
July '97 .... 120.00

Dan Majerle (R)
July '93 .... 12.00
July '95 .... 15.00
July '97 .... 15.00

Karl Malone
July '93 .... 10.00
July '95 .... 12.00
July '97 .... 20.00

Reggie Miller
July '93 .... 10.00
July '95 .... 16.00
July '97 .... 42.00

Chris Mullin
July '93 .... 10.00
July '95 .... 14.00
July '97 .... 20.00

Dikembe Mutombo (R)
July '93 ....18.00
July '95 ....18.00
July '97 ....20.00

Hakeem Olajuwon
July '93 ....8.00
July '95 ....25.00
July '97 ....40.00

John Paxson
July '93 ....8.00
July '95 ....12.00
July '97 ....12.00

Scottie Pippen
July '93 ....10.00
July '95 ....12.00
July '97 ....32.00

Mark Price
July '93 ....10.00
July '95 ....12.00
July '97 ....12.00

David Robinson (regular)
July '93 ....10.00
July '95 ....16.00
July '97 ....16.00

David Robinson (warm up)
July '93 ....12.00
July '95 ....20.00
July '97 ....20.00

Dennis Rodman
July '93 ....7.00
July '95 ....12.00
July '97 ....60.00

John Stockton
July '93 ....8.00
July '95 ....12.00
July '97 ....30.00

Isiah Thomas
July '93 ....8.00
July '95 ....10.00
July '97 ....10.00

1993 BASKETBALL

★ **Set Price: $600.00** ★ **Total Figures: 29** ★

The '93 Basketball back (pictured above) offers the first Kenner Club piece, a Shaquille O'Neal Slam Dunk figure. Pictured at left is the rookie piece of O'Neal.

As the Starting Lineup hobby began to boom, Kenner again capitalized on the success of the trading card market by reaching an agreement with Topps. The deal allowed Kenner to include both a regular Topps and a Stadium Club card with each 1993 Basketball figure. Not only did this help draw the attention of SLU collectors in general to basketball, but it also brought more card and memorabilia collectors into the Kenner hobby.

At the time this set appeared, Shaquille O'Neal was taking the NBA by storm. His '93 Stadium Club and Topps cards were selling for $12 and $8, respectively, so it's no wonder that his first Kenner figure was hot right out of the gate. Collectors who were lucky enough to find one of his figures on retail shelves for a mere $5.99 not only got a great Shaq piece, but two Shaq rookie cards bearing a special Kenner stamp. Since Topps produced these cards in much smaller quantities than its regular-set cards, the O'Neal SLU was an instant hit.

Shaq has plenty of good company in this rookie-laden set. Fourteen of the 29 players appear in a Starting Lineup series

for the the first time. Among the new faces are Alonzo Mourning, Shawn Kemp, and Tom Gugliotta.

Three years after it hit the market, this set's biggest star is still Michael Jordan. When Jordan retired just before the '94 season, Kenner lost the right to produce his figures. As no new deal with Jordan has ever been reached, his 1993 SLU just might be the last one ever produced. Despite the fact that Jordan was a two-pack in both the .05 and the .06 cases, most collectors and dealers feel that this is his shortest-printed piece. Add the bonus of the Topps regular and Stadium Club cards and you have one of the most sought-after pieces in the hobby.

Kenner released this set in only two different case assortments, which is great for collectors who buy their figures by the case (you need only two cases vs. four or five in other sets). Unfortunately, this makes several of the pieces extremely hard to find.

While a few star players (O'Neal and Larry Johnson, for example) appeared in both cases, several other players (among them Clyde Drexler and Kemp) were single-packs in just one case and are considered the short-prints in '93 Basketball.

Although the case assortments make some figures difficult to find and the set difficult to complete, this is still a great series for Kenner hobbyists who want to get started in collecting basketball. Great player selection, key rookies, the last Jordan piece, and a reasonable price tag all combine to make '93 basketball an excellent choice for collectors.

Case Assortments

CASE .03		CASE .04	
Stacey Augmon	Patrick Ewing	Kenny Anderson	Shaquille O'Neal (3)
Charles Barkley	Larry Johnson (2)	Charles Barkley	Terry Porter
Brad Daugherty	Michael Jordan (2)	Todd Day	Mark Price
Todd Day	Karl Malone	Horace Grant	Glen Rice
Clyde Drexler	Dan Majerle	Larry Johnson (2)	Mitch Richmond
Horace Grant	Alonzo Mourning	Michael Jordan (2)	David Robinson
Tom Gugliotta	Dikembe Mutombo	Christian Laettner	Detlef Shrempf
Tim Hardaway	Shaquille O'Neal (3)	Karl Malone	Dominique Wilkins
Shawn Kemp	Scottie Pippen	Alonzo Mourning	
Sean Elliott	David Robinson	Dikembe Mutombo	
	John Stockton		

Kenny Anderson (R)

July '94	18.00
July '95	25.00
July '97	20.00

Stacey Augmon (R)
July '94 ....18.00
July '95 ....20.00
July '97 ....15.00

Charles Barkley
July '94 ....20.00
July '95 ....25.00
July '97 ....25.00

Brad Daugherty (R)
July '94......................10.00
July '95 ....12.00
July '97 ....12.00

Todd Day (R)
July '94 ....15.00
July '95 ....22.00
July '97 ....20.00

Clyde Drexler
July '94 ....14.00
July '95 ....18.00
July '97 ....20.00

Sean Elliott (R)
July '94 ....15.00
July '95 ....15.00
July '97 ....15.00

Patrick Ewing
July '94 ....16.00
July '95 ....25.00
July '97 ....25.00

Horace Grant (R)
July '94 ....12.00
July '95 ....15.00
July '97 ....25.00

Tom Gugliotta (R)
July '94 ....34.00
July '95 ....42.00
July '97 ....40.00

Tim Hardaway
July '94......................10.00
July '95 ....15.00
July '97 ....20.00

Larry Johnson
July '94 ....12.00
July '95 ....15.00
July '97 ....15.00

Michael Jordan
July '94 ....30.00
July '95 ....45.00
July '97 ....140.00

Shawn Kemp (R)
July '94......................15.00
July '95 ....24.00
July '97 ....40.00

Christian Laettner (R)
July '94 ....35.00
July '95 ....48.00
July '97 ....30.00

Dan Majerle
July '94......................10.00
July '95 ....10.00
July '97 ....10.00

Karl Malone
July '94......................12.00
July '95......................14.00
July '97 ....15.00

Alonzo Mourning (R)
July '94 ....75.00
July '95 ....65.00
July '97 ....80.00

Dikembe Mutombo
July '94 ....7.00
July '95 ....8.00
July '97 ....10.00

Shaquille O'Neal (R)
July '94 ....45.00
July '95 ....45.00
July '97 ....90.00

Scottie Pippen
July '94 ....10.00
July '95 ....12.00
July '97 ....30.00

Terry Porter
July '94 ....10.00
July '95 ....10.00
July '97 ....10.00

Mark Price
July '94 ....8.00
July '95 ....12.00
July '97 ....12.00

Glen Rice (R)
July '94 ....14.00
July '95 ....15.00
July '97 ....20.00

Mitch Richmond (R)
July '94 ....14.00
July '95 ....16.00
July '97 ....25.00

David Robinson
July '94 ....14.00
July '95 ....15.00
July '97 ....15.00

Detlef Schrempf (R)
July '94 ....10.00
July '95 ....12.00
July '97 ....15.00

John Stockton
July '94 ....14.00
July '95 ....15.00
July '97 ....20.00

Dominique Wilkins
July '94 ....14.00
July '95 ....16.00
July '97 ....15.00

1994 BASKETBALL

★ Set Price: $450.00 ★ Total Figures: 27 ★

This turned out to be another great year for Starting Lineup basketball. The simple design of the pieces in this set combined with a SkyBox Hoops card helped make 1994 Basketball a winner from the start. Since then, two key figures have helped it maintain its popularity.

The first is the rookie piece of Anfernee "Penny" Hardaway. In just three short years, Penny has developed into a bona fide superstar. With Shaquille O'Neal's defection to the Los Angeles Lakers, Hardaway is now the leader of the Orlando Magic, and his excellence on the court and winning personality have made him a fan favorite. At $100, his rookie SLU is expensive, but there's little doubt he'll be a force in the NBA for many years.

The hottest piece from the '94 set, however, is the Dennis Rodman hair-color variation. Kenner wanted to make this figure as real as possible, so when Rodman changed his hair color from blond to red, Kenner stopped production on his figure and made the switch. The blond figures were issued in the early .09 and .10 cases. The "red" Rodman was included only in the .11 case, which was released last. When collectors first learned of this variation, many thought it might be a mistake like the "yellow" Magic Johnson, and the price quickly rose to $150. Since then, some of the initial excitement has waned, but this piece still trades for an impressive $125.

The Hardaway rookie and "red" Rodman are the most hyped pieces in this set, but the real strength of '94 Basketball might be several sleeper figures, including the rookie pieces of Latrell Sprewell and Chris Webber. After a stellar 1996-97 season, which included a selection to the All-Star team, Sprewell is on the verge of stardom. If he continues to play well, look for his piece to rise in value. At $20, he could be the biggest steal in this set.

Webber has been injury-prone for most of his career; he missed more than 100 games in his first three years. Healthy for most of the '96-'97 season, however, he emerged as one of the elite power forwards in the game. If he can stay healthy and continue to post

The '94 Basketball back (above) is the last hoop package to provide a checklist of players. Like many other backs, this one listed a few figures that were never actually produced. At left is the only piece of Stacey Augmon.

impressive numbers, his piece could be a bargain at $20. Just remember that it was packed four to a case in the .09 and .10 assortments.

This set isn't too hard to complete, but finding figures in mint condition can be a problem. Kenner introduced a new packing method in 1994, but because of some initial problems, many of this set's pieces were damaged before they were shipped from the factory. Still, this remains a strong issue and (except for the Penny rookie and "red" Rodman) a relatively inexpensive one.

Case Assortments

CASE .08		CASE .10	CASE .11
Charles Barkley	Dominique Wilkins (2)	B.J. Armstrong	Charles Barkley (2)
Stacey Augmon		Charles Barkley (2)	Shawn Bradley (2)
Shawn Bradley	CASE .09	LaPhonso Ellis (2)	Calbert Cheaney (2)
Calbert Cheaney	B.J. Armstrong (3)	Anfernee Hardaway	LaPhonso Ellis (2)
Derrick Coleman	Charles Barkley	Jimmy Jackson (2)	Patrick Ewing (2)
Sean Elliott	LaPhonso Ellis	Larry Johnson (2)	Jimmy Jackson (2)
Patrick Ewing	Anfernee Hardaway (3)	Shawn Kemp	Larry Johnson (2)
Larry Johnson (2)	Jimmy Jackson	Jamal Mashburn (2)	Shawn Kemp (2)
Karl Malone	Larry Johnson	Alonzo Mourning (2)	Jamal Mashburn (2)
Harold Miner	Shawn Kemp (3)	Shaquille O'Neal	Hakeem Olajuwon (2)
Alonzo Mourning (2)	Jamal Mashburn	Dennis Redman	Dennis Rodman (red) (2)
Chris Mullin	Alonzo Mourning	(blond) (2)	Latrell Sprewell (2)
Hakeem Olajuwon	Shaquille O'Neal (3)	Latrell Sprewell (2)	
Shaquille O'Neal (3)	Dennis Rodman (blond)	Chris Webber (4)	
Scottie Pippen (2)	Latrell Sprewell		
David Robinson (2)	Chris Webber (4)		

B.J. Armstrong (R)
July '95 ....12.00
July '96 ....12.00
July '97 ....10.00

Stacey Augmon
July '95 ....10.00
July '96 ....10.00
July '97 ....10.00

Charles Barkley
July '95 ....18.00
July '96 ....20.00
July '97 ....25.00

Shawn Bradley (R)
July '95 ....35.00
July '96 ....15.00
July '97 ....15.00

Calbert Cheaney (R)
July '95 ....35.00
July '96 ....15.00
July '97 ....15.00

Derrick Coleman
July '95 ....12.00
July '96 ....12.00
July '97 ....12.00

Sean Elliott
July '95 ....10.00
July '96 ....10.00
July '97 ....10.00

LaPhonzo Ellis (R)
July '95 ....25.00
July '96 ....20.00
July '97 ....15.00

Patrick Ewing
July '95 ....12.00
July '96 ....12.00
July '97 ....12.00

Anfernee Hardaway (R)
July '95 ....35.00
July '96 ....75.00
July '97 ....100.00

Jimmy Jackson (R)
July '95 ....38.00
July '96 ....40.00
July '97 ....30.00

Larry Johnson
July '95 ....12.00
July '96 ....12.00
July '97 ....12.00

Shawn Kemp
July '95 ....15.00
July '96 ....15.00
July '97 ....24.00

Karl Malone
July '95 ....12.00
July '96 ....12.00
July '97 ....12.00

Jamal Mashburn (R)
July '95 ....38.00
July '96 ....35.00
July '97 ....25.00

Harold Miner (R)
July '95 ....32.00
July '96 ....30.00
July '97 ....25.00

Alonzo Mourning
July '95 ....15.00
July '96 ....15.00
July '97 ....15.00

Chris Mullin
July '95 ....10.00
July '96 ....10.00
July '97 ....10.00

Hakeem Olajuwon
July '95 ....15.00
July '96 ....20.00
July '97 ....20.00

Shaquille O'Neal
July '95 ....22.00
July '96 ....35.00
July '97 ....50.00

Scottie Pippen
July '95 ....10.00
July '96 ....10.00
July '97 ....24.00

David Robinson
July '95 ....10.00
July '96 ....10.00
July '97 ....10.00

Dennis Rodman (blond)
July '95 ....10.00
July '96 ....30.00
July '97 ....50.00

Dennis Rodman (red)
July '95 ....75.00
July '96 ....120.00
July '97 ....125.00

Latrell Sprewell (R)
July '95 ....35.00
July '96 ....25.00
July '97 ....22.00

Chris Webber (R)
July '95 ....30.00
July '96 ....24.00
July '97 ....30.00

Dominique Wilkins
July '95 ....10.00
July '96 ....10.00
July '97 ....10.00

1995 BASKETBALL

★ Set Price: $450.00 ★ Total Figures: 33 ★

Kenner issued 1995 Basketball with only two different case assortments—the .02 and .03 cases. Each player in the set appears in only one case except for Grant Hill, who is featured in both. Although Kenner won't release exact production numbers, it's logical to assume that the company produced the two cases in similar quantities. Since no player appears more than once per case, there are twice as many Hill pieces as there are other players. With all players—except for Hill—produced in equal quantities, player ability and rookie status drive the prices for this set.

The rookie selection in 1995 Basketball isn't bad. Jason Kidd, despite a poor season, is still an All-Star, and his recent trade to the Phoenix Suns appears to have given him new life. With the return of Kevin Johnson in 1997, the Suns will have the best two-guard tandem in the league. Look for Kidd to return to All-Star form.

Glenn Robinson has quietly put up good numbers since joining the NBA in the 1994-95 season. Playing in Milwaukee doesn't give him a lot of media attention, but if he continues to post big numbers, the "Big Dog" will show up the want list of most collectors.

Most basketball experts expect Hill to become the next Michael Jordan (if such a thing is possible), but Hill's rookie SLU piece doesn't carry quite the same potential. After most of the '95 Basketball cases had already sold out at retail outlets, several cases of Hill figures began showing up at Kmart stores across the country. The department store chain had an agreement with Kenner to distribute a special Hill piece, but instead of a different figure, Kenner reissued the regular '95 Hill with a "Rookie of the Year/Kmart Exclusive" sticker. This overabundance of Hill rookies quickly led to a sharp decline in secondary-market values—and much frus-

Pictured above is the back of the '95 Basketball package. It shows only some of the players actually produced.

tration from collectors.

Hobbyists shouldn't give up on these Hill pieces too quickly, however. Remember that Kenner produced most of Jordan's figures in double or triple quantities, but it's still virtually impossible to find any Jordan figure for less than $100. If Hill indeed emerges as the NBA's biggest star in the league's post-Michael years, his figures could escalate to Jordanian levels, and you might find yourself wishing you had more than just one of his rookie pieces.

Case Assortments

CASE .02		CASE .03	
Patrick Ewing	Alonzo Mourning	Charles Barkley	Hakeem Olajuwon
Anfernee Hardaway	Robert Pack (R)	Muggsy Bogues (R)	Shaquille O'Neal
Grant Hill (R)	Glenn Robinson (R)	Horace Grant	Scottie Pippen
Jeff Hornacek	Steve Smith (R)	Grant Hill (R)	Mark Price
Jason Kidd (R)	Latrell Sprewell	Jimmy Jackson (R)	Cliff Robinson (R)
Karl Malone	Nick Van Exel (R)	Shawn Kemp	David Robinson
Reggie Miller	Chris Webber	Toni Kukoc (R)	John Starks (R)
Eric Montross (R)	Dominique Wilkins	Dan Majerle	Clarence Weatherspoon (R)

Charles Barkley
July '95 ....—
July '96 ....15.00
July '97 ....20.00

Muggsy Bogues (R)
July '95 ....—
July '96 ....15.00
July '97 ....12.00

Patrick Ewing
July '95 ....—
July '96 ....12.00
July '97 ....12.00

Horace Grant (blue goggles)
July '95 ....—
July '96 ....20.00
July '97 ....20.00

Horace Grant (black goggles)
July '95 ....—
July '96 ....30.00
July '97 ....30.00

Anfernee Hardaway
July '95 ....—
July '96 ....25.00
July '97 ....50.00

Grant Hill (R) (regular)
July '95 ....—
July '96 ....35.00
July '97 ....20.00

Grant Hill (R) (Kmart)
July '95 ....—
July '96 ....35.00
July '97 ....20.00

Jeff Hornacek
July '95 ....—
July '96 ....12.00
July '97 ....10.00

Jimmy Jackson
July '95 ....—
July '96 ....15.00
July '97 ....12.00

Shawn Kemp
July '95 ....—
July '96 ....12.00
July '97 ....15.00

Jason Kidd (R)
July '95 ....—
July '96 ....60.00
July '97 ....60.00

Tony Kukoc (R)
July '95 ....—
July '96 ....15.00
July '97 ....20.00

Dan Majerle
July '95 ....—
July '96 ....12.00
July '97 ....10.00

Karl Malone
July '95 ....—
July '96 ....12.00
July '97 ....15.00

Reggie Miller
July '95 ....—
July '96 ....15.00
July '97 ....15.00

Eric Montross (R)
July '95 ....—
July '96 ....15.00
July '97 ....15.00

Alonzo Mourning
July '95 ....—
July '96 ....12.00
July '97 ....15.00

Shaquille O'Neal
July '95 ....—
July '96 ....30.00
July '97 ....35.00

Hakeem Olajuwon
July '95 ....—
July '96 ....15.00
July '97 ....15.00

Robert Pack (R)
July '95 ....—
July '96 ....15.00
July '97 ....12.00

Scottie Pippen
July '95 ....—
July '96 ....12.00
July '97 ....24.00

Mark Price
July '95 ....—
July '96 ....12.00
July '97 ....10.00

Cliff Robinson (R)
July '95 ....—
July '96 ....12.00
July '97 ....10.00

David Robinson
July '95 ....—
July '96 ....12.00
July '97 ....12.00

Glenn Robinson (R)
July '95 ....—
July '96 ....40.00
July '97 ....30.00

Steve Smith (R)
July '95 ....—
July '96 ....15.00
July '97 ....15.00

Latrell Sprewell
July '95 ....—
July '96 ....12.00
July '97 ....12.00

John Starks (R)
July '95 ....—
July '96 ....15.00
July '97 ....15.00

Nick Van Exel (R)
July '95 ....—
July '96 ....30.00
July '97 ....20.00

Clarence Weatherspoon (R)
July '95 ....—
July '96 ....15.00
July '97 ....15.00

Chris Webber
July '95 ....—
July '96 ....12.00
July '97 ....12.00

Dominique Wilkins
July '95 ....—
July '96 ....12.00
July '97 ....10.00

1996 BASKETBALL

★ **Set Price: $500.00** ★ **Total Figures: 37** ★
★ **Extended Set Price: $250.00** ★ **Total Figures: 8** ★
★ **Far East Set Price: $550.00** ★ **Total Figures: 13** ★

This may be the best Kenner basketball set since the company's 1993 issue. Rookie selection is fantastic, the three different Dennis Rodman hair color variations are hot, and the first Extended set has breathed new life into the basketball hobby. Plus the set features several short-printed pieces, making it a great chase for collectors.

The rookies of Kevin Garnett, Juwan Howard, Eddie Jones, and Antonio McDyess were all short-prints. As these players develop into All-Stars, their pieces should become hot commodities in the hobby.

As for Gary Payton's piece, it's hard to believe it took seven years for Kenner to produce a figure of the Seattle superstar. He's considered by most NBA observers to be the top point guard in the game today, and his rookie SLU should be another strong seller.

Other great rookies in this set include young stars Vin Baker, Joe Smith, and Damon Stoudamire. Their pieces weren't short-printed, but look for these fan favorites to rank high on collector want lists anyway.

While the rookies have generated their share of collector interest, the hottest-selling pieces have been the green, yellow, and orange hair-color variations of Rodman. Kenner apparently produced the three versions in equal quantities. As long as Rodman remains a center of attention, his SLUs will continue to generate strong

collector interest.

One interesting note: Kenner had started production of this set when the NBA requested that its 50th Anniversary logo be added on the front of the packaging. Kenner complied by adding the logo via a sticker on those figures it had already produced and by printing the logo on subsequent packages. It appears that most figures ended up with one treatment or the other. Currently, there's no price difference between the variations.

While 1996 Basketball is already a strong issue, the addition of the Extended series makes it a can't-miss. This particular Extended set was the most anticipated Kenner has ever issued. Dealers were preselling sets and cases for more than five times the wholesale cost. When these figures started to hit store shelves,

The '96 back (above) shows just a few team logos and no figures. Pictured at left is the Grant Hill piece from the regular set.

the prices were still rising.

The Kobe Bryant and Allen Iverson rookie pieces have led the way so far. While Iverson posted impressive numbers (including five straight 40-point games) in 1996-97, Bryant has yet to make much of an impact on the court. Occasional flashes of brilliance along with a healthy dose of media hype have combined to drive the price of each player's rookie piece through the roof. Only time will tell if each player can move into the ranks of the NBA elite—and keep their SLU values high.

Case Assortments

CASE .03		
Sean Elliott	Scottie Pippen (3)	Mitch Richmond	Jerry Stackhouse
Anfernee Hardaway (2)	Cliff Robinson	Joe Smith	Pooh Richardson
Reggie Miller (2)	David Robinson	Rik Smits	Glenn Robinson
Alonzo Mourning (2)	Dennis Rodman (2)	Jerry Stackhouse	Dennis Rodman
Shaquille O'Neal (2)	Damon Stoudamire (2)	Damon Stoudamire (2)	Joe Smith
Hakeem Olajuwon			
Scottie Pippen (2)	**CASE .09**	**CASE .10**	**EXTENDED**
Cliff Robinson	Vin Baker	Clyde Drexler	Charles Barkley (2)
David Robinson	Charles Barkley	Kevin Garnett (2)	Kobe Bryant (2)
Dennis Rodman (2)	Patrick Ewing	Anfernee Hardaway	Grant Hill (2)
	Anfernee Hardaway	Grant Hill	Allen Iverson (2)
CASE .06	Grant Hill	Juwan Howard	Larry Johnson (2)
Anfernee Hardaway (2)	Tyrone Hill	Larry Johnson	Dikembe Mutombo (2)
Reggie Miller (2)	Jamal Mashburn	Eddie Jones	Shaquille O'Neal (2)
Shaquille O'Neal (2)	Gary Payton	Jason Kidd	Damon Stoudamire (2)
Hakeem Olajuwon	Dino Radja	Karl Malone	
	Bryant Reeves	Antonio McDyess	

Vin Baker (R)

July '95 ....—
July '96 ....—
July '97 ....30.00

Charles Barkley

July '95 ....—
July '96 ....—
July '97 ....18.00

Clyde Drexler

July '95 ....—
July '96 ....—
July '97 ....16.00

Sean Elliot

July '95 ....—
July '96 ....—
July '97 ....10.00

Patrick Ewing

July '95 ....—
July '96 ....—
July '97 ....10.00

Kevin Garnett (R)

July '95 ....—
July '96 ....—
July '97 ....50.00

Anfernee Hardaway

July '95 ....—
July '96 ....—
July '97 ....25.00

Grant Hill (dribbling)

July '95 ....—
July '96 ....—
July '97 ....15.00

Grant Hill (Pistons)

July '95 ....—
July '96 ....—
July '97 ....20.00

Tyrone Hill (R)

July '95 ....—
July '96 ....—
July '97 ....10.00

Juwan Howard (R)

July '95 ....—
July '96 ....—
July '97 ....50.00

Larry Johnson

July '95 ....—
July '96 ....—
July '97 ....15.00

Eddie Jones (R)

July '95 ....—
July '96 ....—
July '97 ....30.00

Jason Kidd

July '95 ....—
July '96 ....—
July '97 ....20.00

Karl Malone

July '95 ....—
July '96 ....—
July '97 ....15.00

Jamal Mashburn

July '95 ....—
July '96 ....—
July '97 ....15.00

Antonio McDyess (R)
July '95 ....—
July '96 ....—
July '97 ....25.00

Reggie Miller
July '95 ....—
July '96 ....—
July '97 ....10.00

Alonzo Mourning
July '95 ....—
July '96 ....—
July '97 ....10.00

Hakeem Olajuwon
July '95 ....—
July '96 ....—
July '97 ....15.00

Shaquille O'Neal
July '95 ....—
July '96 ....—
July '97 ....25.00

Gary Payton (R)
July '95 ....—
July '96 ....—
July '97 ....25.00

Scottie Pippen
July '95 ....—
July '96 ....—
July '97 ....12.00

Dino Radja (R)
July '95 ....—
July '96 ....—
July '97 ....10.00

Bryant Reeves (R)
July '95 ....—
July '96 ....—
July '97 ....15.00

Pooh Richardson (R)
July '95 ....—
July '96 ....—
July '97 ....10.00

Mitch Richmond
July '95 ....—
July '96 ....—
July '97 ....10.00

Cliff Robinson
July '95 ....—
July '96 ....—
July '97 ....10.00

David Robinson
July '95 ....—
July '96 ....—
July '97 ....10.00

Glenn Robinson
July '95 ....—
July '96 ....—
July '97 ....12.00

Dennis Rodman (green hair)
July '95 ....—
July '96 ....—
July '97 ....40.00

Dennis Rodman (orange hair)
July '95 ....—
July '96 ....—
July '97 ....40.00

Dennis Rodman (yellow hair)

July '95 ....—
July '96 ....—
July '97 ....40.00

Joe Smith (R)

July '95 ....—
July '96 ....—
July '97 ....25.00

Rik Smits (R)

July '95 ....—
July '96 ....—
July '97 ....15.00

Jerry Stackhouse (R)

July '95 ....—
July '96 ....—
July '97 ....28.00

Damon Stoudamire

July '95 ....—
July '96 ....—
July '97 (R) 30.00

Charles Barkley

July '95 ....—
July '96 ....—
July '97 ....20.00

Kobe Bryant (R)

July '95 ....—
July '96 ....—
July '97 ....65.00

Grant Hill

July '95 ....—
July '96 ....—
July '97 ....35.00

Allen Iverson (R)

July '95 ....—
July '96 ....—
July '97 ....80.00

Larry Johnson

July '95 ....—
July '96 ....—
July '97 ....15.00

Dikembe Mutombo

July '95 ....—
July '96 ....—
July '97 ....15.00

Shaquille O'Neal

July '95 ....—
July '96 ....—
July '97 ....40.00

Damon Stoudamire

July '95 ....—
July '96 ....—
July '97 ....25.00

Magic Johnson

July '95 ....—
July '96 ....—
July '97 ....—

1992 HEADLINE

★ Set Price: $400 ★ Total Figures: 8 ★

This is the only basketball headline set Kenner ever issued. Like the Headline series from other sports, the basketball version never caught on with collectors. It's hard to understand why these pieces aren't more popular, especially since they're easy to display, whether the box is opened or not.

If you open a Basketball Headline package—and you can do it without ruining the box—you're rewarded with an eye-catching piece. Each package contains a figure and a newspaper article about the featured player. When assembled on the black stand, the Headline piece makes an attractive display item. In unopened form, the pictures on the box allow you to see exactly how each piece looks. The boxes store well and are relatively easy to keep in mint condition, since their sturdy construction makes them resistant to scratches and dings.

Until recently, most collectors have overlooked the Headline series, concentrating instead on Kenner regular issues. As more hobbyists discover how limited the production on this series was, however, these pieces are becoming harder to find. And with Kenner increasing its output of regular SLUs, the Headline series are attracting collectors searching for unique items. As time goes on, this one should continue to increase in popularity.

The back of the '92 Basketball Headline box (above) shows all eight pieces in the set. This is the only Basketball Headline set Kenner has issued.

Case Assortments

CASE	CASE
Larry Bird	Charles Barkley
Patrick Ewing	Larry Bird
Magic Johnson (2)	Patrick Ewing
Michael Jordan (4)	Magic Johnson (2)
Dikembe Mutombo	Michael Jordan (4)
Scottie Pippen (2)	Dikembe Mutombo
David Robinson	Scottie Pippen
	David Robinson

Charles Barkley
July '93..................................23.00
July '95 .....48.00   July '97 ....80.00

Larry Bird
July '93..................................20.00
July '95 .....55.00   July '97 ....80.00

Patrick Ewing
July '93 ....16.00
July '95 .....32.00   July '97 ....40.00

Magic Johnson
July '93 ....18.00
July '95 .....35.00   July '97 ....70.00

Michael Jordan
July '93 ....15.00
July '95 .....48.00   July '97 ...125.00

Dikembe Mutombo
July '93...................................17.00
July '95 .....22.00   July '97 ....25.00

Scottie Pippen
July '93 ....14.00
July '95 .....20.00   July '97 ....50.00

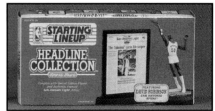

David Robinson
July '93 ....14.00
July '95 .....20.00   July '97 ....30.00

1989 SLAM DUNK

★ **Red Box Set Price: $700.00** ★ **Total Figures: 6** ★
★ **White Box Set Price: $400.00** ★ **Total Figures: 6** ★

One of the most widely known and popular of Kenner's "non-regular" issues is its 1989 Basketball Slam Dunk series. Initially offered to collectors via a mail-in promotion, the figures in this series of six were available for five SLU proofs of purchase each.

Originally, Slam Dunks were packaged in a plain white cardboard box, so collectors were forced to open the package in order to see which figure they had. Consequently, few of these figures remain in mint-in-box condition. The promotion was unsuccessful, and Kenner repackaged the surplus figures in a more attractive red box (with each player's picture on the front) and sold them through retail outlets across the nation. Most of these figures sat on store shelves for more than a year. During the past two or three years, however, collector interest in Slam Dunks has revived, and they are currently some of the hottest pieces on the secondary market.

Experts estimate that Kenner actually issued fewer than 2,000 of each red-box Slam Dunk figure, but it's unknown as to how many white-box figures came out. The look of the red packaging has helped it to become more popular than the plain white box. Great player selection and limited print run should keep this set popular for many years to come.

Note: We've pictured only one red and white Slam Dunk Superstars box. All of the red boxes are identical except for the sticker which indicates the player. All of the white boxes have a mailing label

Above is the back of a Slam Dunk package. Below is the front with a sticker indicating a Patrick Ewing figure. Also pictured: a white Slam Dunk box mailed to a collector (below left) and an opened Michael Jordan figure (left).

addressed to a collector. A letter code is used to identify the player in the package.

Case Assortments

This information applies to red-box figures only, since Kenner didn't issue white-box Slam Dunks via normal retail channels.

Larry Bird (2)	Michael Jordan (3)
Patrick Ewing (2)	Isiah Thomas (3)
Magic Johnson	Dominique Wilkins

Red Box

Larry Bird		Michael Jordan	
July '91	30.00	July '91	70.00
July '94	90.00	July '94	130.00
July '97	175.00	July '97	275.00

Patrick Ewing		Isiah Thomas	
July '91	30.00	July '91	30.00
July '94	70.00	July '94	42.00
July '97	100.00	July '97	60.00

Magic Johnson		Dominique Wilkins	
July '91	70.00	July '91	35.00
July '94	130.00	July '94	62.00
July '97	175.00	July '97	70.00

White Box

Larry Bird		Michael Jordan	
July '91	30.00	July '91	70.00
July '94	45.00	July '94	52.00
July '97	100.00	July '97	175.00

Patrick Ewing		Isiah Thomas	
July '91	30.00	July '91	30.00
July '94	36.00	July '94	34.00
July '97	60.00	July '97	40.00

Magic Johnson		Dominique Wilkins	
July '91	70.00	July '91	35.00
July '94	54.00	July '94	30.00
July '97	100.00	July '97	40.00

1988 FOOTBALL

★ **Set Price: $7,000.00** ★ **Total Figures: 137** ★

Kenner's 1988 Football ranks as one of the crown jewels of the Starting Lineup collecting hobby. Like Kenner's initial issues in other sports, '88 Football is extremely large, very difficult to complete, and very popular with collectors.

The largest football series Kenner has ever issued, this one is loaded with stars and future Hall of Famers. And thanks to the set's status, collectors are finding it tougher and tougher to locate '88 Football figures in mint condition.

The hardest pieces to find in this early release are not the stars, but the lesser-known regional players. Kenner used its original distribution scheme for '88 Football, shipping superstars nationally in AFC and NFC All-Pro cases and the lesser-known players in regional team cases. This latter type of distribution presents a challenge for the collector, turning players few would consider huge names into some of the most desirable—and expensive—pieces in the hobby. Players like Rod Woodson of the Steelers and the Cowboys' Randy White are almost impossible to find in decent condition, and truly mint pieces of either are rarely—if ever—seen on the market.

Kenner issued '88 Football figures 24 per case, but the company produced star players in

Pictured above is the back of the '88 Football package. At left is Tony Dorsett.

larger quantities and regional players in much smaller numbers. The short-printed pieces usually are the offensive and defensive linemen for each team. Typically, they were issued one or two per team case, and it's these figures that most collectors need in order to complete their sets.

Case Assortments

ALL-STAR CASE
Brian Bosworth (2)
Eric Dickerson (2)
Dan Marino (3)
John Elway (2)
Marcus Allen (2)
Joe Montana (2)
Herschel Walker (2)
Phil Simms (2)
Jim McMahon (3)
Lawrence Taylor (3)
Reggie White (1)

Note: At press time team case assortments were unavailable.

TEAM CASES
Atlanta Falcons
Aundray Bruce
Scott Campbell
Tony Casillas
Floyd Dixon
Gerald Riggs

Buffalo Bills
Cornelius Bennett
Chris Burkett
Ronnie Harmon
Jim Kelly
Bruce Smith

Chicago Bears
Neal Anderson
Richard Dent
Willie Gault
Jim McMahon
Mike Singletary

Cincinnati Bengals
James Brooks
Eddie Brown
Chris Collinsworth
Boomer Esiason
Tim Krumrie

Cleveland Browns
Brian Brennan
Bob Golic
Bernie Kosar
Kevin Mack
Ozzie Newsome

Dallas Cowboys
Doug Cosbie
Tony Dorsett
Ed Jones
Herschel Walker
Danny White
Randy White

Denver Broncos
John Elway

Vance Johnson
Rulon Jones
Karl Mecklenburg
Sammy Winder

Detroit Lions
Jeff Chadwick
James Jones
Chuck Long
Reggie Rogers

Green Bay Packers
Ken Davis
Phillip Epps
Brent Fullwood
Mark Lee
Randy Wright

Houston Oilers
Ray Childress
Alonzo Highsmith
Drew Hill
Warren Moon
Mike Rozier

Indianapolis Colts
Albert Bentley
Duane Bickett
Bill Brooks
Eric Dickerson
Jack Trudeau

Kansas City Chiefs
Carlos Carson
Deron Cherry
Bill Kenney
Christian Okoye

Los Angeles Raiders
Marcus Allen
Todd Christiansen
Howie Long
Marc Wilson

Los Angeles Rams
Carl Ekern
Henry Ellard
Jim Everett
Jerry Gray
Charles White

Miami Dolphins
Mark Clayton
Mark Duper
Dan Marino
John Offerdahl
Troy Stradford

Minnesota Vikings
Joey Browner
Anthony Carter

Steve Jordan
Tommy Kramer
Darrin Nelson

New England Patriots
Tony Eason
Steve Grogan
Ronnie Lippett
Stanley Morgan
Andre Tippett

New Orleans Saints
Bobby Hebert
Rickey Jackson
Eric Martin
Rueben Mayes
Dave Waymer

New York Giants
Mark Bavaro
Harry Carson
Joe Morris
Phil Simms
Lawrence Taylor

New York Jets
Mark Gastineau
Freeman McNeil
Ken O'Brien
Mickey Shuler
Al Toon

Philadelphia Eagles
Keith Byars
Randall Cunningham
Mike Quick
Anthony Toney
Reggie White

Pittsburgh Steelers
Todd Blackledge
Earnest Jackson
Louis Lipps
Mike Merriweather
Rod Woodson

San Diego Chargers
Chip Banks
Mark Malone
Billy Ray Smith
Kellen Winslow

San Francisco 49ers
Michael Carter
Roger Craig
Ronnie Lott
Joe Montana
Jerry Rice

Seattle Seahawks
Brian Bosworth
Jacob Green
Dave Krieg
Curt Warner

Phoenix Cardinals
Roy Green
E. J. Junior
Neil Lomax
Stump Mitchell
J. T. Smith

Tampa Bay Buccaneers
Gerald Carter
Jeff Davis
Rod Jones
Vinnie Testaverde
James Wilder

Washington Redskins
Gary Clark
Darrell Green
Dexter Manley
Art Monk
Jay Schroeder
Doug Williams

Another interesting aspect of this issue is the rare "snapping" pose Kenner used for some of the quarterbacks. The company produced just 10 such figures in '88, and except for the 1990 Doug Flutie, the pose never showed up again. Because of the small number of these pieces, many collectors try to put together a set of snapping QBs only—a much more attainable goal than completing the entire 1988 series.

Collectors who love a challenge can't ask for a better one than this release. There are countless short-printed pieces that are nearly impossible to find in any condition let alone in mint. SLUs were originally marketed as a toy to be opened and played with; as a result, mint-condition examples of all of the early releases are scarce. The fact that SLUs in general sold poorly in the early years also makes certain pieces that much more rare, as relatively unknown players sat on store shelves and unsold pieces were either returned to Kenner (and presumably destroyed) or simply thrown out. Due to all of these factors, it can take years to complete an '88 Football.

Marcus Allen

July '91......................12.00
July '94 ....40.00
July '97 ....80.00

Neal Anderson

July '91.....................20.00
July '94 ....18.00
July '97 ....35.00

Chip Banks

July '91......................12.00
July '94 ....40.00
July '97.....................75.00

Mark Bavaro

July '91.....................20.00
July '94 ....25.00
July '97 ....50.00

Cornelius Bennett

July '91......................12.00
July '94 ....75.00
July '97 ....150.00

Albert Bentley

July '91.....................12.00
July '94 ....20.00
July '97 ....35.00

Duane Bickett

July '91.....................12.00
July '94 ....28.00
July '97 ....50.00

Todd Blackledge

July '91.....................12.00
July '94 ....20.00
July '97 ....35.00

Brian Bosworth

July '91.....................20.00
July '94 ....20.00
July '97 ....35.00

Brian Brennan

July '91.....................12.00
July '94 ....22.00
July '97 ....35.00

Bill Brooks

July '91.....................12.00
July '94 ....24.00
July '97 ....50.00

James Brooks

July '91......................12.00
July '94 ....40.00
July '97 ....55.00

Eddie Brown
July '91.......................12.00
July '94.....................40.00
July '97 ....55.00

Joey Browner
July '91.......................12.00
July '94.....................25.00
July '97 ....50.00

Aundray Bruce
July '91.......................15.00
July '94.....................20.00
July '97 ....50.00

Chris Burkett
July '91.......................12.00
July '94.....................50.00
July '97 ....125.00

Keith Byars
July '91.......................12.00
July '94.....................25.00
July '97 ....35.00

Scott Campbell
July '91.......................12.00
July '94.....................22.00
July '97 ....35.00

Carlos Carson
July '91.......................12.00
July '94.....................24.00
July '97 ....35.00

Harry Carson
July '91.......................12.00
July '94.....................26.00
July '97 ....35.00

Anthony Carter
July '91.......................12.00
July '94.....................55.00
July '97.......................75.00

Gerald Carter
July '91.......................12.00
July '94.....................18.00
July '97 ....35.00

Michael Carter
July '91.......................12.00
July '94.....................40.00
July '97 ....65.00

Tony Casillas
July '91.......................12.00
July '94.....................23.00
July '97 ....35.00

Jeff Chadwick
July '91.......................12.00
July '94.....................20.00
July '97 ....35.00

Deron Cherry
July '91.......................12.00
July '94.....................25.00
July '97 ....35.00

Ray Childress
July '91.......................12.00
July '94.....................30.00
July '97.......................70.00

Todd Christiansen
July '91.......................12.00
July '94.....................30.00
July '97 ....85.00

Gary Clark

July '91......................12.00
July '94 ....40.00
July '97 ....50.00

Mark Clayton

July '91......................12.00
July '94 ....40.00
July '97 ....60.00

Chris Collinsworth

July '91......................25.00
July '94 ....45.00
July '97 ....90.00

Doug Cosbie

July '91......................12.00
July '94 ....25.00
July '97......................75.00

Roger Craig

July '91......................12.00
July '94 ....30.00
July '97 ....40.00

Randall Cunningham

July '91......................35.00
July '94 ....40.00
July '97 ....54.00

Jeff Davis

July '91......................18.00
July '94 ....20.00
July '97 ....40.00

Ken Davis

July '91......................12.00
July '94 ....40.00
July '97 ....90.00

Richard Dent

July '91......................12.00
July '94 ....30.00
July '97 ....45.00

Eric Dickerson

July '91......................38.00
July '94 ....50.00
July '97......................75.00

Floyd Dixon

July '91......................12.00
July '94 ....20.00
July '97 ....35.00

Tony Dorsett

July '91......................50.00
July '94 ....130.00
July '97 ....260.00

Mark Duper

July '91......................12.00
July '94 ....25.00
July '97......................75.00

Tony Eason

July '91......................12.00
July '94 ....25.00
July '97 ....35.00

Carl Ekern

July '91......................12.00
July '94 ....20.00
July '97 ....40.00

Henry Ellard

July '91......................12.00
July '94 ....24.00
July '97 ....40.00

John Elway

July '91......................18.00
July '94 ....45.00
July '97 ....150.00

Phillip Epps

July '91......................12.00
July '94 ....25.00
July '97 ....40.00

Boomer Esiason

July '91......................30.00
July '94 ....45.00
July '97 ....75.00

Jim Everett

July '91......................25.00
July '94 ....30.00
July '97 ....50.00

Brent Fullwood

July '91......................18.00
July '94 ....28.00
July '97 ....40.00

Mark Gastineau

July '91......................12.00
July '94 ....18.00
July '97 ....35.00

Willie Gault

July '91......................35.00
July '94 ....50.00
July '97 ....110.00

Bob Golic

July '91......................12.00
July '94 ....20.00
July '97 ....35.00

Jerry Gray

July '91......................12.00
July '94 ....20.00
July '97 ....35.00

Darrell Green

July '91......................12.00
July '94 ....38.00
July '97 ....50.00

Jacob Green

July '91......................12.00
July '94 ....25.00
July '97 ....35.00

Roy Green

July '91......................12.00
July '94 ....30.00
July '97 ....35.00

Steve Grogan

July '91......................12.00
July '94 ....20.00
July '97 ....40.00

Ronnie Harmon

July '91......................25.00
July '94 ....50.00
July '97 ....125.00

Bobby Hebert

July '91......................20.00
July '94 ....30.00
July '97 ....40.00

Alonzo Highsmith

July '91......................12.00
July '94 ....25.00
July '97 ....35.00

Drew Hill
July '91.....................12.00
July '94.....................28.00
July '97.....................35.00

Earnest Jackson
July '91.....................12.00
July '94.....................18.00
July '97.....................35.00

Rickey Jackson
July '91.....................12.00
July '94.....................18.00
July '97.....................35.00

Vance Johnson
July '91.....................12.00
July '94.....................24.00
July '97.....................35.00

Ed Jones
July '91.....................18.00
July '94.....................24.00
July '97...................100.00

James Jones
July '91.....................12.00
July '94.....................20.00
July '97.....................35.00

Rod Jones
July '91.....................18.00
July '94.....................18.00
July '97.....................35.00

Rulon Jones
July '91.....................12.00
July '94.....................20.00
July '97.....................40.00

Steve Jordan
July '91.....................12.00
July '94.....................30.00
July '97.....................35.00

E.J. Junior
July '91.....................25.00
July '94.....................40.00
July '97.....................35.00

Jim Kelly
July '91.....................12.00
July '94...................110.00
July '97...................200.00

Bill Kenney
July '91.....................12.00
July '94.....................27.00
July '97.....................35.00

Bernie Kosar
July '91.....................15.00
July '94.....................21.00
July '97.....................35.00

Tommy Kramer
July '91.....................12.00
July '94.....................32.00
July '97.....................45.00

Dave Krieg
July '91.....................12.00
July '94.....................24.00
July '97.....................65.00

Tim Krumrie
July '91.....................12.00
July '94.....................45.00
July '97.....................65.00

Mark Lee
July '91......................12.00
July '94 ....35.00
July '97 ....40.00

Ronnie Lippett
July '91......................12.00
July '94 ....28.00
July '97 ....35.00

Louis Lipps
July '91......................12.00
July '94 ....25.00
July '97 ....35.00

Neil Lomax
July '91......................12.00
July '94 ....25.00
July '97 ....35.00

Chuck Long
July '91......................12.00
July '94 ....20.00
July '97 ....35.00

Howie Long
July '91......................20.00
July '94 ....40.00
July '97 ....120.00

Ronnie Lott
July '91......................12.00
July '94 ....52.00
July '97 ....140.00

Kevin Mack
July '91......................12.00
July '94 ....20.00
July '97 ....35.00

Mark Malone
July '91......................18.00
July '94 ....35.00
July '97......................70.00

Dexter Manley
July '91......................12.00
July '94 ....22.00
July '97 ....35.00

Dan Marino
July '91......................18.00
July '94....................110.00
July '97 ....300.00

Eric Martin
July '91......................12.00
July '94 ....24.00
July '97 ....35.00

Rueben Mayes
July '91......................12.00
July '94 ....24.00
July '97 ....35.00

Jim McMahon
July '91......................12.00
July '94 ....24.00
July '97 ....35.00

Freeman McNeil
July '91......................12.00
July '94 ....18.00
July '97 ....35.00

Karl Mecklenburg
July '91......................12.00
July '94 ....20.00
July '97 ....50.00

Mike Merriweather

July '91......................12.00
July '94......................18.00
July '97......................35.00

Stump Mitchell

July '91......................12.00
July '94......................24.00
July '97......................35.00

Art Monk

July '91......................12.00
July '94....................100.00
July '97....................250.00

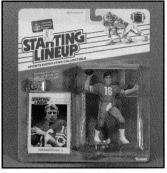

Joe Montana

July '91......................70.00
July '94....................115.00
July '97....................240.00

Warren Moon

July '91......................25.00
July '94......................45.00
July '97......................80.00

Stanley Morgan

July '91......................12.00
July '94......................20.00
July '97......................35.00

Joe Morris

July '91......................12.00
July '94......................20.00
July '97......................35.00

Darrin Nelson

July '91......................12.00
July '94......................21.00
July '97......................35.00

Ozzie Newsome

July '91......................20.00
July '94......................23.00
July '97......................45.00

Ken O'Brien

July '91......................12.00
July '94......................20.00
July '97......................35.00

John Offerdahl

July '91......................20.00
July '94......................24.00
July '97......................60.00

Christian Okoye

July '91......................40.00
July '94......................40.00
July '97......................40.00

Mike Quick

July '91......................12.00
July '94......................20.00
July '97......................35.00

Jerry Rice

July '91......................45.00
July '94....................110.00
July '97....................350.00

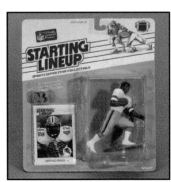

Gerald Riggs

July '91......................12.00
July '94......................20.00
July '97......................35.00

Reggie Rogers

July '91......................12.00
July '94......................18.00
July '97......................35.00

Mike Rozier
July '91......................12.00
July '94 ....25.00
July '97 ....35.00

Jay Schroeder
July '91......................12.00
July '94 ....35.00
July '97 ....35.00

Mickey Shuler
July '91......................12.00
July '94 ....19.00
July '97 ....35.00

Phil Simms
July '91......................15.00
July '94 ....25.00
July '97 ....45.00

Mike Singletary
July '91......................25.00
July '94 ....30.00
July '97 ....40.00

Billy Ray Smith
July '91......................12.00
July '94 ....40.00
July '97 ....90.00

Bruce Smith
July '91......................12.00
July '94 ....75.00
July '97 ....140.00

J.T. Smith
July '91......................12.00
July '94 ....28.00
July '97 ....35.00

Troy Stradford
July '91......................12.00
July '94 ....19.00
July '97 ....45.00

Lawrence Taylor
July '91......................12.00
July '94 ....28.00
July '97 ....80.00

Vinnie Testaverde
July '91......................18.00
July '94 ....17.00
July '97 ....40.00

Andre Tippett
July '91......................12.00
July '94 ....22.00
July '97 ....35.00

Anthony Toney
July '91......................12.00
July '94 ....20.00
July '97 ....35.00

Al Toon
July '91......................12.00
July '94 ....22.00
July '97 ....35.00

Jack Trudeau
July '91......................18.00
July '94 ....20.00
July '97 ....40.00

Herschel Walker
July '91......................12.00
July '94 ....20.00
July '97 ....35.00

Curt Warner

July '91......................12.00
July '94 ....22.00
July '97 ....35.00

Dave Waymer

July '91......................12.00
July '94 ....24.00
July '97 ....35.00

Charles White

July '91......................12.00
July '94 ....22.00
July '97 ....35.00

Danny White

July '91......................12.00
July '94 ....25.00
July '97 ....100.00

Randy White

July '91......................12.00
July '94 ....34.00
July '97 ....150.00

Reggie White

July '91......................18.00
July '94 ....32.00
July '97 ....100.00

James Wilder

July '91......................12.00
July '94 ....20.00
July '97 ....35.00

Doug Williams

July '91......................12.00
July '94 ....25.00
July '97 ....40.00

Marc Wilson

July '91......................55.00
July '94 ....70.00
July '97 ....140.00

Sammy Winder

July '91......................12.00
July '94 ....20.00
July '97 ....35.00

Kellen Winslow

July '91......................12.00
July '94 ....65.00
July '97 ....350.00

Rod Woodson

July '91......................12.00
July '94 ....25.00
July '97 ....300.00

Randy Wright

July '91......................12.00
July '94 ....25.00
July '97 ....60.00

1989 FOOTBALL

★ **Set Price: $6,000.00** ★ **Total Figures: 123** ★

The 1989 Kenner Football issue contains 14 fewer players than the 1988 version, but many collectors consider it more difficult to complete than the inaugural release. Due to slow sales the previous year, Kenner cut back production on several team cases, making the sets for these teams almost impossible to assemble. Poor sales also led the company to cancel production of several team cases, including the Phoenix Cardinals, Green Bay Packers, Kansas City Chiefs, Los Angeles Rams, Miami Dolphins, San Diego Chargers, and Tampa Bay Buccaneers. But scaled-back production quantities make up just one of the many challenges facing the collector attempting to complete this set.

Again, the offensive and defensive linemen are among the rarest and most sought-after pieces in the set. Because the linemen were not the most popular players on their teams, Kenner packed them only one or two per case. Players like Dave Cadigan, Bryan Hinkle, Jerome Brown, and Bill Bates are usually the last pieces most collectors need to complete a set.

While the linemen are the hardest 1989 figures to find, most of the star players are extremely popular and difficult to obtain as well. Like the 1988 figures, many of these pieces were opened and played with by kids. And it can be a long, frustrating search to find them in

The '89 Football set lists several players that weren't produced. At left is Danny Noonan.

anything resembling mint condition.

Most of Kenner's '89 Football figures are fairly scarce, but one piece that isn't too hard to find is the Jerry Rice. The NFL handed out hundreds of '89 Rice figures at the second NFL Experience, which was

Case Assortments

AFC ALL-STAR CASE		Dennis McKinnon	Denver Broncos	Vann McElroy	Jim Burt	Louis Lipps
Cornelius Bennett	Jerry Rice	Jim McMahon	Tony Dorsett	Jay Schroeder	Lionel Manuel	Rod Woodson
Bubby Brister (2)	Phil Simms (2)	Steve McMichael	John Elway		Leonard Marshall	
Eddie Brown	Mike Singletary	Mike Singletary	Rickey Nattiel	Minnesota	Joe Morris	San Francisco
Tim Brown	Lawrence Taylor			Vikings	Phil Simms	49ers
John Elway (2)	Vinny Testaverde (2)	Cincinnati	Detroit Lions	Joey Browner	Lawrence Taylor	Michael Carter
Boomer Esiason (2)	Herschel Walker	Bengals	Bennie Blades	Anthony Carter		Roger Craig
Bernie Kosar (2)	Reggie White	James Brooks	Gary James	Chris Doleman	New York Jets	Charles Haley
James Lofton		Eddie Brown	Chuck Long	Keith Millard	Dave Cadigan	Ronnie Lott
Howie Long	*Note: At press time*	Boomer Esiason	Pete Mandley	Darrin Nelson	Alex Gordon	Joe Montana
Dan Marino (2)	*team case assort-*	David Fulcher	Chris Spielman	Wade Wilson	Johnny Hector	Jerry Rice
Freeman McNeil	*ments were unavail-*	Joe Kelly			Eric McMillan	Steve Young
Warren Moon (2)	*able.*	Tim Krumrie	Houston	New England	Freeman McNeil	
Ken O'Brien (2)		Anthony Munoz	Oilers	Patriots	Ken O'Brien	Seattle
John Stephens	TEAM CASES	Ickey Woods	Ernest Givins	Sean Farrell	Mickey Shuler	Seahawks
Andre Tippett	Atlanta Falcons		Drew Hill	Irving Fryar	Al Toon	Kelly Stouffer
Al Toon	Bill Fralic	Cleveland	Sean Jones	John Stephens		Curt Warner
Curt Warner	Chris Miller	Browns	Warren Moon	Andre Tippett	Philadelphia	John Williams
	John Settle	Hanford Dixon	Mike Rozier	Garin Veris	Eagles	
NFC		Bernie Kosar			Jerome Brown	Washington
ALL-STAR CASE	Buffalo Bills	Kevin Mack	Indianapolis	New Orleans	Keith Byars	Redskins
Neal Anderson	Cornelius Bennett	Frank Minnifield	Colts	Saints	Randall Cunningham	Kelvin Bryant
Mark Bavaro	Shane Conlan	Webster Slaughter	Duane Bickett	Bobby Hebert	Keith Jackson	Gary Clark
Roger Craig	Jim Kelly		Bill Brooks	Dalton Hilliard	Mike Quick	Dexter Manley
Randall Cunningham (2)	Andre Reed	Dallas Cowboys	Chris Chandler	Eric Martin	Anthony Toney	Charles Mann
Jim Everett (2)	Bruce Smith	Bill Bates		Ruben Mayes	Reggie White	Art Monk
Keith Jackson	Thurman Thomas	Michael Irvin	Los Angeles	Pat Swilling		Doug Williams
Neil Lomax		Eugene Lockhart	Raiders		Pittsburgh	
Dexter Manley	Chicago Bears	Danny Noonan	Marcus Allen	New York	Steelers	
Jim McMahon (2)	Neal Anderson	Steve Pelleur	Tim Brown	Giants	Bubby Brister	
Joe Montana (2)	Jimbo Covert	Herschel Walker	James Lofton	Carl Banks	Thomas Everett	
	Richard Dent		Howie Long	Mark Bavaro	Bryan Hinkle	
	Dave Duerson					

held in January 1993 in conjunction with Super Bowl XXVII in Pasadena, Calif. But the abundance of these pieces on the market doesn't stop the NFL's most prolific receiver from being a popular—and relatively expensive—choice for collectors.

One of Kenner's first error pieces appeared in this set: the Ken O'Brien figure. The card front incorrectly listed his name as "O'Brian." Once Kenner realized its mistake, it quickly corrected it. As a result, the error version is much more difficult to find than the corrected version and commands a premium on the secondary market.

The increasing popularity of the NFL in the sports collectibles hobby and the relative scarcity of most of these pieces should keep collector demand for '89 Football strong for years to come. Many collectors continue the search for one or two elusive figures they lack. Since several of the rarer figures seldom, if ever, show up in the marketplace, the price collectors might be willing to pay for mint specimens is unknown. And the passage of time will only ensure that this series—already extremely difficult to complete—will become close to impossible to put together.

Marcus Allen

July '91	8.00
July '94	20.00
July '97	45.00

Neal Anderson

July '91	15.00
July '94	14.00
July '97	30.00

Carl Banks (R)

July '91	8.00
July '94	14.00
July '97	40.00

Bill Bates (R)

July '91	8.00
July '94	15.00
July '97	240.00

Mark Bavaro

July '91	8.00
July '94	15.00
July '97	40.00

Cornelius Bennett

July '91	8.00
July '94	30.00
July '97	75.00

Duane Bickett

July '91	8.00
July '94	12.00
July '97	30.00

Bennie Blades (R)

July '91	8.00
July '94	14.00
July '97	60.00

Bubby Brister (R)

July '91	8.00
July '94	15.00
July '97	30.00

Bill Brooks

July '91	8.00
July '94	12.00
July '97	40.00

James Brooks

July '91	8.00
July '94	14.00
July '97	30.00

Eddie Brown

July '91	8.00
July '94	14.00
July '97	30.00

Jerome Brown (R)
July '91 ....8.00
July '94 ....45.00
July '97 ....225.00

Tim Brown (R)
July '91 ....8.00
July '94 ....15.00
July '97 ....75.00

Joey Browner
July '91 ....8.00
July '94 ....15.00
July '97 ....30.00

Kelvin Bryant (R)
July '91 ....8.00
July '94 ....15.00
July '97 ....30.00

Jim Burt (R)
July '91 ....8.00
July '94 ....18.00
July '97 ....30.00

Keith Byars
July '91 ....8.00
July '94 ....18.00
July '97 ....30.00

Dave Cadigan (R)
July '91 ....8.00
July '94 ....14.00
July '97 ....60.00

Anthony Carter
July '91 ....8.00
July '94 ....15.00
July '97 ....30.00

Michael Carter
July '91 ....8.00
July '94 ....24.00
July '97 ....40.00

Chris Chandler (R)
July '91 ....8.00
July '94 ....13.00
July '97 ....30.00

Gary Clark
July '91 ....8.00
July '94 ....30.00
July '97 ....35.00

Shane Conlan (R)
July '91 ....8.00
July '94 ....40.00
July '97 ....100.00

Jimbo Covert (R)
July '91 ....15.00
July '94 ....30.00
July '97 ....30.00

Roger Craig
July '91 ....8.00
July '94 ....14.00
July '97 ....30.00

Randall Cunningham
July '91 ....20.00
July '94 ....15.00
July '97 ....30.00

Richard Dent
July '91 ....8.00
July '94 ....14.00
July '97 ....30.00

Hanford Dixon (R)
July '91........................8.00
July '94........................12.00
July '97.......................30.00

Chris Doleman (R)
July '91.......................15.00
July '94.......................16.00
July '97.......................30.00

Tony Dorsett (HOF)
July '91.......................28.00
July '94.......................54.00
July '97......................140.00

Dave Duerson (R)
July '91........................8.00
July '94.......................14.00
July '97.......................30.00

John Elway
July '91........................8.00
July '94.......................25.00
July '97......................100.00

Boomer Esiason
July '91........................8.00
July '94.......................20.00
July '97.......................30.00

Jim Everett
July '91........................8.00
July '94.......................15.00
July '97.......................30.00

Thomas Everett (R)
July '91........................8.00
July '94.......................13.00
July '97.......................30.00

Sean Farrell (R)
July '91........................8.00
July '94.......................14.00
July '97.......................30.00

Bill Fralic (R)
July '91.......................15.00
July '94.......................16.00
July '97.......................30.00

Irving Fryar (R)
July '91........................8.00
July '94.......................18.00
July '97.......................80.00

David Fulcher (R)
July '91........................8.00
July '94.......................14.00
July '97.......................30.00

Ernest Givins (R)
July '91........................8.00
July '94.......................18.00
July '97.......................30.00

Alex Gordon (R)
July '91........................8.00
July '94.......................13.00
July '97.......................30.00

Charles Haley (R)
July '91........................8.00
July '94.......................22.00
July '97......................180.00

Bobby Hebert
July '91........................8.00
July '94.......................30.00
July '97.......................35.00

Johnny Hector (R)
July '91........................8.00
July '94......................14.00
July '97 ....30.00

Drew Hill
July '91........................8.00
July '94......................18.00
July '97 ....30.00

Dalton Hilliard (R)
July '91........................8.00
July '94......................18.00
July '97 ....30.00

Bryan Hinkle (R)
July '91........................8.00
July '94......................12.00
July '97 ....50.00

Michael Irvin (R)
July '91........................8.00
July '94......................45.00
July '97 ....125.00

Keith Jackson (R)
July '91........................8.00
July '94......................22.00
July '97 ....40.00

Gary James (R)
July '91........................8.00
July '94......................12.00
July '97 ....30.00

Sean Jones (R)
July '91........................8.00
July '94......................13.00
July '97 ....30.00

Jim Kelly
July '91......................25.00
July '94 ....75.00
July '97 ....225.00

Joe Kelly (R)
July '91........................8.00
July '94......................10.00
July '97 ....30.00

Bernie Kosar
July '91........................8.00
July '94......................12.00
July '97 ....30.00

Tim Krumrie
July '91........................8.00
July '94......................20.00
July '97 ....30.00

Louis Lipps
July '91......................20.00
July '94......................16.00
July '97 ....30.00

Eugene Lockhart (R)
July '91........................8.00
July '94......................14.00
July '97 ....75.00

James Lofton (R)
July '91......................15.00
July '94 ....34.00
July '97 ....75.00

Neil Lomax
July '91........................8.00
July '94......................12.00
July '97 ....30.00

Chuck Long
July '91.......................8.00
July '94.....................12.00
July '97 ....30.00

Howie Long
July '91.......................8.00
July '94.....................14.00
July '97.....................55.00

Ronnie Lott
July '91.......................8.00
July '94 ....34.00
July '97 ....80.00

Kevin Mack
July '91.......................8.00
July '94.....................12.00
July '97 ....30.00

Pete Mandley (R)
July '91.......................8.00
July '94.....................12.00
July '97 ....30.00

Dexter Manley
July '91.......................8.00
July '94.....................14.00
July '97 ....30.00

Charles Mann (R)
July '91.......................8.00
July '94.....................14.00
July '97 ....30.00

Lionel Manuel (R)
July '91.......................8.00
July '94.....................15.00
July '97 ....30.00

Dan Marino
July '91.....................15.00
July '94 ....74.00
July '97 ....300.00

Leonard Marshall (R)
July '91.......................8.00
July '94.....................13.00
July '97 ....30.00

Eric Martin
July '91.......................8.00
July '94.....................15.00
July '97 ....30.00

Rueben Mayes
July '91.......................8.00
July '94.....................13.00
July '97 ....30.00

Vann McElroy (R)
July '91.......................8.00
July '94.....................14.00
July '97 ....40.00

Dennis McKinnon (R)
July '91.......................8.00
July '94.....................12.00
July '97 ....30.00

Jim McMahon
July '91.......................8.00
July '94.....................14.00
July '97 ....30.00

Steve McMichael (R)
July '91.......................8.00
July '94.....................20.00
July '97 ....50.00

Eric McMillan (R)
July '91 ....8.00
July '94 ....12.00
July '97 ....30.00

Freeman McNeil
July '91 ....8.00
July '94 ....10.00
July '97 ....30.00

Keith Millard (R)
July '91 ....20.00
July '94 ....16.00
July '97 ....30.00

Chris Miller (R)
July '91 ....8.00
July '94 ....25.00
July '97 ....30.00

Frank Minnifield (R)
July '91 ....8.00
July '94 ....12.00
July '97 ....30.00

Art Monk
July '91 ....8.00
July '94 ....44.00
July '97 ....80.00

Joe Montana
July '91 ....35.00
July '94 ....58.00
July '97 ....140.00

Warren Moon
July '91 ....8.00
July '94 ....28.00
July '97 ....70.00

Joe Morris
July '91 ....8.00
July '94 ....14.00
July '97 ....30.00

Anthony Munoz (R)
July '91 ....8.00
July '94 ....22.00
July '97 ....140.00

Rickey Nattiel (R)
July '91 ....8.00
July '94 ....12.00
July '97 ....35.00

Darrin Nelson
July '91 ....8.00
July '94 ....10.00
July '97 ....30.00

Danny Noonan (R)
July '91 ....8.00
July '94 ....12.00
July '97 ....75.00

Ken O'Brian (error)
July '91 ....50.00
July '94 ....50.00
July '97 ....75.00

Ken O'Brien (correct spelling)
July '91 ....8.00
July '94 ....14.00
July '97 ....30.00

Steve Pelleur (R)
July '91 ....15.00
July '94 ....11.00
July '97 ....70.00

Mike Quick

July '91 ....8.00
July '94 ....12.00
July '97 ....30.00

Andre Reed (R)

July '91 ....8.00
July '94 ....60.00
July '97 ....125.00

Jerry Rice

July '91 ....18.00
July '94 ....52.00
July '97 ....50.00

Mike Rozier

July '91 ....8.00
July '94 ....17.00
July '97 ....30.00

Jay Schroeder

July '91 ....15.00
July '94 ....14.00
July '97 ....30.00

John Settle (R)

July '91 ....8.00
July '94 ....11.00
July '97 ....30.00

Mickey Shuler

July '91 ....8.00
July '94 ....12.00
July '97 ....30.00

Phil Simms

July '91 ....8.00
July '94 ....12.00
July '97 ....30.00

Mike Singletary

July '91 ....8.00
July '94 ....16.00
July '97 ....30.00

Webster Slaughter (R)

July '91 ....15.00
July '94 ....15.00
July '97 ....30.00

Bruce Smith

July '91 ....8.00
July '94 ....42.00
July '97 ....150.00

Chris Spielman (R)

July '91 ....18.00
July '94 ....20.00
July '97 ....200.00

John Stephens (R)

July '91 ....8.00
July '94 ....12.00
July '97 ....30.00

Kelly Stouffer (R)

July '91 ....18.00
July '94 ....20.00
July '97 ....30.00

Pat Swilling (R)

July '91 ....8.00
July '94 ....24.00
July '97 ....30.00

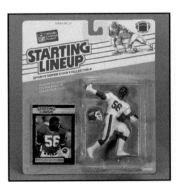

Lawrence Taylor

July '91 ....8.00
July '94 ....20.00
July '97 ....60.00

Vinny Testaverde

July '91......................15.00
July '94......................16.00
July '97......................30.00

Thurman Thomas (R)

July '91......................25.00
July '94......................72.00
July '97....................175.00

Andre Tippett

July '91........................8.00
July '94......................15.00
July '97......................30.00

Anthony Toney

July '91........................8.00
July '94......................18.00
July '97......................30.00

Al Toon

July '91........................8.00
July '94......................14.00
July '97......................30.00

Garin Veris (R)

July '91........................8.00
July '94......................13.00
July '97......................30.00

Herschel Walker

July '91........................8.00
July '94......................11.00
July '97......................30.00

Curt Warner

July '91........................8.00
July '94......................16.00
July '97......................30.00

Reggie White

July '91........................8.00
July '94......................20.00
July '97......................60.00

Doug Williams

July '91........................8.00
July '94......................12.00
July '97......................30.00

John Williams (R)

July '91......................18.00
July '94......................16.00
July '97......................30.00

Wade Wilson (R)

July '91........................8.00
July '94......................18.00
July '97......................30.00

Ickey Woods (R)

July '91......................20.00
July '94......................17.00
July '97......................30.00

Rod Woodson

July '91........................8.00
July '94......................16.00
July '97....................200.00

Steve Young (R)

July '91......................20.00
July '94......................64.00
July '97....................375.00

1990 FOOTBALL

★ Set Price: $2,000.00 ★ Total Figures: 75 ★

Because Kenner's 1988 and '89 Football sets are becoming increasingly difficult and expensive to complete, many SLU collectors are turning to the 1990 issue. Most of the 1990 Football pieces still cost less than $25 and with only 66 different players, the set is a manageable size. It offers a good crop of rookies in Troy Aikman, Barry Sanders, Jim Harbaugh, and Cris Carter. Plus there are a few short-prints that make completing this release a challenge.

The Doug Flutie is one such short-print. It was released only in the New England Patriots team case, and it's highly sought by collectors trying to assemble the only 10 quarterbacks Kenner ever made in the "snapping" pose—crouched under center. The Flutie piece is considered one of the hardest to find in this set.

Another curious feature involves its uniform variations. Kenner issued nine players wearing two different jersey colors. The variations are actually '89 figures in the '90 package. After producing its '89 Football set, Ken-

ner had an unknown quantity of figures left over, so the company repackaged them in the '90 set. To finish the production run, Kenner manufactured additional figures in a different color uniform. Each figure has the year of production stamped on the bottom. Interestingly, every Dan Marino and Jim Everett in the '90 release is an '89 figure. Kenner never produced a "1990" Marino or Everett figure (see sidebar).

Again, poor sales of the prior year's figures prompted Kenner to cut back the number of team cases. The toymaker issued just 14 team cases in limited quantities. Most of the "'89" figures were issued in the all-star cases while the "'90" figures were released in the team cases.

Collectors disagree on whether or not you need the variations to assemble a complete '90 set.

Pictured above is the back of the '90 Football package. At left is Michael Irvin.

Whether you decide to seek out those extra pieces or not, '90 Football is an exciting set that is well worth collecting.

Leftovers?

Below is a list of players whose 1990 package includes either a 1989 or a '90 figure. Generally, the white-jersey version is a player's 1989 figure and the color-uniform piece is his '90 figure. The only exception: Boomer Esiason.

Neal Anderson	blue '90	white '89
Roger Craig	red '90	white '89
Randall Cunningham	green '90	white '89
John Elway	orange '90	white '89
Boomer Esiason	black '89	white '90
Bernie Kosar	orange '90	white '89
Joe Montana	red '90	white '89
Mike Singletary	blue '90	white '89
Reggie White	green '90	white '89

Case Assortments

AFC ALL-STAR CASE						
Boomer Esiason	Jim Everett (1)	Mike Hampton (2)	Felix Wright (4)		Phil Simms (4)	Roger Craig (3)
John Elway (2)	Don Majkowski (1)	Jim Harbaugh (2)			Odessa Turner (4)	Tom Rathman (4)
Bo Jackson (4)	Keith Millard (1)	Mike Singletary (2)	**Dallas Cowboys**	**Minnesota**	**Philadelphia**	John Taylor (4)
Jim Kelly (2)	Joe Montana (1)	Mike Tomczak (3)	Troy Aikman (7)	**Vikings**	**Eagles**	
Bernie Kosar (1)	Deion Sanders (1)	Donell Woolford (2)	Michael Irvin (5)	Keith Millard (4)	Cris Carter (1)	**Washington**
Dan Marino (1)	Barry Sanders (1)		Steve Walsh (4)	Mike Merriweather (4)	Randall Cunningham (6)	**Redskins**
Warren Moon (1)	Mike Singletary (1)	**Cincinnati**		Herschel Walker (5)	Keith Jackson (2)	Charles Mann (3)
Christian Okoye (1)	Herschel Walker (2)	**Bengals**	**Denver Broncos**	Wade Wilson (3)	Clyde Simmons (3)	Gerald Riggs (4)
Bruce Smith (1)	Reggie White (1)	James Brooks (3)	John Elway (5)		Reggie White (4)	Mark Rypien (5)
Ickey Woods (2)		Boomer Esiason (4)	Simon Fletcher (4)	**New England**		Ricky Sanders (4)
	TEAM CASES	Rodney Holman (2)	Bobby Humphrey (4)	**Patriots**	**Pittsburgh**	
	Buffalo Bills	Tim McGee (3)	Vance Johnson (3)	Doug Flutie (4)	**Steelers**	
NFC	Jim Kelly (6)	Ickey Woods (4)		Hart Lee Dykes (6)	Bubby Brister (6)	
ALL-STAR CASE	Andre Reed (5)		**Los Angeles**	John Stephens (6)	Louis Lipps (5)	
Troy Aikman (1)	Thurman Thomas (5)	**Cleveland**	**Raiders**		Tim Worley (5)	
Neal Anderson (1)		**Browns**	Steve Beurlein (4)	**New York Giants**		
Roger Craig (1)	**Chicago Bears**	Eric Metcalf (3)	Tim Brown (3)	Mark Bavaro (2)	**San Francisco**	
Randall Cunningham (2)	Neal Anderson (3)	Bernie Kosar (5)	Bo Jackson (6)	Lionel Manuel (2)	**49ers**	
	Dennis Gentry (2)	Webster Slaughter (4)	Greg Townsend (4)	Dave Meggett (4)	Joe Montana (5)	

Troy Aikman (R)
July '91 ....12.00
July '94 ....42.00
July '97 ....75.00

Neal Anderson (blue)
July '91 ....6.00
July '94 ....14.00
July '97 ....20.00

Neal Anderson (white)
July '91 ....6.00
July '94 ....14.00
July '97 ....20.00

Mark Bavaro
July '91 ....6.00
July '94 ....20.00
July '97 ....25.00

Steve Beurlein (R)
July '91 ....6.00
July '94 ....16.00
July '97 ....20.00

Bubby Brister
July '91 ....6.00
July '94 ....15.00
July '97 ....20.00

James Brooks
July '91 ....6.00
July '94 ....13.00
July '97 ....20.00

Tim Brown
July '91 ....6.00
July '94 ....11.00
July '97 ....40.00

Cris Carter (R)
July '91 ....25.00
July '94 ....20.00
July '97 ....125.00

Roger Craig (red)
July '91 ....15.00
July '94 ....10.00
July '97 ....20.00

Roger Craig (white)
July '91 ....15.00
July '94 ....10.00
July '97 ....20.00

Randall Cunningham (green)
July '91 ....6.00
July '94 ....14.00
July '97 ....20.00

Randall Cunningham (white)
July '91 ....6.00
July '94 ....14.00
July '97 ....20.00

Hart Lee Dykes (R)
July '91 ....6.00
July '94 ....15.00
July '97 ....20.00

John Elway (orange)
July '91 ....6.00
July '94 ....15.00
July '97 ....50.00

John Elway (white)
July '91 ....6.00
July '94 ....22.00
July '97 ....50.00

Boomer Esiason (black)

July '91........................6.00
July '94......................16.00
July '97......................20.00

Boomer Esiason (white)

July '91........................6.00
July '94......................16.00
July '97......................20.00

Jim Everett

July '91......................15.00
July '94......................14.00
July '97......................15.00

Simon Fletcher (R)

July '91........................6.00
July '94......................10.00
July '97......................15.00

Doug Flutie (R)

July '91......................25.00
July '94......................22.00
July '97....................140.00

Dennis Gentry (R)

July '91........................6.00
July '94......................12.00
July '97......................20.00

Dan Hampton (R)

July '91........................6.00
July '94......................18.00
July '97......................25.00

Jim Harbaugh (R)

July '91......................15.00
July '94......................20.00
July '97......................70.00

Rodney Holman (R)

July '91......................15.00
July '94......................15.00
July '97......................15.00

Bobby Humphrey (R)

July '91......................25.00
July '94......................16.00
July '97......................18.00

Michael Irvin

July '91........................6.00
July '94......................35.00
July '97......................60.00

Bo Jackson (R)

July '91......................20.00
July '94......................16.00
July '97......................16.00

Keith Jackson

July '91........................6.00
July '94......................12.00
July '97......................18.00

Vance Johnson

July '91........................6.00
July '94......................14.00
July '97......................18.00

Jim Kelly

July '91........................6.00
July '94......................20.00
July '97......................30.00

Bernie Kosar (orange)

July '91........................6.00
July '94......................14.00
July '97......................20.00

Bernie Kosar (white)
July '91 ....6.00
July '94 ....14.00
July '97 ....20.00

Louis Lipps
July '91 ....6.00
July '94 ....12.00
July '97 ....15.00

Dan Majkowski (R)
July '91 ....18.00
July '94 ....13.00
July '97 ....15.00

Charles Mann
July '91 ....6.00
July '94 ....12.00
July '97 ....16.00

Lionel Manuel
July '91 ....6.00
July '94 ....10.00
July '97 ....16.00

Dan Marino
July '91 ....12.00
July '94 ....42.00
July '97 ....250.00

Tim McGee (R)
July '91 ....6.00
July '94 ....12.00
July '97 ....16.00

Dave Meggett (R)
July '91 ....25.00
July '94 ....15.00
July '97 ....18.00

Mike Merriweather
July '91 ....6.00
July '94 ....12.00
July '97 ....16.00

Eric Metcalf (R)
July '91 ....20.00
July '94 ....14.00
July '97 ....25.00

Keith Millard
July '91 ....6.00
July '94 ....10.00
July '97 ....16.00

Joe Montana (red)
July '91 ....18.00
July '94 ....30.00
July '97 ....75.00

Joe Montana (white)
July '91 ....18.00
July '94 ....30.00
July '97 ....75.00

Warren Moon
July '91 ....6.00
July '94 ....24.00
July '97 ....32.00

Christian Okoye
July '91 ....15.00
July '94 ....18.00
July '97 ....16.00

Tom Rathman (R)
July '91 ....6.00
July '94 ....18.00
July '97 ....30.00

Andre Reed

July '91 ....6.00
July '94 ....20.00
July '97 ....30.00

Gerald Riggs

July '91 ....6.00
July '94 ....14.00
July '97 ....15.00

Mark Rypien (R)

July '91 ....15.00
July '94 ....24.00
July '97 ....20.00

Barry Sanders (R)

July '91 ....30.00
July '94 ....60.00
July '97 ....80.00

Deion Sanders (R)

July '91 ....15.00
July '94 ....30.00
July '97 ....50.00

Rickey Sanders (R)

July '91 ....6.00
July '94 ....15.00
July '97 ....15.00

Clyde Simmons (R)

July '91 ....6.00
July '94 ....16.00
July '97 ....20.00

Phil Simms

July '91 ....6.00
July '94 ....11.00
July '97 ....15.00

Mike Singletary (blue)

July '91 ....6.00
July '94 ....12.00
July '97 ....20.00

Mike Singletary (white)

July '91 ....6.00
July '94 ....12.00
July '97 ....20.00

Webster Slaughter

July '91 ....6.00
July '94 ....10.00
July '97 ....15.00

Bruce Smith

July '91 ....6.00
July '94 ....18.00
July '97 ....30.00

John Stephens

July '91 ....6.00
July '94 ....12.00
July '97 ....15.00

John Taylor (R)

July '91 ....6.00
July '94 ....20.00
July '97 ....20.00

Thurman Thomas

July '91 ....25.00
July '94 ....40.00
July '97 ....40.00

Mike Tomczak (R)

July '91 ....6.00
July '94 ....14.00
July '97 ....15.00

Greg Townsend (R)
July '91 ....20.00
July '94 ....12.00
July '97 ....15.00

Odessa Turner (R)
July '91 ....6.00
July '94 ....11.00
July '97 ....15.00

Herschel Walker
July '91 ....6.00
July '94 ....11.00
July '97 ....15.00

Steve Walsh (R)
July '91 ....20.00
July '94 ....18.00
July '97 ....16.00

Reggie White (green)
July '91 ....6.00
July '94 ....16.00
July '97 ....30.00

Reggie White (white)
July '91 ....6.00
July '94 ....16.00
July '97 ....30.00

Wade Wilson
July '91 ....6.00
July '94 ....14.00
July '97 ....15.00

Ickey Woods (R)
July '91 ....6.00
July '94 ....11.00
July '97 ....15.00

Donnell Woolford (R)
July '91 ....6.00
July '94 ....20.00
July '97 ....20.00

Tim Worley (R)
July '91 ....20.00
July '94 ....14.00
July '97 ....15.00

Felix Wright (R)
July '91 ....6.00
July '94 ....12.00
July '97 ....15.00

1991 FOOTBALL

★ Set Price: $650.00 ★ Total Figures: 26 ★

This is one of the smallest football issues Kenner has produced. The company distributed most of its 1991 Football pieces through its all-star cases; hence they're not hard to find. Except for the big three—Troy Aikman, Dan Marino, and Emmitt Smith—this series is relatively inexpensive and easy to complete. Most of the pieces go for less than $30.

Because of continued slow sales with most of its team cases, Kenner issued just two of them in 1991—the Cincinnati Bengals and New York Giants. These would be the final team cases Kenner would ever issue, as the company moved away from regional distribution.

Like Kenner's other sets from that year, the '91 Football figures came with the less-than-popular coin insert. During production, Kenner made the switch from a steel coin to an aluminum one, and most of the figures can be found with either coin. Whether one coin version is scarcer than the other is unknown. But a lack of collector interest in these premiums

means there's no variation in price.

The Smith rookie figure is the premier piece in the set. Because he's established himself as one of the game's greatest running backs, Smith is extremely popular with collectors. Plus, the '91 Emmitt SLU is fairly scarce—Kenner packed it in only one of the two case assortments.

The second-year Aikman is actually harder to find than his 1990 rookie piece. Aikman was a one-pack in just one of the two case assortments in 1991. His rookie piece was packed one per NFC All-Pro case and seven per Cowboys team case. The '91 piece is already valued above Aikman's rookie, and its rarity makes it one to keep an eye on.

The last of the big three figures is Marino, the most popular football player Kenner has ever issued. Despite the fact that Kenner usually produces Marino figures in greater quantities than most of the other figures in a set, he still ranks among the most expensive pieces.

If you can afford the Smith, Aikman, and Marino figures, completing this set shouldn't be too difficult.

Above is the '91 package back. It is the last football checklist Kenner included on a package. At left is the popular Troy Aikman figure.

Case Assortments

ALL-STAR CASE
Flipper Anderson (2)
Neal Anderson (2)
Jeff George (2)
Jim Harbaugh (2)
Bobby Humphrey (1)
Don Majkowski (1)
Dan Marino (4)
Warren Moon (3)
Andre Rison (1)
Emmitt Smith (1)
Thurman Thomas (3)
Herschel Walker (2)

ALL-STAR CASE
Troy Aikman (1)
Mark Carrier (1)
Boomer Esiason (3)
Bobby Humphrey (1)
Don Majkowski (1)

Joe Montana (4)
Christian Okoye (2)
Jerry Rice (3)
Andre Rison (1)
Barry Sanders (5)
Phil Simms (1)
Herschel Walker (1)

Cincinnati Bengals
Eddie Brown (4)
James Brooks (4)
James Francis (3)
Boomer Esiason (5)

New York Giants
Mike Hampton (4)
Jeff Hostetler (4)
Dave Meggett (4)
Phil Simms (4)

Troy Aikman

July '92	15.00
July '94	32.00
July '97	100.00

Flipper Anderson (R)

July '92	10.00
July '94	10.00
July '97	15.00

Neal Anderson

July '92	15.00
July '94	18.00
July '97	15.00

James Brooks

July '92	10.00
July '94	14.00
July '97	15.00

Eddie Brown

July '92 ....10.00
July '94 ....12.00
July '97 ....15.00

Mark Carrier (R)

July '92 ....20.00
July '94 ....16.00
July '97 ....15.00

Boomer Esiason

July '92 ....7.00
July '94 ....10.00
July '97 ....15.00

James Francis (R)

July '92 ....16.00
July '94 ....20.00
July '97 ....20.00

Jeff George (R)

July '92 ....21.00
July '94 ....22.00
July '97 ....20.00

Rodney Hampton (R)

July '92 ....15.00
July '94 ....22.00
July '97 ....25.00

Jim Harbaugh

July '92 ....14.00
July '94 ....18.00
July '97 ....40.00

Jeff Hostetler (R)

July '92 ....20.00
July '94 ....22.00
July '97 ....25.00

Bobby Humphrey

July '92 ....8.00
July '94 ....10.00
July '97 ....15.00

Don Majkowski

July '92 ....9.00
July '94 ....12.00
July '97 ....15.00

Dan Marino

July '92 ....15.00
July '94 ....35.00
July '97 ....140.00

Dave Meggett

July '92 ....10.00
July '94 ....10.00
July '97 ....14.00

Joe Montana

July '92 ....8.00
July '94 ....22.00
July '97 ....30.00

Warren Moon

July '92 ....12.00
July '94 ....18.00
July '97 ....24.00

Christian Okoye

July '92 ....8.00
July '94 ....10.00
July '97 ....10.00

Jerry Rice

July '92 ....9.00
July '94 ....18.00
July '97 ....35.00

Andre Rison (R)
July '92 ....25.00
July '94 ....25.00
July '97 ....25.00

Barry Sanders
July '92 ....12.00
July '94 ....12.00
July '97 ....25.00

Phil Simms
July '92 ....8.00
July '94 ....10.00
July '97 ....15.00

Emmitt Smith (R)
July '92 ....45.00
July '94 ....85.00
July '97 ....300.00

Thurman Thomas
July '92 ....20.00
July '94 ....25.00
July '97 ....24.00

Herschel Walker
July '92 ....12.00
July '94 ....10.00
July '97 ....10.00

1992 FOOTBALL

★ Set Price: $500 ★ Total Figures: 26 ★

Kenner's '92 Football issue is one of its least collectible sets. Yes, it contains a sensible selection of stars—Troy Aikman, Dan Marino, Emmitt Smith, Steve Young, Jerry Rice, Barry Sanders, and Joe Montana. But the rookie crop is downright weak. Kenner produced only five rookies for this set: Earnest Byner, Haywood Jeffires, Seth Joyner, Rob Moore, and Derrick Thomas. Among them, only the Thomas is noteworthy.

Kenner issued its 1992 Football set in three different all-star case assortments. Byner, Pat Swilling, and Seth Joyner are the short-printed pieces, but their relative scarcity hasn't led to a corresponding increase in price, due mainly to collector indifference.

Like the previous year's baseball issue, this one's hottest piece at the time of its release was Bo Jackson. Although not nearly as overproduced as his 1991 Baseball figure, Jackson's second-year football piece suffered the same fate. When Jackson's career ended, the value of his figures fell, dragging down an already mediocre set.

As with other '92 issues, Kenner includ-ed a poster with each '92 Football figure as a premium, but they proved less than popular. Unless the package is opened, you cannot see the poster, and even when it's unfolded, the many creases detract from its appearance. After 1992, Kenner ceased its flirtation with such premiums as posters and coins and went back to cards—which most collectors seem to prefer.

While this set certainly isn't Kenner's best football effort, it does contain some affordable pieces of several great players. The second-year figures of Young and Smith and the Marino piece are expensive, but most of the other pieces can be found for less than $20. The small size, low price tag, and ready availability of these pieces make this set a good one for collectors just breaking in to the hobby. More experienced hobbyists, however, will want a series with a little more substance.

The back of the '92 package shows collectors an unfolded poster of Mark Rypien. At left is Emmitt Smith.

Case Assortments

ALL-STAR CASE	
Troy Aikman (2)	Seth Joyner
Michael Irvin	Jim Kelly
Haywood Jeffires	Jerry Rice (2)
Ronnie Lott	Mark Rypien
Dan Marino	Deion Sanders (2)
Joe Montana	Emmitt Smith (3)
Mark Rypien	Derrick Thomas
Barry Sanders (2)	Thurman Thomas
Deion Sanders	
Emmitt Smith (3)	**ALL-STAR CASE**
Derrick Thomas	R. Cunningham (2)
Thurman Thomas	Rodney Hampton
	Bobby Hebert
ALL-STAR CASE	Bo Jackson (3)
Earnest Byner	Warren Moon (3)
Bobby Hebert	Rob Moore
Jeff Hostetler	Andre Rison (2)
Haywood Jeffires	Pat Swilling
	Steve Young (2)

Troy Aikman

July '93		16.00
July '95		30.00
July '97		45.00

Earnest Byner (R)

July '93		10.00
July '95		9.00
July '97		15.00

Randall Cunningham

July '93		13.00
July '95		12.00
July '97		15.00

Rodney Hampton

July '93		12.00
July '95		12.00
July '97		15.00

Bobby Hebert

July '93	10.00
July '95	10.00
July '97	15.00

Jeff Hostetler

July '93	10.00
July '95	10.00
July '97	15.00

Michael Irvin

July '93	16.00
July '95	24.00
July '97	18.00

Bo Jackson

July '93	10.00
July '95	10.00
July '97	15.00

Haywood Jeffires (R)

July '93	10.00
July '95	12.00
July '97	15.00

Seth Joyner (R)

July '93	10.00
July '95	10.00
July '97	15.00

Jim Kelly

July '93	12.00
July '95	14.00
July '97	15.00

Ronnie Lott

July '93	10.00
July '95	18.00
July '97	25.00

Dan Marino

July '93	20.00
July '95	50.00
July '97	100.00

Joe Montana

July '93	10.00
July '95	24.00
July '97	40.00

Warren Moon

July '93	11.00
July '95	15.00
July '97	20.00

Rob Moore (R)

July '93	10.00
July '95	10.00
July '97	12.00

Jerry Rice

July '93	12.00
July '95	20.00
July '97	35.00

Andre Rison

July '93	12.00
July '95	12.00
July '97	15.00

Mark Rypien

July '93	10.00
July '95	10.00
July '97	10.00

Barry Sanders

July '93	10.00
July '95	18.00
July '97	20.00

Deion Sanders
July '93 ....15.00
July '95 ....18.00
July '97 ....20.00

Emmitt Smith
July '93 ....18.00
July '95 ....30.00
July '97 ....80.00

Pat Swilling
July '93 ....10.00
July '95 ....12.00
July '97 ....12.00

Derrick Thomas (R)
July '93 ....18.00
July '95 ....28.00
July '97 ....25.00

Thurman Thomas
July '93 ....10.00
July '95 ....12.00
July '97 ....15.00

Steve Young
July '93 ....15.00
July '95 ....30.00
July '97 ....60.00

1993 FOOTBALL

★ Set Price: $350.00 ★ Total Figures: 28 ★

Kenner's 1993 Football features the introduction of some new poses, including the first-ever kicker pose. Created for Chip Lohmiller and Pete Stoyanovich, the new pose adds significance to this set. Even so, it failed to inspire collectors—mainly because there's a general lack of excitement surrounding real NFL kickers.

The rookie crop isn't much of an improvement over '92 Football. Sterling Sharpe and Ricky Watters lead the way, and watch out for Anthony Miller, too. His recent move to Dallas, where he could become the primary receiver, makes his rookie a sleeper piece. Unfortunately, Sharpe's early retirement due to a neck injury following the 1995 season has taken some of the luster from his piece. And the disappointing on-field performances of such players as Barry Foster and David Klingler keep '92 Football in the mediocre category.

The set does, however, include an interesting variation. Kenner issued Warren Moon with blue or white pants. The white pants were found in the first case (.08) and the "blue" Moon was found in the second case. Although Moon was packed just one to a case in both instances, it appears the second case was produced in smaller quantities than the first. Consequently, the "blue" Moon is worth slightly more than the white one.

Another highlight from this set is the Joe Montana piece; '93 Football marks his first

The back of the '93 package (above) is interesting because it shows figures from the '93 Basketball and Hockey sets. At left is Junior Seau.

SLU appearance in a Kansas City Chiefs uniform.

Not even Joe, though, can make up for this otherwise lackluster set.

Case Assortments

CASE .08		CASE .09	
Troy Aikman (2)	Andre Reed	Troy Aikman (2)	Joe Montana (2)
Cornelius Bennett	Barry Sanders	Randall Cunningham	Warren Moon (blue)
Randall Cunningham	Deion Sanders (2)	Chris Doleman	Deion Sanders (2)
Chris Doleman	Junior Seau	John Elway	Junior Seau
John Elway	Sterling Sharpe	Michael Irvin (2)	Emmitt Smith (2)
Barry Foster	Emmitt Smith (2)	Cortez Kennedy	Ricky Watters
Michael Irvin	Neil Smith	Chip Lohmiller	Rod Woodson
Rickey Jackson	Pete Stoyanovich	Russell Maryland	Steve Young (2)
David Klingler	Ricky Watters	Anthony Miller	
Warren Moon (white)	Steve Young (2)	Chris Miller	

Troy Aikman

July '94	16.00
July '95	20.00
July '97	30.00

Cornelius Bennett

July '94	7.00
July '95	8.00
July '97	10.00

Randall Cunningham

July '94	6.00
July '95	10.00
July '97	10.00

Chris Doleman

July '94	7.00
July '95	8.00
July '97	10.00

John Elway
July '94 ....13.00
July '95 ....16.00
July '97 ....40.00

Barry Foster (R)
July '94 ....18.00
July '95 ....25.00
July '97 ....12.00

Michael Irvin
July '94 ....12.00
July '95 ....14.00
July '97 ....15.00

Rickey Jackson
July '94 ....6.00
July '95 ....8.00
July '97 ....8.00

Cortez Kennedy (R)
July '94 ....12.00
July '95 ....14.00
July '97 ....15.00

David Klingler (R)
July '94 ....18.00
July '95 ....16.00
July '97 ....15.00

Chip Lohmiller (R)
July '94 ....15.00
July '95 ....15.00
July '97 ....15.00

Russell Maryland (R)
July '94 ....12.00
July '95 ....12.00
July '97 ....12.00

Anthony Miller (R)
July '94 ....12.00
July '95 ....12.00
July '97 ....12.00

Chris Miller
July '94 ....8.00
July '95 ....9.00
July '97 ....10.00

Joe Montana
July '94 ....28.00
July '95 ....40.00
July '97 ....50.00

Warren Moon (white)
July '94 ....8.00
July '95 ....14.00
July '97 ....14.00

Warren Moon (blue)
July '94 ....8.00
July '95 ....15.00
July '97 ....20.00

Andre Reed
July '94 ....6.00
July '95 ....8.00
July '97 ....12.00

Barry Sanders
July '94 ....8.00
July '95 ....12.00
July '97 ....18.00

Deion Sanders
July '94 ....6.00
July '95 ....10.00
July '97 ....15.00

Junior Seau (R)
July '94 ....10.00
July '95 ....10.00
July '97 ....10.00

Sterling Sharpe (R)
July '94 ....28.00
July '95 ....45.00
July '97 ....20.00

Emmitt Smith
July '94 ....11.00
July '95 ....15.00
July '97 ....30.00

Neil Smith (R)
July '94 ....6.00
July '95 ....8.00
July '97 ....10.00

Pete Stoyanovich (R)
July '94 ....15.00
July '95 ....15.00
July '97 ....15.00

Ricky Watters (R)
July '94 ....16.00
July '95 ....24.00
July '97 ....25.00

Rod Woodson
July '94 ....8.00
July '95 ....10.00
July '97 ....15.00

Steve Young
July '94 ....7.00
July '95 ....14.00
July '97 ....30.00

1994 FOOTBALL

★ **Set Price: $550.00** ★ **Total Figures: 32** ★

In contrast to the rather weak efforts of the previous two years, Kenner's 1994 Football issue is one of the best series the company has ever released. Player selection is outstanding; it features a quality assortment of veteran favorites and an excellent crop of rookies.

Super Bowl XXXI featured a showdown between the two hot rookies from this set— Brett Favre and Drew Bledsoe. Favre—the NFL's MVP in 1995 and '96—broke his own NFC record with 39 TD passes in '96 in leading the Green Bay Packers to the title. Bledsoe set numerous New England Patriots passing records on the road to the Super Bowl, showing the talent and poise that made him the first overall pick in the 1993 draft. Both quarterbacks are entering their prime and should carry the NFL well into the next century. It's no wonder that collectors are clamoring for their first SLUs.

As an added twist, Kenner chose to depict this set's veteran quarterbacks in their practice uniforms—a new pose

intended to generate interest from collectors who had been less than impressed with the previous two football series. Initially, the pose didn't catch on. A few years later, however, some collectors have found the practice uniforms to be a nice change of pace, and interest in the quarterbacks— especially Dan Marino and Joe Montana—is picking up.

Kenner released '94 Football in just two different case assortments of 24 players each—the final time the company would produce 24-figure assortments. There are a handful of players issued in only one of the two cases and are therefore consid-

Pictured above is the back of the '94 Football package. Left is Troy Aikman in the practice uniform.

ered short-prints. The biggest names are Favre and Chris Warren. But if Garrison Hearst and Rick Mirer ever live up to their potential, their short-printed '94 rookie pieces could become some of the most expensive figures in the set.

Case Assortments

CASE .04		CASE.05	
Troy Aikman	Joe Montana	Troy Aikman	Joe Montana
Drew Bledsoe	Jerry Rice	Jerome Bettis (2)	Ken Norton
Randall Cunningham	Barry Sanders	Drew Bledsoe	Jerry Rice
Boomer Esiason	Deion Sanders	Boomer Esiason	Andre Rison
Barry Foster	Junior Seau	Brett Favre	Barry Sanders
Garrison Hearst	Phil Simms	Barry Foster	Deion Sanders
Brent Jones	Emmitt Smith	Rodney Hampton	Junior Seau
Cortez Kennedy	Lawrence Taylor	Ronnie Harmon	Phil Simms
Nick Lowery	Chris Warren	Raghib Ismail	Emmitt Smith
Dan Marino	Reggie White	Dan Marino	Lawrence Taylor
Rick Mirer	Rod Woodson	Eric Metcalf	Lorenzo White
	Steve Young (2)		Rod Woodson

Troy Aikman

July '95	16.00
July '96	20.00
July '97	25.00

Jerome Bettis (R)

July '95	25.00
July '96	15.00
July '97	30.00

Drew Bledsoe (R)

July '95	50.00
July '96	70.00
July '97	75.00

Randall Cunningham

July '95	10.00
July '96	10.00
July '97	10.00

Boomer Esiason
July '95 ....10.00
July '96 ....10.00
July '97 ....10.00

Brett Favre (R)
July '95 ....38.00
July '96 ....80.00
July '97 ....130.00

Barry Foster
July '95 ....10.00
July '96 ....10.00
July '97 ....10.00

Rodney Hampton
July '95 ....10.00
July '96 ....10.00
July '97 ....10.00

Ronnie Harmon
July '95 ....8.00
July '96 ....8.00
July '97 ....8.00

Garrison Hearst (R)
July '95 ....18.00
July '96 ....20.00
July '97 ....15.00

Raghib Ismail (R)
July '95 ....18.00
July '96 ....15.00
July '97 ....15.00

Brent Jones (R)
July '95 ....12.00
July '96 ....12.00
July '97 ....12.00

Cortez Kennedy
July '95 ....8.00
July '96 ....10.00
July '97 ....10.00

Nick Lowery (R)
July '95 ....12.00
July '96 ....12.00
July '97 ....12.00

Dan Marino
July '95 ....30.00
July '96 ....35.00
July '97 ....45.00

Eric Metcalf
July '95 ....14.00
July '96 ....14.00
July '97 ....14.00

Rick Mirer (R)
July '95 ....32.00
July '96 ....30.00
July '97 ....24.00

Joe Montana
July '95 ....28.00
July '96 ....35.00
July '97 ....42.00

Ken Norton (R)
July '95 ....15.00
July '96 ....15.00
July '97 ....15.00

Jerry Rice
July '95 ....20.00
July '96 ....20.00
July '97 ....20.00

Andre Rison

July '95 ....10.00
July '96 ....10.00
July '97 ....10.00

Barry Sanders

July '95 ....14.00
July '96 ....14.00
July '97 ....14.00

Deion Sanders

July '95 ....10.00
July '96 ....10.00
July '97 ....10.00

Junior Seau

July '95 ....10.00
July '96 ....10.00
July '97 ....10.00

Phil Simms

July '95 ....10.00
July '96 ....10.00
July '97 ....10.00

Emmitt Smith

July '95 ....12.00
July '96 ....18.00
July '97 ....42.00

Lawrence Taylor

July '95 ....15.00
July '96 ....15.00
July '97 ....15.00

Chris Warren (R)

July '95 ....12.00
July '96 ....16.00
July '97 ....20.00

Lorenzo White (R)

July '95 ....10.00
July '96 ....10.00
July '97 ....10.00

Reggie White

July '95 ....16.00
July '96 ....18.00
July '97 ....20.00

Rod Woodson

July '95 ....10.00
July '96 ....10.00
July '97 ....15.00

Steve Young

July '95 ....15.00
July '96 ....30.00
July '97 ....30.00

1995 FOOTBALL

★ Set Price: $500.00 ★ Total Figures: 33 ★

Kenner's 1995 Football set has a lot to offer SLU collectors: a good overall selection of players, including affordable second-year pieces of top quarterbacks Brett Favre and Drew Bledsoe; all of the NFL's elite veterans; and a great batch of rookies. But the collector favorite—the piece that drives this set—is the Joe Montana retirement figure.

While collectors have long prized the rookie figures of top players, recently they have been pursuing the last-year pieces of legendary athletes with almost equal frenzy. The trend started with the wildly successful Nolan Ryan retirement piece (1993 Baseball) and continued with the last figure of Michael Jordan (1993 Basketball). With Montana, the craze came to football.

When Montana hung up the cleats after the 1994 season, Kenner decided to commemorate one of the greatest quarterbacks of all time by issuing his final piece with a special retirement sticker. The Montana figure isn't considered a short-print (he was shipped one to a pack in both the .07 and

.09 cases), but has become the most expensive figure in the set. If history repeats itself, this could become one of his most valuable figures and a definite asset to any collection.

This release is rich with rookies. Almost half of the players in the set (15 of 33) make their Kenner Starting Lineup debut. Many of them haven't made an impact in the NFL, but a few players have stepped up. Ben Coates and Shannon Sharpe are considered the top tight ends in the game. Marshall Faulk has shown flashes of brilliance and could become one of the league's top running backs.

This is the first football package to offer a Kenner Club membership. Pictured at left is Steve Christie in the kicking pose.

And Natrone Means turned in a strong finish to his '96 season.

The stature of '95 Football will depend on how many of the rookies emerge as stars to complement Montana's "last stand."

Case Assortments

CASE .07	Barry Sanders	Natrone Means	Stan Humphries
Troy Aikman	Deion Sanders	Scott Mitchell	Johnny Johnson
Jerome Bettis	Chris Zorich	Hardy Nickerson	Dan Marino
Drew Bledsoe		Jerry Rice	Terry McDaniel
Jim Everett	**CASE .08**	Shannon Sharpe	Joe Montana
Marshall Faulk	Troy Aikman	Emmitt Smith	Michael Dean Perry
Irving Fryar	Jerome Bettis	Steve Young	Barry Sanders
Stan Humphries	Steve Christie		Deion Sanders
Michael Irvin	Ben Coates	**CASE .09**	Emmitt Smith
Greg Lloyd	Randall Cunningham	Drew Bledsoe	Dan Wilkinson
Dan Marino	Brett Favre	Randall Cunningham	Steve Young
Joe Montana	Marshall Faulk	Willie Davis	
Warren Moon	Jeff George	Brett Favre	
Jerry Rice	Seth Joyner	Marshall Faulk	

Troy Aikman
July '95 ....—
July '96 ....18.00
July '97 ....25.00

Jerome Bettis
July '95 ....—
July '96 ....10.00
July '97 ....20.00

Drew Bledsoe
July '95 ....—
July '96 ....25.00
July '97 ....35.00

Steve Christie (R)
July '95 ....—
July '96 ....12.00
July '97 ....12.00

Ben Coates (R)
July '95 ....—
July '96 ....20.00
July '97 ....25.00

Randall Cunningham
July '95 ....—
July '96 ....10.00
July '97 ....10.00

Willie Davis (R)
July '95 ....—
July '96 ....10.00
July '97 ....10.00

Jim Everett
July '95 ....——
July '96 ....10.00
July '97 ....10.00

Marshall Faulk (R)
July '95 ....—
July '96 ....36.00
July '97 ....35.00

Brett Favre
July '95 ....—
July '96 ....25.00
July '97 ....35.00

Irving Fryar
July '95 ....—
July '96 ....12.00
July '97 ....15.00

Jeff George
July '95 ....——
July '96 ....10.00
July '97 ....10.00

Stan Humphries (R)
July '95 ....—
July '96 ....14.00
July '97 ....14.00

Michael Irvin
July '95 ....—
July '96 ....12.00
July '97 ....18.00

Johnny Johnson (R)
July '95 ....—
July '96 ....10.00
July '97 ....10.00

Seth Joyner (R)
July '95 ....—
July '96 ....10.00
July '97 ....10.00

Greg Lloyd (R)
July '95 ....—
July '96 ....12.00
July '97 ....16.00

Dan Marino
July '95 ....—
July '96 ....32.00
July '97 ....45.00

Terry McDaniel (R)
July '95 ....—
July '96 ....10.00
July '97 ....10.00

Natrone Means (R)
July '95 ....—
July '96 ....35.00
July '97 ....30.00

Scott Mitchell (R)

July '95 ....—
July '96 ....14.00
July '97 ....14.00

Joe Montana

July '95 ....—
July '96 ....75.00
July '97 ....75.00

Warren Moon

July '95 ....—
July '96 ....10.00
July '97 ....10.00

Hardy Nickerson (R)

July '95 ....—
July '96 ....12.00
July '97 ....12.00

Michael Dean Perry (R)

July '95 ....—
July '96 ....12.00
July '97 ....12.00

Jerry Rice

July '95 ....—
July '96 ....12.00
July '97 ....15.00

Barry Sanders

July '95 ....—
July '96 ....12.00
July '97 ....15.00

Deion Sanders

July '95 ....—
July '96 ....10.00
July '97 ....12.00

Shannon Sharpe (R)

July '95 ....—
July '96 ....16.00
July '97 ....20.00

Emmitt Smith

July '95 ....—
July '96 ....20.00
July '97 ....30.00

Dan Wilkinson (R)

July '95 ....—
July '96 ....12.00
July '97 ....12.00

Steve Young

July '95 ....—
July '96 ....15.00
July '97 ....15.00

Chris Zorich (R)

July '95 ....—
July '96 ....10.00
July '97 ....10.00

1996 FOOTBALL

★ Set Price: $600.00 ★ Total Figures: 41 ★

With this 1996 release, Kenner made it three successful football series in a row. The set's excellent rookie selection is led by quarterback phenoms Mark Brunell and Kerry Collins, two difficult-to-find regional pieces, and a hot rare variation. All this makes 1996 Football a winner.

The first regional piece is the Shopko Brett Favre. Kenner didn't include Favre in the regular set, instead issuing his figure exclusively through Shopko stores in Wisconsin and environs. As a result, the Favre piece has been difficult to find and relatively expensive.

Kenner took a different tack with the 1996 Troy Aikman figure, including one version in the regular set but also releasing a regional piece and a rare variation. The regular Aikman figure features the standard white Dallas Cowboys uniform. The Albertson's figure, released only in Texas via the grocery chain, has Aikman wearing a throwback jersey with blue shirt, white sleeves, and double star. Meanwhile, the rare variation—shipped in the nationally distributed cases as opposed to the regional Albertson's cases—has Aikman in the throwback jersey, but with opposite colors from the Albertson's figure: a white shirt with blue sleeves and a star on each shoulder. Interestingly, the backs of all 1996 Football packages picture Aikman in the variation uniform and not in the traditional one issued in the set.

The 1996 Football release is tough to complete because it contains a number of short-printed pieces. The last case—.04—includes several players issued at one per case. That's why the Kordell Stewart rookie piece has become so expensive. Although Stewart is popular with football fans, he has yet to become a certified NFL star. If he does,

The back of the '96 package (above) shows the rare Troy Aikman variation. Pictured at left is the popular rookie piece of Kordell Stewart.

watch the value of his figure soar. If he falls short, Stewart's piece could become the next Bo Jackson.

With all of the buzz surrounding the Stewart rookie and the Aikman variation, there's one '96 Football figure many collectors have overlooked: Emmitt Smith. This may be Smith's sixth figure, but he's still one of the NFL's top running backs. Like Stewart, he was only a one-pack in the last case assortment. But unlike Stewart, if Smith stops playing tomorrow, he can still count on a place in Canton. Wise collectors will pick up his '96 piece while it's still affordable.

Case Assortments

CASE .05			
Troy Aikman (2)	Marshall Faulk	Junior Seau	**CASE .04**
Jeff Blake (2)	Joey Galloway (2)	Harvey Williams	Terry Allen
Drew Bledsoe (2)	Kevin Greene	Steve Young (2)	Steve Bono
Robert Brooks	Dan Marino (2)		Dave Brown
Mark Carrier	Eric Metcalf	**CASE .08**	Mark Brunell
Marshall Faulk	Frank Reich	Kyle Brady	Kerry Collins
Joey Galloway	Deion Sanders (2)	Isaac Bruce	John Elway
Kevin Greene		Mark Brunell	Steve McNair
Dan Marino (2)	**CASE .07**	Cris Carter	Carl Pickens
Eric Metcalf	Steve Beuerlein	Kerry Collins	Errict Rhett
Deion Sanders (2)	Kyle Brady	Kevin Greene	Jerry Rice
	Isaac Bruce	Jay Novacek (2)	Rashan Salaam
CASE .06	Cris Carter	Bryce Paup	Emmitt Smith
Troy Aikman (2)	Kerry Collins	Jerry Rice	Chris Spielman
Jeff Blake	Kevin Greene	Rashan Salaam	Kordell Stewart
Drew Bledsoe	Jay Novacek (2)	Barry Sanders	Ricky Watters
Robert Brooks	Bryce Paup	Junior Seau	Reggie White
Mark Carrier	Jerry Rice (2)	Harvey Williams	
	Barry Sanders	Steve Young (2)	

Troy Aikman (regular)

July '95	—
July '96	—
July '97	20.00

Troy Aikman (Albertson's)
July '95 ....—
July '96 ....—
July '97 ....28.00

Troy Aikman
(blue sleeves w/stars)
July '95 ....—
July '96 ....—
July '97 ....300.00

Terry Allen (R)
July '95 ....—
July '96 ....—
July '97 ....25.00

Steve Beuerlein
July '95 ....—
July '96 ....—
July '97 ....15.00

Jeff Blake (R)
July '95 ....—
July '96 ....—
July '97 ....15.00

Drew Bledsoe
July '95 ....—
July '96 ....—
July '97 ....15.00

Steve Bono (R)
July '95 ....—
July '96 ....—
July '97 ....12.00

Kyle Brady (R)
July '95 ....—
July '96 ....—
July '97 ....12.00

Robert Brooks (R)
July '95 ....—
July '96 ....—
July '97 ....15.00

Dave Brown (R)
July '95 ....—
July '96 ....—
July '97 ....10.00

Isaac Bruce (R)
July '95 ....—
July '96 ....—
July '97 ....15.00

Mark Brunell (R)
July '95 ....—
July '96 ....—
July '97 ....40.00

Mark Carrier (R)
July '95 ....—
July '96 ....—
July '97 ....10.00

Cris Carter
July '95 ....—
July '96 ....—
July '97 ....15.00

Kerry Collins (R)
July '95 ....—
July '96 ....—
July '97 ....40.00

John Elway
July '95 ....—
July '96 ....—
July '97 ....24.00

Brett Favre (Shopko)
July '95 ....—
July '96 ....—
July '97 ....40.00

Marshall Faulk
July '95 ....—
July '96 ....—
July '97 ....12.00

Joey Galloway (R)
July '95 ....—
July '96 ....—
July '97 ....18.00

Kevin Greene (R)
July '95 ....—
July '96 ....—
July '97 ....15.00

Dan Marino
July '95 ....—
July '96 ....—
July '97 ....30.00

Steve McNair (R)
July '95 ....—
July '96 ....—
July '97 ....25.00

Eric Metcalf
July '95 ....—
July '96 ....—
July '97 ....10.00

Jay Novacek (R)
July '95 ....—
July '96 ....—
July '97 ....14.00

Bryce Paup (R)
July '95 ....—
July '96 ....—
July '97 ....14.00

Carl Pickens (R)
July '95 ....—
July '96 ....—
July '97 ....15.00

Frank Reich (R)
July '95 ....—
July '96 ....—
July '97 ....20.00

Errict Rhett (R)
July '95 ....—
July '96 ....—
July '97 ....15.00

Jerry Rice
July '95 ....—
July '96 ....—
July '97 ....12.00

Rashan Salaam (R)
July '95 ....—
July '96 ....—
July '97 ....15.00

Barry Sanders
July '95 ....—
July '96 ....—
July '97 ....12.00

Deion Sanders
July '95 ....—
July '96 ....—
July '97 ....10.00

Junior Seau

July '95 ....—
July '96 ....—
July '97 ....10.00

Emmitt Smith

July '95 ....—
July '96 ....—
July '97 ....40.00

Chris Spielman

July '95 ....—
July '96 ....—
July '97 ....20.00

Kordell Stewart (R)

July '95 ....—
July '96 ....—
July '97 ....50.00

Ricky Watters

July '95 ....—
July '96 ....—
July '97 ....15.00

Reggie White

July '95 ....—
July '96 ....—
July '97 ....25.00

Harvey Williams (R)

July '95 ....—
July '96 ....—
July '97 ....15.00

Steve Young

July '95 ....—
July '96 ....—
July '97 ....12.00

1989 FOOTBALL HELMETS

★ **Set Price: $275.00** ★ **Total Pieces: 4** ★

Because Kenner originally conceived of Starting Lineups as toys, the company designed its football players with helmets that could easily be removed. Knowing that kids would inevitably lose some of the tiny helmets while playing, the company introduced separate packages of spares to be used as replacements. There are four different helmet packages—an offensive and defensive pack for both the American Football Conference and National Football Conference. The offensive helmets have one horizontal bar across the face while the defensive helmets have two.

Kenner issued the helmets in 12-count cases—and only to retail stores. Initially, the helmets didn't sell well, possibly due to the way they were packaged. Someone who had all of the members of the Dallas Cowboys and needed two or three replacement helmets, for instance, would be forced to buy multiple complete packages of NFC helmets. Because of the dismal sales, most of the helmets found their way to close-out shelves, and many wound up in discount stores at $1 per package.

Due to the fact that the helmet packages were intended to be opened, it has become increasingly difficult to find them in mint condition—especially the NFC defensive package which was the shortest-printed of the four. As these pieces have become more and more popular with Kenner football collectors who are rounding out their collections, the value

The Helmet Collection package back (above) shows a different player checklist than the '89 Football package. Both checklists are incorrect.

of the helmets has risen considerably and they are quickly disappearing from the secondary marketplace.

Case Assortments

AFC Offensive (4)	NFC Offensive (3)
AFC Defensive (3)	NFC Defensive (2)

AFC Offensive
July '95	—
July '96	75.00
July '97	80.00

AFC Defensive
July '95	—
July '96	75.00
July '97	80.00

NFC Offensive
July '95	—
July '96	75.00
July '97	80.00

NFC Defensive
July '95	—
July '96	75.00
July '97	80.00

FOOTBALL HEADLINE

★ **1991 Set Price: $275.00** ★ **Total Figures: 6** ★
★ **1992 Set Price: $125.00** ★ **Total Figures: 6** ★

Kenner issued only two sets of Football Headlines—the first in 1991, another in '92. Each series consists of six pieces. The format was the same as the Headline series in the other sports and proved to be just as unpopular with collectors. Poor sales convinced the company to cease production of the series fairly quickly.

Case Assortments

1991 HEADLINE	1992 HEADLINE
John Elway	Note: Case assortment information was not available at press time.
Boomer Esiason (2)	
Dan Marino	
Joe Montana (4)	
Jerry Rice	
Barry Sanders (3)	

Recently, many collectors who have already completed most of their football sets—or those who have given up on the '88 and '89 issues—have given the Headlines a second look. With just six figures per set, they aren't too difficult to complete. The player selection is great, with most of the NFL's big guns—minus Troy Aikman and Brett Favre—represented. Both Joe Montana and Barry Sanders are featured in each set, and even though there's no Aikman, there is an Emmitt Smith. Since these figures have never been all that popular, most are relatively inexpensive and readily available.

As with the Headlines from other sports, these figures make great display

The '91 Headline Collection box back shows all six players in the set.

pieces—especially when opened and removed from the box. As more and more collectors complete their older sets and begin to look for something different, the Headline series should continue to draw more interest.

'91 John Elway
July '93	25.00
July '95	36.00
July '97	55.00

'91 Boomer Esiason
July '93	15.00
July '95	18.00
July '97	18.00

'91 Dan Marino
July '93	24.00
July '95	63.00
July '97	110.00

'91 Joe Montana
July '93	15.00
July '95	35.00
July '97	50.00

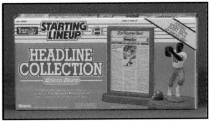

'91 Jerry Rice
July '93	26.00
July '95	32.00
July '97	50.00

'91 Barry Sanders
July '93	22.00
July '95	30.00
July '97	40.00

'92 Joe Montana

July '93 ....14.00
July '95....................................20.00
July '97....................................30.00

'92 Warren Moon

July '93 ....16.00
July '95....................................16.00
July '97....................................18.00

'92 Mark Rypien

July '93 ....14.00
July '95 ....12.00
July '97....................................12.00

'92 Barry Sanders

July '93 ....14.00
July '95 ....16.00
July '97....................................25.00

'92 Emmitt Smith

July '93...................................20.00
July '95...................................40.00
July '97....................................60.00

'92 Thurman Thomas

July '93 ....14.00
July '95....................................20.00
July '97....................................25.00

1993 HOCKEY

★ **American Set Price: $600.00** ★ **Total Figures: 12** ★
★ **Canadian Set Price: $275.00** ★ **Total Figures: 11** ★

Traditionally, the inaugural set of every sport is the most popular. Just look at Kenner's 1988 Baseball, Basketball, and Football sets. Even non-hockey collectors have gone after this set—especially if they missed the boat with the other sets. Today, the set remains a big hit; in fact, it's still the most popular Hockey issue by far.

Kenner issued just 12 players in two different case assortments in '93. The Ed Belfour, Pat LaFontaine, and Grant Fuhr figures are the shortprints of the set. Kenner produced the second case assortment, which has the Fuhr figure but no Belfour or LaFontaine, in smaller quantities than the first, which is why the Fuhr has become the most expensive piece here.

Just like they chase quarterbacks in football, many collectors go for goalies in hockey. Recently, Patrick Roy—who many feel is the best goaltender in the game today—has

become one of the hottest pieces in this set. After sitting in the $50 range for a while, it skyrocketed to $100 after the Colorado Avalanche won the 1996 Stanley Cup.

Hasboro of Canada issued a set similar to this one, but it included only 11 players, omitting Fuhr. Initially, the price for these pieces was higher than the American versions. But today, collectors generally go for only the American versions instead of trying to complete both sets. Even though the Canadian pieces had a smaller print run than the American pieces, they sell for the same or less than their U.S. counterparts.

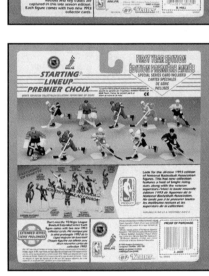

Pictured above is '93 American (top) and Canadian package backs. At left is the rookie piece of Eric Lindros.

Case Assortments

1993 AMERICAN CASE	CASE	Ray Bourque	Eric Lindros (2)
Ed Belfour	Ray Bourque	Brett Hull (3)	Mark Messier (2)
Ray Bourque	Grant Fuhr	Jaromir Jagr	Jeremy Roenick (2)
Brett Hull (3)	Brett Hull (3)	Pat LaFontaine	Partrick Roy (2)
Jaromir Jagr	Jaromir Jagr (2)	Mario Lemieux (3)	Steve Yzerman (2)
Pat LaFontaine	Mario Lemieux (3)	Eric Lindros (2)	
Mario Lemieux (3)	Eric Lindros (2)	Mark Messier	**CASE .92b**
Eric Lindros (2)	Mark Messier	Jeremy Roenick	Ed Belfour (3)
Mark Messier	Jeremy Roenick	Patrick Roy	Ray Bourque (2)
Jeremy Roenick	Patrick Roy	Steve Yzerman	Jaromir Jagr (2)
Patrick Roy	Steve Yzerman		Pat LaFontaine (3)
Steve Yzerman		**CASE .92a**	Mark Messier (3)
	1993 CANADIAN	Ray Bourque (2)	Jeremy Roenick (3)
	CASE .05	Brett Hull (2)	
	Ed Belfour	Pat LaFontaine (2)	

Ed Belfour

July '94	....	75.00
July '95	....	90.00
July '97	....	130.00

Ray Bourque
July '94......................20.00
July '95......................20.00
July '97......................20.00

Grant Fuhr
July '94....................110.00
July '95....................160.00
July '97....................180.00

Brett Hull
July '94......................12.00
July '95......................12.00
July '97......................10.00

Jaromir Jagr
July '94......................20.00
July '95......................24.00
July '97......................35.00

Pat LaFontaine
July '94......................62.00
July '95......................75.00
July '97......................80.00

Mario Lemieux
July '94......................22.00
July '95......................18.00
July '97......................20.00

Eric Lindros
July '94......................35.00
July '95......................38.00
July '97......................45.00

Mark Messier
July '94......................20.00
July '95......................25.00
July '97......................35.00

Jeremy Roenick
July '94......................22.00
July '95......................22.00
July '97......................25.00

Patrick Roy
July '94......................40.00
July '95......................50.00
July '97....................100.00

Steve Yzerman
July '94......................20.00
July '95......................20.00
July '97......................25.00

Ed Belfour
July '94...........................—
July '95......................60.00
July '97......................65.00

Ray Bourque
July '94...........................—
July '95......................18.00
July '97......................18.00

Brett Hull
July '94...........................—
July '95......................10.00
July '97......................10.00

Jaromir Jagr
July '94...........................—
July '95......................20.00
July '97......................20.00

Pat LaFontaine
July '94...........................—
July '95......................40.00
July '97......................40.00

Mario Lemieux

July '94 ....—
July '95 ....20.00
July '97 ....20.00

Eric Lindros

July '94 ....—
July '95 ....32.00
July '97 ....32.00

Mark Messier

July '94 ....—
July '95 ....22.00
July '97 ....25.00

Jeremy Roenick

July '94 ....—
July '95 ....20.00
July '97 ....20.00

Patrick Roy

July '94 ....—
July '95 ....45.00
July '97 ....50.00

Steve Yzerman

July '94 ....—
July '95 ....20.00
July '97 ....20.00

1994 HOCKEY

★ **American Set Price: $400.00** ★ **Total Figures: 20** ★
★ **Canadian Set Price: $250.00** ★ **Total Figures: 13** ★

Although this issue has several more players and a quality crop of rookies, it isn't as popular as Kenner's inaugural hockey series of '93. There just aren't as many hockey collectors as there are baseball, basketball and football. And even though Kenner's hockey sets are smaller and the production runs shorter than those for the other three sports, the hockey SLU market remains relatively soft.

Back in 1994, most dealers reportedly received only the first case assortments, which contained no rookies—just repeat players from the 1993 set. The second and third cases—which did contain rookie pieces—didn't hit store shelves until much later. Initially, this distribution quirk led to extremely low values for the repeat players, while prices for the rookies remained high. Since then, however, it has become apparent that the first case had a much shorter production run than the two "rookie" cases, and secondary market values have adjusted themselves accordingly. The Mark Messier figure is only a single-pack in the first case

and is actually harder to find than his 1993 rookie piece.

Hasbro of Canada again issued a set similar to Kenner's U.S. release—and again with fewer players. Collectors were disappointed that there hadn't been a Grant Fuhr figure in the '93 Canadian set. To satisfy those fans, Hasbro did get Fuhr into the 1994 set, and it's a more realistic version that depicts him with darker skin to reflect his African-American heritage. Ironically, there is no Fuhr in the 1994 U.S. release. The Canadian Fuhr is a short-print. That status, coupled with the lack of a '94 American Fuhr, has made Fuhr's the most expensive piece in either set.

Pictured above are the '94 American and Canadian backs. The latter includes a checklist of players. Only Grant Fuhr is missing. At left is Adam Oates from the American set.

Case Assortments

1994 AMERICAN CASE .02		Brian Leetch (3)	Grant Fuhr
Ray Bourque	Alexander Mogilny	Mario Lemieux (2)	Doug Gilmour (3)
Brett Hull (2)	Adam Oates	Alexander Mogilny (2)	Brian Leetch
Jaromir Jagr (2)	Mike Richter (2)	Adam Oates (2)	Mario Lemieux
Pat LaFontaine (2)	Luc Robitaille	Teemu Selanne	Eric Lindros
Mario Lemieux (3)	Teemu Selanne	Steve Yzerman (3)	Alexander Mogilny
Eric Lindros (2)			Adam Oates
Mark Messier	**CASE .04**	**CASE .02**	Mike Richter
Jeremy Roenick	Tom Barrasso (2)	Pavel Bure (2)	Teemu Selanne
Steve Yzerman (2)	Pavel Bure (2)	Grant Fuhr	Steve Yzerman
	Doug Gilmour (2)	Doug Gilmour (3)	
CASE .03	Arturs Irbe (2)	Brian Leetch (2)	**CASE .92D**
Tom Barrasso	Brian Leetch (2)	Eric Lindros (3)	Doug Gilmour (3)
Pavel Bure (2)	Alexander Mogilny (2)	Adam Oates (2)	Brian Leetch
Sergei Fedorov (2)	Adam Oates (2)	Mike Richter	Alexander Mogilny (2)
Doug Gilmour	Mike Richter (2)	Teemu Selanne (2)	Adam Oates (2)
Arturs Irbe			Mike Richter (2)
Brian Leetch	**1994 CANADIAN**	**CASE .92**	Luc Robitaille (4)
Mario Lemieux (2)	**CASE .01**	Pavel Bure (2)	Teemu Selanne (2)
	Pavel Bure	Sergei Fedorov (2)	
	Sergei Fedorov (2)		

Tom Barrasso (R)
July '95 .... 55.00
July '96 .... 40.00
July '97 .... 40.00

Ray Bourque
July '95 .... 24.00
July '96 .... 30.00
July '97 .... 30.00

Pavel Bure (R)
July '95 .... 25.00
July '96 .... 18.00
July '97 .... 18.00

Sergei Fedorov (R)
July '95 .... 25.00
July '96 .... 18.00
July '97 .... 18.00

Doug Gilmour (R)
July '95 .... 25.00
July '96 .... 15.00
July '97 .... 15.00

Brett Hull
July '95 .... 12.00
July '96 .... 12.00
July '97 .... 12.00

Arturs Irbe (R)
July '95 .... 60.00
July '96 .... 45.00
July '97 .... 45.00

Jaromir Jagr
July '95 .... 18.00
July '96 .... 20.00
July '97 .... 25.00

Pat LaFontaine
July '95 .... 16.00
July '96 .... 18.00
July '97 .... 18.00

Brian Leetch (R)
July '95 .... 25.00
July '96 .... 20.00
July '97 .... 20.00

Mario Lemieux
July '95 .... 12.00
July '96 .... 12.00
July '97 .... 16.00

Eric Lindros
July '95 .... 20.00
July '96 .... 30.00
July '97 .... 30.00

Mark Messier
July '95 .... 25.00
July '96 .... 40.00
July '97 .... 55.00

Alexander Mogilny (R)
July '95 .... 20.00
July '96 .... 20.00
July '97 .... 20.00

Adam Oates (R)
July '95 .... 20.00
July '96 .... 15.00
July '97 .... 15.00

Mike Richter (R)
July '95 .... 40.00
July '96 .... 25.00
July '97 .... 25.00

Luc Robitaille (R)
July '95 .... 28.00
July '96 .... 28.00
July '97 .... 28.00

Jeremy Roenick
July '95 ....18.00
July '96 ....24.00
July '97 ....25.00

Teemu Selanne (R)
July '95 ....25.00
July '96 ....25.00
July '97 ....25.00

Steve Yzerman
July '95 ....15.00
July '96 ....15.00
July '97 ....15.00

Pavel Bure (R)
July '95 ....22.00
July '96 ....16.00
July '97 ....16.00

Sergei Fedorov (R)
July '95 ....22.00
July '96......................16.00
July '97 ....16.00

Grant Fuhr
July '95 ....75.00
July '96 ....75.00
July '97 ....75.00

Doug Gilmour (R)
July '95 ....20.00
July '96.....................15.00
July '97 ....15.00

Brian Leetch (R)
July '95 ....25.00
July '96.....................15.00
July '97 ....15.00

Mario Lemieux
July '95......................14.00
July '96......................14.00
July '97 ....15.00

Eric Lindros
July '95 ....20.00
July '96 ....20.00
July '97 ....20.00

Alexander Mogilny (R)
July '95 ....20.00
July '96 ....15.00
July '97 ....15.00

Adam Oates (R)
July '95 ....20.00
July '96 ....14.00
July '97 ....14.00

Mike Richter (R)
July '95 ....35.00
July '96 ....30.00
July '97 ....30.00

Luc Robitaille (R)
July '95 ....30.00
July '96 ....30.00
July '97 ....30.00

Teemu Selanne (R)
July '95 ....22.00
July '96.....................16.00
July '97 ....16.00

Steve Yzerman
July '95......................16.00
July '96......................16.00
July '97 ....16.00

1995 HOCKEY

★ **American Set Price: $200.00** ★ **Total Figures: 19** ★
★ **Canadian Set Price: $200.00** ★ **Total Figures 13** ★

Kenner's 1995 Hockey set saw another influx of rookie figures. Despite the great player selection and the fact that only four of the 19 players were repeated, hockey continues to lag behind in popularity compared to Kenner's other sets. Some of the game's biggest stars made their debut in this issue, yet it's drawn little interest from collectors. Only the three big goalies—Martin Brodeur, Dominik Hasek, and Felix Potvin—trade for more than $20. If you're interested in starting a hockey SLU collection, this is the place to start.

Kenner issued this set in two different case assortments. There are a handful of players that were one-packs in just one of the two case assortments. But a lack of collector activity makes completing this set easy and inexpensive.

The Canadian version includes the Brodeur, Hasek, and Potvin figures from the American series plus goalies Tom Barrasso and Arturs Irbe, who were omit-ted from the '94 Canadian Hockey set. Like the American set, this one has received little attention from collectors.

The '95 Canadian back (above) shows eight figures and has a correct checklist. Pictured at left is New Jersey Devil Martin Brodeur.

Case Assortments

1995 AMERICAN CASE .00	CASE .01	1995 CANADIAN Case 68720A	Case 68720B
Martin Brodeur (2)	Rob Blake (2)	Tom Barrasso (2)	Rob Blake
Pavel Bure	Bob Corkum	Rob Blake	Martin Brodeur (2)
Chris Chelios (2)	Sergei Fedorov	Martin Brodeur	Chris Chelios (2)
Bob Corkum (2)	Thoren Fleury	Chris Chelios	Thereon Fleury
Sergei Fedorov	Dominik Hasek (2)	Thereon Fluery	Adam Graves (2)
Adam Graves (2)	Brett Hull	Adam Graves	Dominik Hasek (2)
Brett Hull	Kirk Muller	Arturs Irbe (2)	Mike Modano (2)
Mike Modano (2)	Cam Neely	Mike Modano	Cam Neely
Cam Neely	Sandis Ozolinsh	Cam Neely (2)	Felix Potvin
Felix Potvin	Felix Potvin	Felix Potvin (2)	Brendan Shanahan
Luc Robitaille	Luc Robitaille	Brendan Shanahan	Scott Stevens
	Brendan Shanahan	Scott Stevens	
	Scott Stevens		
	Pierre Turgeon		

Rob Blake (R)
July '95 ....—
July '96 ....12.00
July '97 ....10.00

Martin Brodeur (R)
July '95 ....—
July '96 ....30.00
July '97 ....30.00

Pavel Bure
July '95 ....—
July '96 ....12.00
July '97 ....18.00

Chris Chelios (R)
July '95 ....—
July '96 ....12.00
July '97 ....10.00

Bob Corkum (R)
July '95 ....—
July '96 ....12.00
July '97 ....10.00

Sergei Fedorov
July '95 ....—
July '96 ....12.00
July '97 ....10.00

Theoren Fleury (R)
July '95 ....—
July '96 ....15.00
July '97 ....10.00

Adam Graves (R)
July '95 ....—
July '96 ....12.00
July '97 ....10.00

Dominik Hasek (R)
July '95 ....—
July '96 ....30.00
July '97 ....30.00

Brett Hull
July '95 ....—
July '96 ....10.00
July '97 ....10.00

Mike Modano (R)
July '95 ....—
July '96 ....16.00
July '97 ....10.00

Kirk Muller (R)
July '95 ....—
July '96 ....12.00
July '97 ....10.00

Cam Neely (R)
July '95 ....—
July '96 ....12.00
July '97 ....12.00

Sandis Ozolinsh (R)
July '95 ....—
July '96 ....15.00
July '97 ....12.00

Felix Potvin (R)
July '95 ....—
July '96 ....25.00
July '97 ....25.00

Luc Robitaille
July '95 ....—
July '96 ....10.00
July '97 ....10.00

Brendan Shanahan (R)
July '95 ....—
July '96 ....18.00
July '97 ....10.00

Scott Stevens (R)
July '95 ....—
July '96 ....15.00
July '97 ....10.00

Pierre Turgeon (R)
July '95 ....—
July '96 ....16.00
July '97 ....10.00

Tom Barrasso
July '95 ....—
July '96 ....25.00
July '97 ....25.00

Rob Blake (R)
July '95 ....—
July '96 ....15.00
July '97 ....10.00

Martin Brodeur (R)
July '95 ....—
July '96 ....30.00
July '97 ....30.00

Chris Chelios (R)
July '95 ....—
July '96 ....15.00
July '97 ....12.00

Theoren Fleury (R)
July '95 ....—
July '96 ....15.00
July '97 ....12.00

Adam Graves (R)
July '95 ....—
July '96 ....15.00
July '97 ....12.00

Dominik Hasek (R)
July '95 ....—
July '96 ....30.00
July '97 ....30.00

Arturs Irbe
July '95 ....—
July '96 ....35.00
July '97 ....35.00

Mike Modano (R)
July '95 ....—
July '96 ....15.00
July '97 ....12.00

Cam Neely (R)
July '95 ....—
July '96 ....12.00
July '97 ....10.00

Felix Potvin (R)
July '95 ....—
July '96 ....25.00
July '97 ....25.00

Brendan Shanahan (R)
July '95 ....—
July '96 ....15.00
July '97 ....12.00

Scott Stevens (R)
July '95 ....—
July '96 ....15.00
July '97 ....10.00

1996 HOCKEY

★ **American Set Price: $250.00** ★ **Total Figures: 24** ★
★ **Canadian Set Price: $200.00** ★ **Total Figures: 15** ★

This was the year Kenner issued its first regional hockey pieces. Pat LaFontaine and Tom Barrasso were distributed only via Hill's department stores. Kenner's orginal plan was to issue these players to those stores surrounding their respective cities; however, both pieces could be found at most Hill's locations up and down the East Coast.

Kenner also issued a special case of Philadelphia's "Legion of Doom" line. The pieces of John LeClair, Eric Lindros, and Mikael Renberg were the same pieces issued nationally in the regular case assortments. Kenner issued these cases only around the Philly area.

The '96 Hockey set includes a Patrick Roy variation. The corrected version shows Roy with his new goatee, but there are several findings of figures without the painted goatee. Currently, the "beardless" Roy is much harder to find and commands a premium on the secondary market.

The hot rookies in this set are goaltender Jim Carey of the Washington Capitals, center Joe Sakic of the Colorado Avalanche, and young gun Paul Kariya of the Anaheim Mighty Ducks. The other hot pieces are goaltenders Roy and Dominik Hasek.

The Canadian version of this set includes most of the rookies from the American version. Only Paul Coffey and Stephane Richer were omitted. There are no Canadian versions of Hills' special exclusive pieces.

The Canadian version continues to move very slowly in the SLU marketplace. Hasek is the only hot U.S. figure that wasn't issued in the Canadian set.

Like the '96 Basketball set, the '96 American and the Canadian packages show team logos instead of figures. At left is Pat LaFontaine, who was issued only at Hills stores.

Case Assortments

1996 AMERICAN CASE .02	CASE .03	1996 CANADIAN Case 68860A	Case 68860B
Jim Carey (2)	Brian Bradley	Brian Bradley	Brian Bradley
Paul Coffey	Paul Coffey	Sergei Fedorov	Jim Carey
Ron Francis (2)	Sergei Federov	Ron Francis	Sergei Fedorov
John LeClair	Dominik Hasek	Paul Kariya (2)	Ron Francis
Eric Lindros	Paul Kariya (3)	Brian Leetch	Paul Kariya (2)
Al MacInnis	Brian Leetch	Eric Lindros	John LeClair
Mark Messier (2)	Eric Lindros	Al MacInnis	Brian Leetch
Mike Modano	Scott Mellanby	Scott Mellanby	Eric Lindros
Adam Oates	Mark Messier	Mark Messier	Al MacInnis
Jeremy Roenick (2)	Mikael Renberg	Mikael Renberg	Scott Mellanby
Joe Sakic (2)	Stephane Richer	Patrick Roy (2)	Mark Messier
	Patrick Roy	Joe Sakic (2)	Patrick Roy
	Brendan Shanahan	Mats Sundin	Joe Sakic (2)
	Mats Sundin		Mats Sundin

Tom Barrasso (Hills)

July '95 ....—
July '96 ....—
July '97 ....25.00

Brian Bradley (R)
July '95 ....—
July '96 ....—
July '97 ....10.00

Jim Carey (R)
July '95 ....—
July '96 ....—
July '97 ....30.00

Paul Coffey (R)
July '95 ....—
July '96 ....—
July '97 ....12.00

Sergei Fedorov
July '95 ....—
July '96 ....—
July '97 ....10.00

Ron Francis (R)
July '95 ....—
July '96 ....—
July '97 ....10.00

Dominik Hasek
July '95 ....—
July '96 ....—
July '97 ....30.00

Paul Kariya (R)
July '95 ....—
July '96 ....—
July '97 ....25.00

Pat LaFontaine (Hills)
July '95 ....—
July '96 ....—
July '97 ....15.00

John LeClair (R)
July '95 ....—
July '96 ....—
July '97 ....15.00

Brian Leetch
July '95 ....—
July '96 ....—
July '97 ....12.00

Eric Lindros
July '95 ....—
July '96 ....—
July '97 ....15.00

Al MacInnis (R)
July '95 ....—
July '96 ....—
July '97 ....10.00

Scott Mellanby (R)
July '95 ....—
July '96 ....—
July '97 ....10.00

Mark Messier
July '95 ....—
July '96 ....—
July '97 ....15.00

Mike Modano
July '95 ....—
July '96 ....—
July '97 ....10.00

Adam Oates
July '95 ....—
July '96 ....—
July '97 ....10.00

Mikael Renberg (R)
July '95 ....—
July '96 ....—
July '97 ....15.00

Stephane Richer (R)
July '95 ....—
July '96 ....—
July '97 ....10.00

Jeremy Roenick
July '95 ....—
July '96 ....—
July '97 ....10.00

Patrick Roy (w/beard)
July '95 ....—
July '96 ....—
July '97 ....50.00

Joe Sakic (R)
July '95 ....—
July '96 ....—
July '97 ....20.00

Brendan Shanahan
July '95 ....—
July '96 ....—
July '97 ....10.00

Mats Sundin (R)
July '95 ....—
July '96 ....—
July '97 ....12.00

Brian Bradley (R)
July '95 ....—
July '96 ....—
July '97 ....10.00

Jim Carey (R)
July '95 ....—
July '96 ....—
July '97 ....30.00

Sergei Fedorov
July '95 ....—
July '96 ....—
July '97 ....10.00

Ron Francis (R)
July '95 ....—
July '96 ....—
July '97 ....12.00

Paul Kariya (R)
July '95 ....—
July '96 ....—
July '97 ....25.00

John LeClair (R)
July '95 ....—
July '96 ....—
July '97 ....15.00

Brian Leetch
July '95 ....—
July '96 ....—
July '97 ....12.00

Eric Lindros
July '95 ....—
July '96 ....—
July '97 ....15.00

Al MacInnis (R)
July '95 ....—
July '96 ....—
July '97 ....12.00

Scott Mellanby (R)
July '95 ....—
July '96 ....—
July '97 ....10.00

Mark Messier
July '95 ....—
July '96 ....—
July '97 ....12.00

Mikael Renberg (R)
July '95 ....—
July '96 ....—
July '97 ....15.00

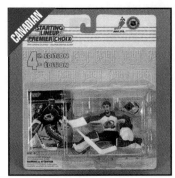

Patrick Roy
July '95 ....—
July '96 ....—
July '97 ....45.00

Joe Sakic (R)
July '95 ....—
July '96 ....—
July '97 ....20.00

Mats Sundin (R)
July '95 ....—
July '96 ....—
July '97 ....12.00

1989 LEGENDS

★ Set Price: $1,250.00 ★ Total Figures: 11 ★

The idea behind this set is similar to that of the Baseball Greats—Kenner tried to expand its audience with the greatest basketball and football players of all time. Unlike Baseball Greats, this set was just one figure per package instead of two. It had the same retail price as the regular SLU figures.

Kenner had announced that there would be a second Legends series that would include Bart Starr, Roger Staubach, and Joe Namath. However, slow sales forced Kenner to drop these figures and issue only the first set—until the recent Timeless Legends series.

Gale Sayers and Johnny Unitas were issued in variations. Sayers appears with or without a mustache, and Unitas is wearing either low- or high-top cleats. There is no price premium for either variation.

The new Timeless Legends series has brought new life to this set. Many collectors who had previously ignored this issue are now trying to complete their set.

Look for this set to continue to be

Case Assortments

Terry Bradshaw (3)
Wilt Chamberlain (3)
Mike Ditka (3)
Julius Erving (4)
Joe Greene (2)
John Havlicek (2)
Oscar Robertson (2)
Gale Sayers (2)
Johnny Unitas (3)

The back of the '89 Legends package shows seven of the nine players issued. Terry Bradshaw and Mike Ditka are not pictured.

more popular as these pieces get harder and harder to find.

Terry Bradshaw
July '91	15.00
July '94	24.00
July '97	75.00

Wilt Chamberlain
July '91	13.00
July '94	28.00
July '97	60.00

Mike Ditka
July '91	10.00
July '94	20.00
July '97	60.00

Julius Erving
July '91	10.00
July '94	24.00
July '97	65.00

Joe Greene
July '91	10.00
July '94	18.00
July '97	65.00

John Havlicek
July '91	10.00
July '94	15.00
July '97	50.00

Oscar Robertson
July '91	10.00
July '94	15.00
July '97	50.00

Gale Sayers (mustache)
July '91	15.00
July '94	22.00
July '97	50.00

Gale Sayers (no mustache)
July '91.......................10.00
July '94 ....20.00
July '97 ....50.00

Johnny Unitas (high tops)
July '91.......................10.00
July '94 ....24.00
July '97 ....60.00

Johnny Unitas (low tops)
July '91.......................15.00
July '94 ....20.00
July '97 ....60.00

TIMELESS LEGENDS

★ **1995 American Set Price : $120.00** ★ **Total Figures: 9** ★
★ **1995 Canadian Set Price : $100.00** ★ **Total Figures: 7** ★
★ **1996 American Set Price : $75.00** ★ **Total Figures: 9** ★
★ **1996 Canadian Set Price : $125.00** ★ **Total Figures: 6** ★

In its 1995 Timeless Legends release, Kenner brought back the concept of producing retired players. Kenner intends for the series to span all of the major sports and to depict the biggest stars.

The first set was initially popular but a higher-than-expected production run pushed values down. The Walter Payton piece appeared in two variations; both are considered to be short-prints. Payton is wearing all black shoes or white shoes with black tips.

The Rocky Marciano piece also has a rare brown-haired variation. It's extremely scarce and a comands a high premium compared to the black-haired piece.

Meanwhile, Hasbro of Canada issued a Canadian version of Timeless Legends, but it didn't include Terry Bradshaw or Walter Payton. Like the Canadian hockey set, this issue has been ignored by American collectors, who generally stick with the U.S. version.

To celebrate the 1996 Summer Olympics held in Atlanta, Kenner issued its '96 Timeless Legends set with nine Olympic athletes. Among them were the first female SLUs. The '96 set has done poorly on the secondary market, and it appears there is considerably more product available than demand.

That same year, Hasbro of Canada issued a completely different set. The company issued six hockey legends, all of whom are in the Hall of Fame. There are no American versions of these figures in this set; consequently, it's sold well on the secondary market.

Overall, though, Timeless Legends haven't been strong with collectors. Just the same, Kenner plans to continue this series with a list of new players for 1997.

Above is the rare brown-haired Rocky Marciano. Pictured at right are the '95 (top) and '96 American Timeless Legends' backs.

'95 Kareem Abdul-Jabbar
July '95 ....—
July '96 ....15.00
July '97 ....15.00

Case Assortments

1995 AMERICAN	Arnold Palmer (3)	Bruce Jenner (2)	Olga Korbut
Case .00	Walter Payton (2)	Michael Johnson (2)	Dan O'Brien
Kareem Abdul-Jabbar (3)		Florence Griffith	Jesse Owens (2)
Gordie Howe (4)	**1995 CANADIAN**	Joyner (2)	Jim Thorpe (2)
Joe Louis (3)	Kareem Abdul-Jabbar (2)	Olga Korbut (2)	
Rocky Marciano (2)	Wilt Chamberlain (2)	Dan O'Brien (2)	**1996 CANADIAN**
Arnold Palmer (4)	Gordie Howe (4)	Jesse Owens (2)	**Case .01**
	Bobby Hull (4)	Jim Thorpe (2)	Gordie Howe (2)
Case .01	Joe Louis (1)		Bobby Hull (2)
Terry Bradshaw (3)	Rocky Marciano (1)	**Case .07**	Phil Esposito (3)
Wilt Chamberlain (3)	Arnold Palmer (2)	Nadia Comaneci (2)	Tony Esposito (3)
Gordie Howe (1)		Bruce Jenner (2)	Jean Beliveau (3)
Bobby Hull (2)	**1996 AMERICAN**	Michael Johnson	Maurice Richard (3)
Joe Louis (1)	**Case .06**	Florence Griffith Joyner	
Rocky Marciano (1)	Nadia Comaneci (2)	Jackie Joyner-Kersee (4)	

'95 Terry Bradshaw
July '95 ....—
July '96 ....20.00
July '97 ....20.00

'95 Wilt Chamberlain
July '95 ....—
July '96 ....18.00
July '97 ....18.00

'95 Gordie Howe
July '95 ....—
July '96 ....15.00
July '97 ....10.00

'95 Bobby Hull
July '95 ....—
July '96 ....25.00
July '97 ....25.00

'95 Joe Louis
July '95 ....—
July '96 ....15.00
July '97 ....12.00

'95 Rocky Marciano
(brown hair)
July '95 ....—
July '96 ....125.00
July '97 ....200.00

'95 Rockey Marciano
(black hair)
July '95 ....—
July '96 ....15.00
July '97 ....15.00

'95 Arnold Palmer
July '95 ....—
July '96 ....10.00
July '97 ....8.00

'95 Walter Payton
(black shoes)
July '95 ....—
July '96 ....50.00
July '97 ....65.00

'95 Walter Payton
(white w/black tips)
July '95 ....—
July '96 ....50.00
July '97 ....65.00

'95 Kareem Abdul-Jabbar
July '95 ....—
July '96 ....15.00
July '97 ....15.00

'95 Wilt Chamberlain
July '95 ....—
July '96 ....15.00
July '97 ....15.00

'95 Gordie Howe
July '95 ....—
July '96 ....15.00
July '97 ....15.00

'95 Bobby Hull
July '95 ....—
July '96 ....15.00
July '97 ....15.00

'95 Joe Louis
July '95 ....—
July '96 ....24.00
July '97 ....24.00

'95 Rocky Marciano
July '95 ....—
July '96 ....24.00
July '97 ....24.00

'95 Arnold Palmer
July '95 ....—
July '96 ....15.00
July '97 ....15.00

'96 Nadia Comaneci
July '95 ....—
July '96 ....—
July '97 ....10.00

'96 Florence Griffith Joyner
July '95 ....—
July '96 ....—
July '97 ....10.00

'96 Bruce Jenner
July '95 ....—
July '96 ....—
July '97 ....10.00

'96 Michael Johnson
July '95 ....—
July '96 ....—
July '97 ....12.00

'96 Jackie Joyner-Kersee
July '95 ....—
July '96 ....—
July '97 ....10.00

'96 Olga Korbut
July '95 ....—
July '96 ....—
July '97 ....10.00

'96 Dan O'Brien
July '95 ....—
July '96 ....—
July '97 ....8.00

'96 Jesse Owens
July '95 ....—
July '96 ....—
July '97 ....8.00

'96 Jim Thorpe
July '95 ....—
July '96 ....—
July '97 ....8.00

'96 Jean Beliveau
July '95 ....—
July '96 ....—
July '97 ....25.00

'96 Tony Esposito
July '95 ....—
July '96 ....—
July '97 ....30.00

'96 Phil Esposito
July '95 ....—
July '96 ....—
July '97 ....25.00

'96 Gordie Howe
July '95 ....—
July '96 ....—
July '97 ....20.00

'96 Bobby Hull
July '95 ....—
July '96 ....—
July '97 ....20.00

'96 Maurice Richard
July '95 ....—
July '96 ....—
July '97 ....25.00

1989 ONE-ON-ONE

★ **Set Price: $1,250.00** ★ **Total Figures: 13** ★

This is one of the more popular non-traditional Starting Lineup sets, but it didn't start out that way. Like many of Kenner's other odd-ball issues, these figures didn't sell well out of the gate. The higher price point and larger size turned off many collectors. By now, all of that has changed, and this is one of the hottest sets in the hobby. The concept obviously appeals to collectors: Kenner took two rival players and pitted them against each other. (Heck, that's what sports are all about.) Kenner issued players from baseball, basketball, and football.

For basketball fans, there's no bigger rivalry than Magic Johnson and Larry Bird. Combined, the Los Angeles Lakers and the Boston Celtics won eight of the 10 NBA championships during the 1980s. And it wasn't just the Lakers fighting the Celtics; it was Magic vs. Bird. These two

players laid the foundation for the NBA today. So their Kenner One-on-One was a can't-miss piece.

In fact, the basketball figures have become the hottest pieces in this set. Kenner issued just four great confrontations. The Michael Jordan vs. Isiah Thomas is the most expensive, but even the "cheapest" combination—Patrick Ewing and Kevin McHale—is more expensive than any piece from any of the other sports except for the John Elway/Howie Long piece.

Speaking of Elway and Long, Denver and Oakland meet twice each year in one of the AFC West's most bitter rivalries. Imagine the number of times defensive end Long tried to sack Elway in the '80s. Recently, there's been a real surge in football pieces among Kenner collectors. Even some of the com-

The package back of the '90 One-on-One series (above) advertises the many different pieces in the set. Pictured at left is the classic basketball confrontation of Larry Bird and Magic Johnson.

mon players rank high on want lists.

The baseball figures, however, are another story. Perhaps it's the less confrontational nature of the game (except in the case of pitcher vs. batter) that has kept baseball One-on-Ones cool. Whatever the reaason, the prices have seen little movement in the past few years. Only the Don Mattingly/Wade Boggs figure has drawn much collector interest.

This is one of the most expensive sets at more than $1,000 for only 13 pieces. If you can afford it, you won't be disappointed.

Charles Barkley/Dominique Wilkins
July '91......................15.00
July '94 ....74.00
July '97 ....150.00

Jose Canseco/Alan Trammell
July '91......................15.00
July '94 ....25.00
July '97 ....35.00

Gary Carter/Eric Davis
July '91......................15.00
July '94 ....20.00
July '97 ....35.00

John Elway/Howie Long
July '91......................15.00
July '94 ....34.00
July '97 ....160.00

Patrick Ewing/Kevin McHale
July '91 ....25.00
July '94 ....40.00
July '97 ....125.00

Magic Johnson/Larry Bird
July '91 ....30.00
July '94 ....125.00
July '97 ....275.00

Michael Jordan/Isiah Thomas
July '91 ....60.00
July '94 ....125.00
July '97 ....300.00

Don Mattingly/Wade Boggs
July '91 ....15.00
July '94 ....38.00
July '97 ....72.00

Jim McMahon/Chris Doleman
July '91 ....15.00
July '94 ....22.00
July '97 ....60.00

Ken O'Brien/Lawrence Taylor
July '91 ....15.00
July '94 ....25.00
July '97 ....60.00

Ryne Sandberg/Vince Coleman
July '91 ....15.00
July '94 ....30.00
July '97 ....40.00

Mike Singletary/Mike Quick
July '91 ....15.00
July '94 ....24.00
July '97 ....65.00

Herschel Walker/Dexter Manley
July '91 ....15.00
July '94 ....24.00
July '97 ....65.00

TEAM LINEUPS

In the late 1980s and early 1990s, Kenner issued several different Team Lineups. The first to appear were the starting lineups of seven Major League Baseball teams. Kenner issued these figures as a test and produced them in much smaller quantities than the other sets. The Oakland Athletics are the shortest-printed team and remain difficult to find in mint condition. The New York Yankees are more plentiful, but strong demand keeps this piece hot.

In 1990 and '91, Kenner issued an Award Winner set that depicts the Most Valuable Player, Cy Young, and Rookie of the Year winners for each league. Both sets had been low on want lists—until Cal Ripken Jr. broke Lou Gehrig's consecutive game streak in 1995. Many Ripken collectors who were trying to add every one of his pieces to their collections simply couldn't find a '91 Award Winner set in mint condition. Almost overnight, that piece went from $20 to $65. The '90 set isn't as popular, but has recently attracted some interest from collectors.

Kenner later issued a figure of the 1992 Olympic basketball "Dream Team." Clyde Drexler and Christian Laettner were omitted from the set because they were added to the team after the figure was already in production.

Kenner followed that release with two sets of the

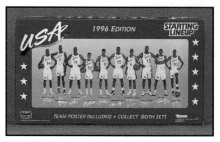

Pictured above is the back of the '91 Award Winner set. Top left is the '89 Baseball team back. The '92 (top right) and '96 (bottom right) Basketball Dream Team backs show all of the players in the set.

'96 Dream Team. Each set has only five players. Again, there were two late additions to the team—Charles Barkley and Mitch Richmond—and neither made it into the

set. Glenn Robinson was injured and later replaced by Gary Payton. Kenner opted to issue the third part of the Dream Team as a Kenner Club piece.

Boston Red Sox
July '91	65.00
July '94	50.00
July '97	65.00

Chicago Cubs
July '91	70.00
July '94	58.00
July '97	65.00

Detroit Tigers
July '91	65.00
July '94	48.00
July '97	65.00

New York Mets

July '91 ....60.00
July '94.....................................50.00
July '97.....................................65.00

New York Yankees

July '91 ....60.00
July '94.....................................75.00
July '97...................................125.00

Oakland Athletics

July '91 ....150.00
July '94...................................170.00
July '97...................................130.00

St. Louis Cardinals

July '91 ....75.00
July '94.....................................70.00
July '97.....................................75.00

1990 Award Winners

July '91 ....—
July '94.....................................20.00
July '97.....................................40.00

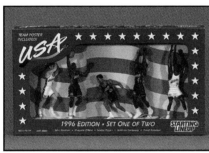

1991 Award Winners

July '91 ....—
July '94.....................................20.00
July '97.....................................65.00

'92 USA Olympic Basketball

July '91 ....—
July '94.....................................32.00
July '97 ....115.00

'96 Basketball (1 of 2)

July '91 ....—
July '94..—
July '97.....................................25.00

'96 Basketball (2 of 2)

July '91 ....—
July '94..—
July '97.....................................25.00

LEGENDS · ONE-ON-ONE · TEAM LINEUPS · CONVENTIONS

KENNER CONVENTIONS

Rob Rogers and Tom Berry held the first all-Kenner convention in Claymont, Del., in July 1993. No one knew what to expect. About 50 dealers with nothing but Starting Lineups set up at the show. Kenner participated by setting up a display booth featuring several new product lines. To everyone's surprise, it was a wonderful weekend. Just like that, the Kenner Convention was born.

As part of the convention, Kenner had several autographed and prototype pieces to be auctioned off for the Make-a-Wish foundation. For attendees, it was exciting to see these one-of-a-kind items available to the hobby. Kenner continued to offer prototype pieces at conventions—until 1995. By that time, the company's executives felt that SLU dealers only were buying the prototypes. Since they wanted to offer something special to convention attendees, they decided on a convention-only figure.

In 1995, Kenner produced a Joe Montana show piece for the Delaware convention, and it was a big hit. In fact, Kenner issued the same figure at all four conventions, with a custom sticker attached to the packages at each site.

When the first convention was over, the Montana figure was one of the hottest pieces in the hobby. Dealers were selling their pieces for as much as $100. Since then, however, the Montana pieces have cooled down considerably; they now sell for about $50.

One interesting note is that a problem developed at the Delaware show. Unfortunately, Kenner didn't have enough stickers on hand for each figure, so the company issued these pieces without a sticker and took the names and addresses of those collectors who didn't get one. Kenner later mailed a sticker to each of the collectors, but there are a considerable number of figures that still don't have a sticker. Currently, there is no price difference between any of the sticker and the "no sticker" Montana.

In 1996, Kenner issued a Cal Ripken Jr. figure with a sticker at each of the conventions. Like the Montana piece, it was hot to start but has since cooled off.

In 1997, Kenner made some changes to its convention-piece program. At each of the four shows, the company planned to issue a Pat McInally piece (with a sticker) plus a regional figure.

In Cincinnati, Kenner issued a Johnny Bench piece—the same one slated for the 1997 Cooperstown Collection. On tap for the Atlanta show in August are Glen Rice and Christian Laettner pieces. In Anaheim, Calif. in September, it'll be Jason Kidd and Shaquille O'Neal. The New Jersey convention in October will feature Larry Johnson and Jerry Stackhouse pieces.

Pictured above are the backs of the Joe Montana and Cal Ripken Jr. convention pieces. Both backs are the same as those on the regular figures from their respective sets. At left is Ripken.

Joe Montana (Cincinnati)

July '95	70.00
July '96	70.00
July '97	45.00

Joe Montana
(Delaware w/sticker)

July '95	70.00
July '96	70.00
July '97	45.00

Joe Montana
(Delaware w/o sticker)

July '95	70.00
July '96	70.00
July '97	45.00

Joe Montana
(Anaheim)

July '95	70.00
July '96	70.00
July '97	45.00

Joe Montana
(New Jersey)

July '95	70.00
July '96	70.00
July '97	45.00

Cal Ripken Jr. (Cincinnati)

July '95	—
July '96	—
July '97	50.00

Cal Ripken Jr. (Dallas)

July '95	—
July '96	—
July '97	50.00

Cal Ripken Jr. (Santa Clara)

July '95	—
July '96	—
July '97	50.00

Cal Ripken Jr. (New Jersey)

July '95	—
July '96	—
July '97	50.00

KENNER CLUB

Kenner started its own collector club in 1991. The idea was simple: Kenner would ship each member a quarterly newsletter that featured an offer to purchase an exclusive, limited-edition figure. The club hit the ground running when Kenner offered a Shaquille O'Neal "slam dunk" figure as its inaugural club piece. The figure was an immediate hit with collectors and it remains one of the most expensive club pieces issued.

Kenner has issued eight more figures. The most recent pieces—from the spring of 1997—include Part 3 of the '96 Dream Team set and a Los Angeles Lakers "Centers" piece. The Dream Team set includes Charles Barkley and Mitch Richmond—late additions to the team—and Gary Payton, who replaced the injured Glenn Robinson. The Lakers' piece depicts three great L.A. pivotmen: Kareem Abdul-Jabbar, Wilt Chamberlain, and Shaquille O'Neal.

Kenner also uses its club to test a number of various products. One example is the Nolan Ryan "Freeze Frame" piece. This figure was so popular that Kenner decided to issue a six-piece Freeze Frame set to Toys R Us stores across the United States. Although these pieces feature three figures per package instead of the four that were used for Ryan, the concept appears to be popular with collectors. Freeze Frames were slated to reach Toys R Us stores in the summer of 1997.

The rest of Kenner's club pieces have been only moderately popular. The "Stadium Star" pieces of baseball Hall of Famers Reggie Jackson and Willie Mays have become slow movers. The same can be said for the two hockey club pieces—John Vanbiesbrouck and the Bobby and Brett Hull combination piece.

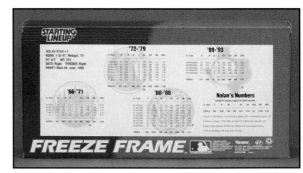

Each of the Kenner Club pieces have a different back. Pictured above is the back of the Nolan Ryan Freeze Frame figure.

Shaquille O'Neal (Slam Dunk)
July '95...75.00
July '96...90.00
July '97...100.00

Nolan Ryan (Freeze Frame)
July '95 ....—
July '96 ....80.00
July '97...110.00

Reggie Jackson (Stad. Star)
July '95 ....45.00
July '96 ....40.00
July '97 ....40.00

Willie Mays (Stad. Star)
July '95 ....35.00
July '96 ....35.00
July '97 ....35.00

Joe Namath
July '95 ....40.00
July '96 ....50.00
July '97 ....50.00

John Vanbiesbrouck
July '95 ....—
July '96 ....35.00
July '97 ....35.00

Bobby & Brett Hull
July '95 ....—
July '96 ....—
July '97 ....35.00

Figure Index

Morris, Hal
(R) 1996 Baseball Extended 69
Morris, Jack
1988 Baseball 17
1989 Baseball 28
Murphy, Dale
1988 Baseball 17
1989 Baseball 28
Murray, Eddie
1988 Baseball 17
1990 Baseball 37
1996 Baseball 67
Musial, Stan
(w/Gibson) 1989 Baseball Greats 71
Mussina, Mike
(R) 1993 Baseball 51
Mussina, Mike
1994 Baseball 56
1995 Baseball 61
Myers, Randy
(R) 1989 Baseball 28
Neagle, Denny
(R) 1996 Baseball Extended 69
Neel, Troy
(R) 1995 Baseball 61
Nied, David
(R) 1993 Baseball Extended 52
Nilsson, Dave
(R) 1995 Baseball 61
Nokes, Matt
1988 Baseball 17
1989 Baseball 28
1990 Baseball 37
Nomo, Hideo
(R, gray) 1996 Baseball 67
(R, white) 1996 Baseball 67
O'Brien, Pete
1988 Baseball 17
O'Neill, Paul
(R) 1990 Baseball 37
1995 Baseball 61
1996 Baseball 67
Oberkfell, Ken
1988 Baseball 18
Olerud, John (R)
1994 Baseball 56
1995 Baseball 61
Oquendo, Jose
(R) 1990 Baseball 37
Ott, Mel
1996 Cooperstown 79
Pagliarulo, Mike
(R) 1989 Baseball 28
Pagnozzi, Tom
(R) 1995 Baseball Extended 62
Paige, Satchel
1995 Cooperstown 79
Palmer, Dean
(R) 1993 Baseball 51
Palmeiro, Rafael
1994 Baseball Extended 57
1996 Baseball Extended 69
Parker, Dave
1988 Baseball 18
1989 Baseball 28
Parrish, Larry
1988 Baseball 18
Pasqua, Dan (R)
1989 Baseball 28
Pena, Tony (R)
1989 Baseball 28
Pendleton, Terry (R)
1989 Baseball 28
1993 Baseball 51
Perez, Melido
(R) 1989 Baseball 28
Perry, Gerald
(R) 1989 Baseball 28
Pettis, Gary
(R) 1990 Baseball 37
Phelps, Ken
1988 Baseball 81
Phillips, Tony
(R) 1994 Baseball 56
Piazza, Mike
(R) 1994 Baseball 56
1995 Baseball 61
1995 Baseball Extended 62
1996 Baseball 67
1996 Baseball Stadium Stars 76
Plesac, Dan
(R) 1989 Baseball 28
Presley, Jim
1988 Baseball 18
Puckett, Kirby
1988 Baseball 18
1989 Baseball 28
1990 Baseball 37
1991 Baseball 43
1992 Baseball Extended 48
1993 Baseball 50
1995 Baseball 51
1996 Baseball 61
1994 Baseball Stadium Stars 75
Quinones, Rey
(R) 1989 Baseball 28
Quisenberry, Dan
1988 Baseball 18
Raines, Tim
1988 Baseball 18
1989 Baseball 29
1991 Baseball Extended 44
Ramirez, Manny
(R) 1995 Baseball Extended 62
Randolph, Willie
1988 Baseball 18
1990 Baseball 38
Rawley, Shane
1988 Baseball 18
Ray, Johnny
(R) 1989 Baseball 29
Reardon, Jeff
1988 Baseball 18
1989 Baseball 29
Redus, Gary
1988 Baseball 18
Reed, Jody
(R) 1990 Baseball 38
Reuschel, Rick
1988 Baseball 18
1990 Baseball 38
Reynolds, Harold
(R) 1989 Baseball 29
Rice, Jim
1988 Baseball 18
1989 Baseball 29
Righetti, Dave
1988 Baseball 18
1989 Baseball 29
1990 Baseball 38
Rijo, Jose
(R) 1994 Baseball 56
Ripken Jr., Cal
1988 Baseball 18
1989 Baseball 29
1990 Baseball 38
1992 Baseball 47
1993 Baseball 51
1994 Baseball 56
1995 Baseball 61
(Streak) 1995 Baseball Extended 63
(diving) 1996 Baseball 67
(diving w/sliding card) 1996 Baseball 67
(sliding) 1996 Baseball 67
(sliding w/diving card) 1996 Baseball 67
1993 Baseball Headline 73
1996 Baseball Stadium Stars 76
(Cincinnati) 1996 Kenner Convention
(Dallas) 1996 Kenner Convention
(New Jersey) 1996 Kenner Convention
(Santa Clara) 1996 Kenner Convention ..181
Roberts, Bip
(R) 1993 Baseball 51
Roberts, Robin
1996 Cooperstown 79
Robinson, Jackie
(#42) 1994 Cooperstown 78
(#44) 1994 Cooperstown 78
1996 Cooperstown 80
Rodriguez, Alex
(R) 1995 Baseball Extended 63
Rodriguez, Ivan
(R) 1994 Baseball 56
1996 Baseball 67
Rose, Pete
1988 Baseball 19
(w/Bench) 1989 Baseball Greats 71
Russell, Jeff
(R) 1989 Baseball 29
Ruth, Babe
(gray/white) 1989 Baseball Greats 71
(white/gray) 1989 Baseball Greats 71
(white/white) 1989 Baseball Greats 71
1994 Cooperstown 78
1995 Cooperstown 79
(Red Sox) 1996 Cooperstown 12" 80
(Yankees) 1996 Cooperstown 12" 80
Ryan, Nolan
1988 Baseball 19
1990 Baseball 38
1990 Baseball Extended 38
1991 Baseball 43
1991 Baseball Extended 44
1991 Baseball Headline 73
1992 Baseball 47
1992 Baseball Headline 73
1993 Baseball 51
(retire) 1993 Baseball Extended 52
1993 Baseball Headline 73
1993 Baseball Stadium Stars 75
(Freeze Frame) 1995 Kenner Club 182
Saberhagen, Bret
1988 Baseball 19
1989 Baseball 29
1992 Baseball Extended 48
Sabo, Chris
(R) 1989 Baseball 29
1990 Baseball 38
1991 Baseball 43
1992 Baseball 47
Salazar, Luis
(R) 1989 Baseball 29
Salmon, Tim
(R) 1994 Baseball 56
1995 Baseball 62
Samuel, Juan
1988 Baseball 19
1989 Baseball 28
1990 Baseball 38
Sandberg, Ryne
1988 Baseball 19
1989 Baseball 29
1990 Baseball 38
1991 Baseball 43
1992 Baseball 47
1992 Baseball Headline 73
1993 Baseball 51
1993 Baseball Stadium Stars 75
1994 Baseball 56
(w/Coleman) One-on-One 177
Sanders, Deion
1993 Baseball Headline 73
1994 Baseball Stadium Stars 75
1995 Baseball 62
1996 Baseball 67
Sanders, Reggie
(R) 1995 Baseball 62
Santiago, Benito
1988 Baseball 19
1989 Baseball 29
1991 Baseball 43
1993 Baseball Extended 52
Sax, Steve
1988 Baseball 19
1990 Baseball 38
1991 Baseball 43
Schilling, Curt
(R) 1994 Baseball 56
Schmidt, Mike
1988 Baseball 19
1989 Baseball 29
1995 Baseball Extended 63
Schofield, Dick
(R) 1989 Baseball 29
Scioscia, Mike
(R) 1989 Baseball 30
Scott, Mike
1988 Baseball 19
1989 Baseball 30
1990 Baseball 38
Seaver, Tom
1992 Baseball Extended 48
Seitzer, Kevin
1988 Baseball 19
1989 Baseball 30
Sheets, Larry
(R) 1989 Baseball 30
Sheffield, Gary
(R) 1990 Baseball 38
1993 Baseball 51
1994 Baseball 56
(power) 1994 Baseball Extended 57
Shelby, John
(R) 1989 Baseball 30
Sierra, Ruben
1988 Baseball 19
1989 Baseball 30
1992 Baseball 48
Slaught, Don
(R) 1989 Baseball 30
Smiley, John
(R) 1990 Baseball 38
Smith, Dave
(R) 1989 Baseball 30
Smith, Lee
(R) 1989 Baseball 30
Smith, Ozzie
1988 Baseball 19
1989 Baseball 30
1990 Baseball 38
1996 Baseball 67
Smith, Zane
1988 Baseball 19
1989 Baseball 30
Smoltz, John
(R) 1993 Baseball 57
Snow, J.T.
(R) 1994 Baseball 57
Snyder, Cory
1988 Baseball 19
1989 Baseball 30
Sosa, Sammy
(R) 1995 Baseball 62
1996 Baseball 68
Stanicek, Pete
(R) 1989 Baseball 30
Stargell, Willie
(w/Clemente) 1989 Baseball Greats 71
Steinbach, Terry
(R) 1989 Baseball 60
1996 Baseball 68
Stewart, Dave
(R) 1989 Baseball 30
1990 Baseball 38
1991 Baseball 43
Stillwell, Kurt
(R) 1989 Baseball 30
Strawberry, Darryl
1988 Baseball 19
1989 Baseball 31
(batting) 1990 Baseball 38
(fielding) 1990 Baseball 39
1991 Baseball 43
1991 Baseball Extended 44
1992 Baseball 48
Stubbs, Franklin
1988 Baseball 19
Surhoff, B.J.
1988 Baseball 20
1989 Baseball 31
Sutcliffe, Rick
1988 Baseball 20
1989 Baseball 31
1990 Baseball 39
Sutter, Bruce
(R) 1989 Baseball 30
Swindell, Greg
(R) 1989 Baseball 30
Tabler, Pat
1988 Baseball 20
1989 Baseball 31
Tartabull, Danny
1988 Baseball 20
1989 Baseball 31
1992 Baseball 48
Tettleton, Mickey
(R) 1990 Baseball 39
1995 Baseball 62
Thigpen, Bobby
(R) 1989 Baseball 31
Thomas, Frank
(fielding) 1992 Baseball 48
(batting) 1992 Baseball Extended 48
1993 Baseball 51
1994 Baseball 57
1995 Baseball 62
1996 Baseball 68
1993 Baseball Headline 73
1993 Baseball Stadium Stars 75
1995 Baseball Stadium Stars 76
Thome, Jim
(R) 1996 Baseball 68
Thompson, Milt
(R) 1989 Baseball 31
Thompson, Robby
(R) 1989 Baseball 31
1994 Baseball 57
Thompson, Ryan
(R) 1996 Baseball 68
Trammell, Alan
1988 Baseball 20
1989 Baseball 31
1990 Baseball 39
1991 Baseball 43
(w/Canseco) 1989 One-on-One 176
Treadway, Jeff
(R) 1989 Baseball 31
Uribe, Jose
(R) 1989 Baseball 31
Valentin, John
(R) 1996 Baseball 68
Valenzuela, Fernando
1988 Baseball 20
1989 Baseball 31
Van Poppel, Todd
1992 Baseball Extended 48
Van Slyke, Andy
1988 Baseball 20
1989 Baseball 31
1990 Baseball 39
1993 Baseball 57
1995 Baseball 62
Vaughn, Greg
(R) 1994 Baseball 57
Vaughn, Mo
(R) 1994 Baseball 57
1995 Baseball 62
1995 Baseball Stadium Stars 76
1996 Baseball 68
Ventura, Robin
(R) 1993 Baseball 52
1994 Baseball 57
1996 Baseball Stadium Stars 76
Viola, Frank
1988 Baseball 20
1989 Baseball 31
1990 Baseball 39
1991 Baseball 43
Virgil, Ozzie
1988 Baseball 20
Wagner, Honus
1994 Cooperstown 78
(Toys R Us) 1996 Cooperstown 12" 80
Walk, Bob
(R) 1989 Baseball 32

FOOTBALL

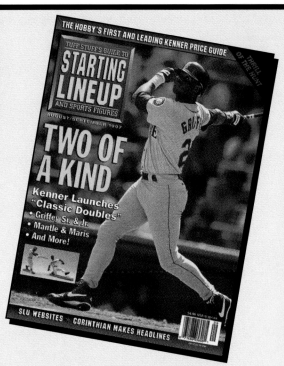

TUFF STUFF
PUBLICATIONS INC.
A Division of Landmark Specialty Publications

Tuff Stuff Publications Inc. is the proud publisher of this exceptional lineup of popular magazines. Each title is written and designed for the avid collector of sports or non-sports trading cards and collectibles. These publications feature the most comprehensive, accurate, and timely price guides on the market. Tuff Stuff also publishes annual fantasy guides for rotisserie football and baseball participants.

COLLECT!

The "bible" of card price guides with over 2,400 sets priced, *COLLECT!* covers the gamut of non-sports and entertainment trading cards. Articles feature popular comic book, movie, and TV character card sets, as well as tobacco cards from the 1800s. *COLLECT!* also boasts excellent coverage of the extremely popular collectible game cards like *Magic: The Gathering.* **Monthly: $3.99 cover price.**

GUIDE TO STARTING LINEUP AND SPORTS FIGURES

Tuff Stuff's Guide to Starting Lineup and Sports Figures features insightful articles and an expanded 24-page price guide covering all Kenner Starting Lineups, as well as Bobbin' Heads, Hartland, Gartlan, and Salvino figures. With more than 2,000 figures priced, we're *"The Kenner Guide"* to the fastest growing segment of sport collectors in the country! **Bimonthly: $4.99 cover price.**

JAM

JAM captures all the action and excitement of the NBA with a leading edge design and a full-color, 32-page price guide. This annual basketball-only special is full of insider features and articles, exclusive interviews, and stunning color photos. **October Annual: $3.99 cover price.**

TUFF STUFF

The #1 Guide to Sports Cards and Collectibles. Sports fans and collectors of trading cards, autographs and memorabilia turn to *Tuff Stuff* every month for the hobby's only all-sport price guide (baseball, football, basketball, hockey, "Kenner," and more!), insightful player profiles, in-depth articles on collecting, and information on what and who's hot and not. Over 250,000 cards priced! **Monthly: $4.99 cover price.**

TUFF STUFF'S CLASSIC COLLECTIBLES

This monthly tabloid supplement offers *Tuff Stuff* subscribers bonus coverage of auctions, autographed memorabilia, shows, and expanded card listings—like boxing and golf. **Monthly: Delivered Free with Subscriber Copies.**

Exclusively endorsed by NFL Players Inc

FANTASY FOOTBALL GUIDE:

Tuff Stuff's Fantasy Football Guide is the definitive resource for fantasy football league players. This 144-page, information-packed special issue provides in-depth numbers on virtually every key position and player in the NFL. Written and designed to do one thing—help fantasy players WIN! **July Annual: $4.99 cover price.**

FANTASY BASEBALL GUIDE:

Designed for the baseball rotisserie league aficionado, *Tuff Stuff's Fantasy Baseball Guide* is the single source guide for all the stats, insider info, and winning strategies. Packed with page after page of in-depth figures and statistics, this fantasy guide gives players the winning edge. **February Annual: $4.99 cover price.**

RPM

Tuff Stuff's RPM—Racing's #1 Guide to Die-Cast, Cards, & Memorabilia—is the most comprehensive guide to the booming NASCAR racing collectibles hobby. For pricing information on die-cast, cards, phone cards, models, knives, and more, *RPM* is the source. Readers get "revved- up" coverage of new product releases, inside track information, and exclusive interviews. **Monthly: $3.99 cover price.**

GAMER

The Collector's Guide to Game Cards, *Tuff Stuff's Gamer* is packed with reviews, previews, and trade news on the latest and greatest collectible card games. Includes exclusive interviews with the industry's top artists and designers, and complete checklists for every game on the market. **Quarterly: $3.99 cover price.**

GRIDIRON

Featuring coverage of today's hottest football collectibles, trading cards, and memorabilia, as well as stories on the game's biggest stars, *Gridiron* is the football fan's *Complete Guide to Football Collectibles.* Season previews, insider interviews, and a full-color price guide. **August Annual: $3.99 cover price.**

Exclusively endorsed by NFL Players Inc

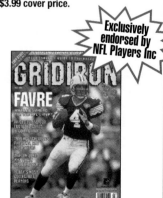

For more information about these great titles call:

(800) 899-8833

About the Author

Jim Warren joined *Tuff Stuff* in 1991 as a big-time hockey card collector. Born in Buffalo, N.Y., he is a die-hard Sabres fan. Although he hasn't lived there for several years, he still has hockey blood running through his veins.

Naturally, his first responsibilities at *Tuff Stuff* involved coordinating the magazine's hockey price guide. In 1992, he added the Starting Lineup price guide to his list of responsibilities. He became the manager of the price guide department in 1994 and senior editor in 1995.

Warren helped put together the second issue of *Tuff Stuff's Guide to Starting Lineup* in 1994. He became the project editor starting with the third issue, published in 1995, and was the driving force in making it a bimonthly magazine. Today, *Tuff Stuff's Guide to Starting Lineup* is the fastest-growing magazine under the *Tuff Stuff* umbrella.

Warren attended the first Starting Lineup convention in 1993 in Claymont, Del., and has been to every one since then. Still a hockey fan at heart, he focuses his SLU collecting on NHL figures only. His prized possession is an opened 1993 Grant Fuhr piece.

THE HUNGERFORD COLLECTION

Almost every Kenner Starting Lineup piece in this book comes from the collection of Charles Hungerford. He first began collecting Starting Lineups back in 1988. It all started when Charles—who at the time was heavy into baseball cards—bought the SLUs for the cards. Charles was on a mission to get every card of every player on the Pittsburgh Pirates. But it didn't take long until he was a bona fide SLU collector.

Almost 10 years later, Charles has put together one of the most impressive SLU collections anyone has ever seen. As we went to press, he is fewer than eight figures away from completing an entire run.

When Charles isn't collecting, he spends his time running the family business. He uses the rest of his spare time looking for opportunities to enjoy his second passion—golf.

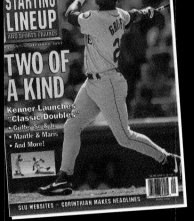

BUSINESS REPLY MAIL
FIRST CLASS MAIL   PERMIT NO. 868   HAGERSTOWN, MD

POSTAGE WILL BE PAID BY ADDRESSEE

TUFF STUFF
PO BOX 5012
HAGERSTOWN, MD 21741-9912

BUSINESS REPLY MAIL
FIRST CLASS MAIL   PERMIT NO. 366   GLEN ALLEN, VA

POSTAGE WILL BE PAID BY ADDRESSEE

TUFF STUFF TOTAL COLLECTORS CLUB
PO BOX 1637
GLEN ALLEN, VA 23060-0637

BUSINESS REPLY MAIL
FIRST CLASS MAIL   PERMIT NO. 868   HAGERSTOWN, MD

POSTAGE WILL BE PAID BY ADDRESSEE

TUFF STUFF'S GUIDE TO STARTING LINEUP
AND SPORT FIGURES
PO BOX 5012
HAGERSTOWN, MD 21741-9912